Does the Investment
Climate Matter?

Does the Investment Climate Matter?

MICROECONOMIC FOUNDATIONS OF GROWTH IN LATIN AMERICA

Edited by

Pablo Fajnzylber, J. Luis Guasch,
and J. Humberto López

A COPUBLICATION OF PALGRAVE MACMILLAN
AND THE WORLD BANK

A copublication of The World Bank and Palgrave Macmillan.

Palgrave Macmillan
Houndmills, Basingstoke, Hampshire RG21 6XS and 175 Fifth Avenue, New York,
N. Y. 10010
Companies and representatives throughout the world

Palgrave Macmillan is the global academic imprint of the Palgrave Macmillan division of
St. Martin's Press, LLC and of Palgrave Macmillan Ltd. Macmillan® is a registered trademark
in the United States, United Kingdom and other countries. Palgrave® is a registered trademark
in the European Union and other countries.

ISBN: 978-0-8213-7411-5 (soft cover) and 978-0-8213-7687-4 (hard cover)
eISBN: 978-0-8213-7412-2
DOI: 10.1596/978-0-8213-7411-5

Library of Congress Cataloging-in-Publication Data
Does the investment climate matter? : microeconomic foundations of growth in Latin America / edited by, Pablo Fajnzylber, Jose Luis Guasch, J. Humberto Lopez.—1st ed.

    p. cm.—(Latin American Development Forum series)
  ISBN 978-0-8213-7411-5 (print)—ISBN 978-0-8213-7412-2 (electronic)
  1. Investments—Latin America. I. Fajnzylber, Pablo. II. Guasch, J. Luis. III. Lopez, J. Humberto.
  HG5160.5.A3D64 2008
  338.5098—dc22

                                         2008024114

Latin American Development Forum Series

This series was created in 2003 to promote debate, disseminate information and analysis, and convey the excitement and complexity of the most topical issues in economic and social development in Latin America and the Caribbean. It is sponsored by the Inter-American Development Bank, the United Nations Economic Commission for Latin America and the Caribbean, and the World Bank. The manuscripts chosen for publication represent the highest quality in each institution's research and activity output and have been selected for their relevance to the academic community, policy makers, researchers, and interested readers.

Advisory Committee Members

Other Titles in the Latin American Development Forum Series

China's and India's Challenge to Latin America: Opportunity or Threat? (forthcoming) Daniel Lederman, Marcelo Olarreaga, and Guillermo E. Perry, editors

Innovative Experiences in Access to Finance: Market-Friendly Roles for the Visible Hand? (forthcoming) by Augusto de la Torre, Juan Carlos Gozzi, and Sergio L. Schmukler

Job Creation in Latin America and the Caribbean: Trends and Policy Challenges (forthcoming) by Carmen Pagés, Gaëlle Pierre, and Stefano Scarpetta

Measuring Inequality of Opportunities in Latin America and the Caribbean (forthcoming) by Ricardo Paes de Barros, Francisco H. G. Ferreira, José R. Molinas Vega, and Jaime Saavedra Chanduvi

The Promise of Early Childhood Development in Latin America (forthcoming) by Emiliana Vegas and Lucrecia Santibáñez

Fiscal Policy, Stabilization, and Growth: Prudence or Abstinence? (2008) Guillermo E. Perry, Luis Servén, and Rodrigo Suescún, editors

The Impact of Private Sector Participation in Infrastructure: Lights, Shadows, and the Road Ahead (2008) by Luis Andres, José Luis Guasch, Thomas Haven, and Vivien Foster

Raising Student Learning in Latin America: Challenges for the 21st Century (2008) by Emiliana Vegas and Jenny Petrow

Remittances and Development: Lessons from Latin America (2008) Pablo Fajnzylber and J. Humberto López, editors

Emerging Capital Markets and Globalization: The Latin American Experience (2007) by Augusto de la Torre and Sergio L. Schmukler

Investor Protection and Corporate Governance: Firm-Level Evidence across Latin America (2007) by Alberto Chong and Florencio López-de-Silanes, editors

Natural Resources: Neither Curse nor Destiny (2007) Daniel Lederman and William F. Maloney, editors

The State of State Reform in Latin America (2007) Eduardo Lora, editor

Beyond Survival: Protecting Households from Health Shocks in Latin America (2006) by Cristian C. Baeza and Truman G. Packard

Beyond Reforms: Structural Dynamics and Macroeconomic Vulnerability (2005) José Antonio Ocampo, editor

Privatization in Latin America: Myths and Reality (2005) Alberto Chong and Florencio López-de-Silanes, editors

Keeping the Promise of Social Security in Latin America (2004) by Indermit S. Gill, Truman G. Packard, and Juan Yermo

Lessons from NAFTA: For Latin America and the Caribbean (2004) by Daniel Lederman, William F. Maloney, and Luis Servén

Globalization and Development: A Latin American and Caribbean Perspective (2003) José Antonio Ocampo and Juan Martin, editors

Is Geography Destiny? Lessons from Latin America (2003) by John Luke Gallup, Alejandro Gaviria, and Eduardo Lora

The Limits of Stabilization: Infrastructure, Public Deficits, and Growth in Latin America (2003) William Easterly and Luis Servén, editors

About the Contributors

Verónica Alaimo, formerly a consultant at the Chief Economist's Office of the Latin America and the Caribbean Region of the World Bank, is an economist at the Inter-American Development Bank. Her areas of expertise include labor markets and applied econometrics.

Carlos Casacuberta is a professor of economics at the Universidad de la República in Montevideo, Uruguay. He has done applied research on firm productivity and the relationship between trade and economic performance.

Pablo Fajnzylber is a senior economist in the Chief Economist's Office of the Latin America and the Caribbean Region of the World Bank. He is the author of numerous articles and books covering a variety of development topics.

Nestor Gandelman is chair of the Economics Department at the ORT University in Uruguay. His research focuses primarily on applied industrial organization and labor economics.

J. Luis Guasch is a senior adviser on competition and regulation in the Latin America and the Caribbean Region of the World Bank. He is also head of the Regulation and Public-Private Partnerships Thematic Group at the World Bank and a professor of economics at the University of California, San Diego. He has written and published extensively in the areas of competitiveness, regulation, infrastructure, the investment climate, and innovation and knowledge transfer.

Daniel Lederman is a senior economist in the World Bank's Development Research Group. He is the author of numerous books and articles on Latin American development.

J. Humberto López is lead economist in the Central America Management Unit of the World Bank's Latin America and the Caribbean Region. He has published numerous articles and books on various development topics.

Inessa Love is a senior economist in the World Bank's Development Research Group. She is the author of numerous articles on access to finance and financial sector development.

Marcelo Olarreaga is a professor of economics at the University of Geneva. His areas of expertise are the political economy of trade policy and the implications of trade reforms for poverty.

Ana María Oviedo is in the Young Professionals Program and works in the Doing Business Reform Unit at the World Bank Group. Her areas of specialization include the determinants of firm productivity, governance, and labor economics.

Guido Porto is a professor of economics at Universidad Nacional de La Plata in Argentina. His area of expertise is the development effects of trade policy and trade reforms, with an emphasis on poverty, distribution, and household behavior.

Eliana Rubiano is a research assistant with Fedesarrollo in Bogotá and a consultant at the World Bank. She specializes in the areas of growth, education, labor markets, and international trade.

Contents

TABLES

Preface

Why do we need a book focusing on the economic performance of Latin America and the Caribbean at a time when growth is at a 30-year high? The truth is that there is little reason to be complacent about the region's recent performance. First, even if Latin America managed to sustain its current trends, the corresponding growth rates would be insufficient to reduce the current share of people living on less than US$2 a day (about 25 percent) over the short run. Second, although the region's recent growth performance is quite impressive by historical standards, so far it is only a three-year run, driven to a significant extent by a number of external factors, such as a favorable global environment, high commodity prices, and the voracious appetite for raw materials and intermediate goods of countries such as China and India. Hence, it is unclear how much longer such a set of favorable conditions will persist. In fact, the 2009 financial crisis, led by the U.S. sub-prime mortgage collapse, is already affecting that favorable environment. Falling commodity prices will have a negative impact on the growth prospects of many developing countries. In such an environment, the prescriptions offered by this book are even more relevant, as it is ever more critical to create a proper investment climate that can increase investor confidence and stimulate investment and economic activity. Third, and perhaps more important in this context, the improvements on the growth front observed in Latin America in recent years are less remarkable when considered in a global context. Indeed, even though the recent growth rates of Latin American and Caribbean countries are the highest of the past three decades, the region is losing ground not only with respect to the world at large but also in comparison with various other reference groups. For instance, Latin American growth rates are still below those of other middle-income countries, the East Asia region, and the group of natural resource–abundant countries.

In this context, the main hypothesis that this book seeks to test is whether the shortcomings in Latin America's growth performance can be dissociated from the microeconomic environment in which the region's firms operate. In other words, the book claims that to achieve even higher and more sustainable rates of economic growth, the region needs to implement important improvements in its investment climate. Some evidence already exists in this respect, including data from various secondary sources suggesting that Latin America is lagging significantly in issues related to the quality of governance and institutions, the availability of physical infrastructure, the development of the financial sector, the enhancement of levels of education of the labor force, and the innovative capacity of the private sector.

Yet there is little empirical evidence to inform the policy agenda or to link the performance of actual firms to the various shortcomings of Latin America's investment climate. This book aims to fill that gap by using extensive and new firm-level data. It provides an alternative, albeit complementary, approach to previous studies of the determinants of the region's growth performance, which are mostly based on cross-country regressions using aggregate data. The microeconomic approach used in this book is motivated by the fact that, after all, aggregate growth and employment creation are driven by the production and investment decisions of firm managers, which in turn are directly affected by the environment in which their firms operate. Using a microeconomic perspective thus allows for a better understanding of the links between the policy environment and the economic performance of firms, which we hope can facilitate the identification of where and how government ought to intervene.

This book uses the information contained in enterprise surveys performed in 16 Latin American and Caribbean countries, covering more than 10,000 firms. These data are complemented with information from household surveys, as well as from enterprise surveys performed in other regions of the world. The analysis in this volume covers topics that have also been stressed by other authors, such as the need to make progress in the areas of financial sector development, export promotion, and innovation policy. The book's contribution in this regard is to inform the corresponding policy debates with evidence on the effect of different policy environments on firm performance. In parallel, the book also stresses other aspects that have received less attention but which we believe contribute to keeping the region behind. They include the need to reduce corruption, to make progress on the governance and regulatory front, and to strengthen the region's judicial systems.

Overall, we hope that this book will contribute to identifying some of the underlying factors that are driving Latin America's lackluster growth performance. In particular, our objective is to improve our understanding of the policies that could have a larger influence on increasing growth and productivity in the region, by means of improving the environment in which firms invest and operate.

Acknowledgments

Does the Investment Climate Matter? Microeconomic Foundations of Growth in Latin America is based on the second volume of the 2007 Latin American and Caribbean Regional Study *Economic Performance in Latin America and the Caribbean: A Microeconomic Perspective* (World Bank Report 40717). That report was the result of a collaborative effort of two units of the Latin America and Caribbean Region of the World Bank: the Office of the Chief Economist and the Finance and Private Sector Development Department.

We are most grateful to the contributors to this book for their efforts in preparing the various versions of the manuscript; to Guillermo Beylis, Edwin Goñi, Tatsuji Hayakawa, Naotaka Sawada, and Denika Torres for their excellent research assistance; to César Calderón, Augusto de la Torre, Makhtar Diop, Álvaro Escribano, Ricardo Hausmann, Danny Leipziger, William Maloney, Guillermo Perry, José Guilherme Reis, Luis Servén, Nick Stern, and especially two anonymous referees, for their very useful comments and advice; and to Elizabeth Kline, Santiago Pombo-Bejarano, and Shana Wagger for their support in the production of this book. We are also indebted to the many colleagues from the World Bank with whom we had opportunities to discuss and bandy ideas on different aspects of the book. The editors alone take responsibility for the content of the book and the views expressed here, which do not necessarily reflect the views of our colleagues in the World Bank Group.

Abbreviations

2SLS	two-stage least squares
ATM	automated teller machine
BEEPS	Business Environment and Enterprise Performance Survey
ENI	Encuesta Nacional Industrial (National Industrial Survey) (Argentina)
ES	Enterprise Survey
FE	fixed effects
GDP	gross domestic product
HIE	high-income exporters
ICOR	incremental capital output ratio
ICRG	*International Country Risk Guide*
INE	Instituto Nacional de Estadística (National Institute of Statistics) (Uruguay)
ISO	International Organization for Standardization
IV	instrumental variable
NBFI	nonbank financial institution
NTB	nontariff barriers
OECD	Organisation for Economic Co-operation and Development
OLS	ordinary least squares
PISA	Programme for International Student Assessment
R&D	research and development
SMEs	small and medium enterprises
TFP	total factor productivity
UN Comtrade	United Nations Commodity Trade Statistics Database
WEF	World Economic Forum

1

Is Another Study of Economic Performance in Latin America and the Caribbean Needed?

Verónica Alaimo, Pablo Fajnzylber,
J. Luis Guasch, J. Humberto López, and
Ana María Oviedo

Per capita growth in the Latin American region between 2004 and 2006 has averaged 2.7 percent and is now at a level not seen since the mid 1970s. Yet there are few reasons to be complacent about the current situation. In particular, despite the positive performance of the region, it appears that Latin America is lagging the rest of the world, that there are issues about the long-term sustainability of such strong performance, and that the region is not fully exploiting the opportunities created by a positive global economic environment. What are the major reasons behind this performance? Is it related to low investment rates, to low returns of investment, or to low total factor productivity? Perhaps more importantly, what policy areas deserve more attention?

Since 2003, Latin America and the Caribbean (Latin America hereafter) has shown signs of significant economic improvement (figure 1.1). Between the end of 2003 and the end of 2006, Chile, the Dominican Republic, Ecuador, and Peru reached per capita growth rates above 3.5 percent, whereas Argentina, Uruguay, and the República Bolivariana de Venezuela grew at annual per capita growth rates above 7 percent. Median per capita growth[1] in the region since 2003 has averaged 2.7 percent and would now be at a level not

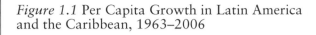

Figure 1.1 Per Capita Growth in Latin America and the Caribbean, 1963–2006

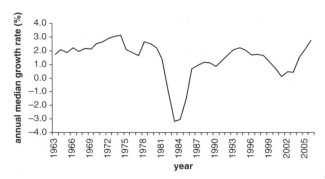

Source: Authors' calculations based on data from World Bank 2007a, 2007b.

Note: The series has been smoothed with a backward-looking three-year moving average.

seen since the mid 1970s, when the region experienced growth rates around 3 percent. Given that since 1970 median per capita growth in the region has rarely averaged more than 2.5 percent over a three-year period, this achievement is nothing short of remarkable and could be interpreted as the result of an acceleration in structural growth rates that is perhaps attributable to the significant reforms implemented by a large number of countries of the region during the 1990s. So does this achievement mean that policy makers and, more generally, development practitioners focusing on Latin America should no longer be concerned about economic growth?

The truth is that there are few reasons to be complacent about the current situation. First, even if the region managed to sustain the current trends, the corresponding growth rates would be insufficient to achieve fast poverty reduction in the short run. According to Perry and others (2007), Latin America's (headcount) poverty rate (using a poverty line of US$2 purchasing power parity per day) is currently close to 25 percent. This finding, together with an average growth elasticity of poverty of around 1.4 for the region (see Gasparini, Gutiérrez, and Tornarolli 2007), would imply that according to current trends, the region would need about 25 years to achieve a poverty rate that is below 10 percent. The need to achieve faster growth rates is even more pressing when national statistics are used to measure poverty: in that case, the current regional poverty rate would be around 40 percent (see figure 2.1 in Perry and others 2007).

Second, although the region's recent performance is quite impressive by historical standards, so far it is only a three-year run, which is driven, to a significant extent, by external factors, such as a favorable global environment, high commodity prices, and the voracious appetite of countries such as China and India for raw materials and intermediate goods from Latin America. It is unclear how much longer such a set of favorable conditions will persist.

Third, and perhaps more important in this context, the improvements on the growth front observed in Latin America are consistent with those observed in the rest of the world. Figure 1.2 plots the deviations of Latin America's annual growth rates with respect to the median growth rate of the world (excluding Latin America).[2] When this deviation is positive (negative) it implies that the region was growing faster (slower) than the typical country in the world (as captured by the median). Thus, figure 1.2 presents Latin American growth estimates from which the effect of the international business cycle has somewhat been eliminated.

Inspection of figure 1.2 suggests several interesting facts. First, even in the 1960s and 1970s, when Latin American growth rates were at historical maxima, the region was falling behind with respect to many other regions (that is, it does not seem to have fully exploited the opportunities presented by the global economy). This point is also made by Perry and others (2007) in their comparison of the performance of the region with that of the Organisation for Economic Co-operation and Development (OECD), East Asia, and the countries of the periphery of Europe. Second, for a number of years during the lost decade of the 1980s, the region experienced growth rates that were 4 to 5 percent lower than those observed globally.

Figure 1.2 Per Capita Growth in Latin America and the Caribbean, Taking into Account Deviations with Respect to Global Trends, 1963–2005

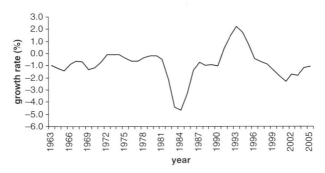

Source: Authors' calculations based on data from World Bank 2007b.
Note: The figure shows the annual median growth rate of the region minus the annual median growth rate of the rest of the world. The series has been smoothed with a backward-looking three-year moving average.

This period of low growth further contributed to the backwardness of the region; such low growth implies a cumulative loss of about 25 percent of per capita gross domestic product (GDP) for the median country in the region with respect to the median country in the world. Third, after the recovery of the early 1990s, the relative performance of the region with respect to the rest of the world has again been disappointing. In fact, since the mid 1990s, Latin America has been losing ground with respect to the median country of the rest of the world at an average of 1 percent per year. In other words, the current situation would somewhat mirror that in the 1960s and 1970s, when despite having high growth rates by historical standards, the region was getting, in relative terms, poorer.

Could this last finding be driven by the choice of the reference group? After all, the "rest of the world" includes developed and developing countries, countries rich in natural resources and net importers of commodities, countries that have experienced important crises over the past decade and economies that have had smooth rides. To further explore this issue, figure 1.3 presents the equivalent to figure 1.2 but uses different reference groups: the OECD (panel a); the group of middle-income countries (panel b); East Asia, a region that went through a profound crisis in the late 1990s (panel c); and a group of economies that are abundant in natural resources[3] outside the Latin American region (panel d). Figure 1.3 suggests that at least for the past few years and for some of the reference groups the picture is more nuanced than the one emerging from figure 1.2.[4] Because Latin America's growth rates have recovered since 2003, the region seems to be closing the existing gap in per capita growth rates with respect to East Asia and the natural resource–abundant economies. In the case of the OECD, it appears to have already closed that gap. Thus, the recent recovery in growth rates has to be recognized. Yet despite these gains, the reading of the different panels in figure 1.3 is that in relative terms (that is, taking into account developments in other regions of the world) the growth rates that are now observed in the region cannot be considered exceptional. There still is ample room for further improvement, particularly given the significant differences in initial conditions.

Clearly, one natural question that arises in this context regards the extent to which Latin American fluctuations are correlated with fluctuations observed elsewhere. That is, to what extent is growth in one region related to developments in another region either because of causality (developments in one region affect GDP outcomes in another) or because of the existence of common factors (such as a global or international business cycle that affects all countries in a similar fashion)?

To somewhat address this question, table 1.1 presents correlation coefficients both contemporaneous and at one- and two-year lag periods[5] (that is, how growth in the reference group one and two years ago correlates

Figure 1.3 Per Capita Growth in Latin America and the Caribbean, Taking into Account Deviations with Respect to Selected Country Groups, 1963–2005

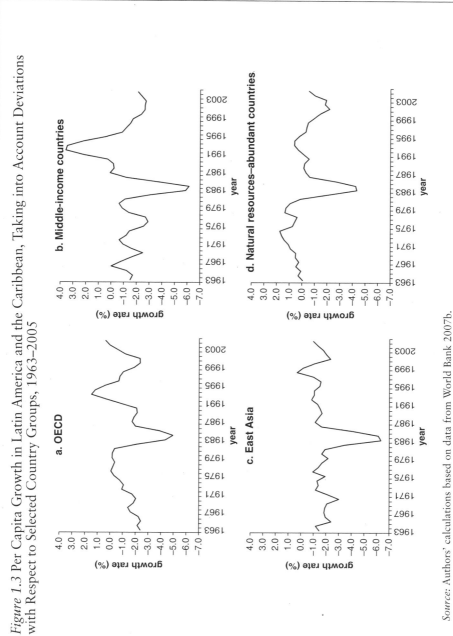

Source: Authors' calculations based on data from World Bank 2007b.
Note: The figure shows the annual median growth rate of the region minus the annual median growth rate of the reference group. The series has been smoothed with a backward-looking three-year moving average.

with observed growth in Latin America today) computed over the period from 1961 to 2005. Inspection of table 1.1 indicates that over the past 45 years, there has been a significant positive correlation between the growth rates observed in Latin America and those in the reference groups under consideration. For example, the contemporaneous correlation coefficient between Latin America's per capita growth and per capita growth series for the world, OECD, and natural resource–abundant groups would be more than 0.4, whereas the correlation coefficient computed with one lag would be around 0.3. When instead middle-income and East Asian countries are used as reference groups, the correlation coefficients are, respectively, 0.6 (at the one lag interval) and 0.3 (contemporaneous). Thus, the evidence that emerges from this basic analysis suggests some degree of business-cycle synchronization between different regions and therefore justifies the comparative analysis in figures 1.2 and 1.3.

However, the significant heterogeneity among the countries in the region must also be recognized. In fact, not all countries are experiencing growth rates lower than those observed in the median country of the rest of the world. Figure 1.4 plots once more per capita growth rates in deviation with respect to global trends, but now at the country level for 20 Latin American economies. In the figure, the countries have been ordered by overall size of the economy (that is, by GDP levels in 2005).

Several aspects emerge from this picture. First, when one looks at the entire period in the different panels, it is difficult to find episodes when a Latin American country has been performing above global trends in a *sustained* fashion. In other words, the lack of growth sustainability has been a trademark of the Latin American region. The only exceptions are Brazil and Paraguay in the 1970s and Chile in the late 1980s and 1990s. Beyond those cases, one observes a tendency to either hover around the global

Table 1.1 Correlations in Per Capita Growth Rates between Latin America and Some Reference Groups, 1961–2005

Reference group	Lag period		
	−2	*−1*	*0*
World	0.21	0.30*	0.41*
OECD	0.2	0.32*	0.42*
United States	0.08	0.43*	0.27*
European Monetary Union	−0.09	−0.08	0.37*
Natural resource–abundant countries	0.24	0.25**	0.44*
Middle-income countries	0.49*	0.61*	0.15
East Asia	0.16	0.17	0.33*

Source: Authors' calculations.
Note: * = significant at the 5 percent level; ** = significant at the 10 percent level.

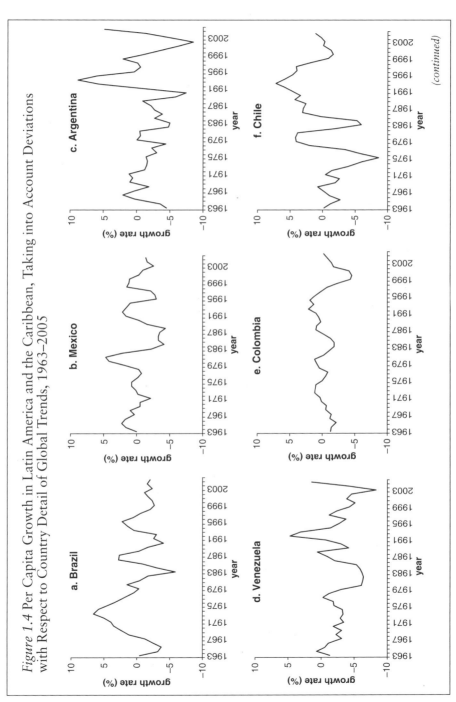

Figure 1.4 Per Capita Growth in Latin America and the Caribbean, Taking into Account Deviations with Respect to Country Detail of Global Trends, 1963–2005

(continued)

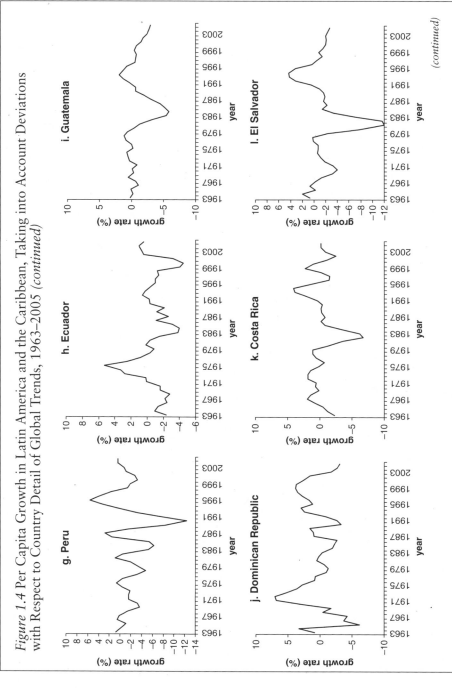

Figure 1.4 Per Capita Growth in Latin America and the Caribbean, Taking into Account Deviations with Respect to Country Detail of Global Trends, 1963–2005 *(continued)*

(continued)

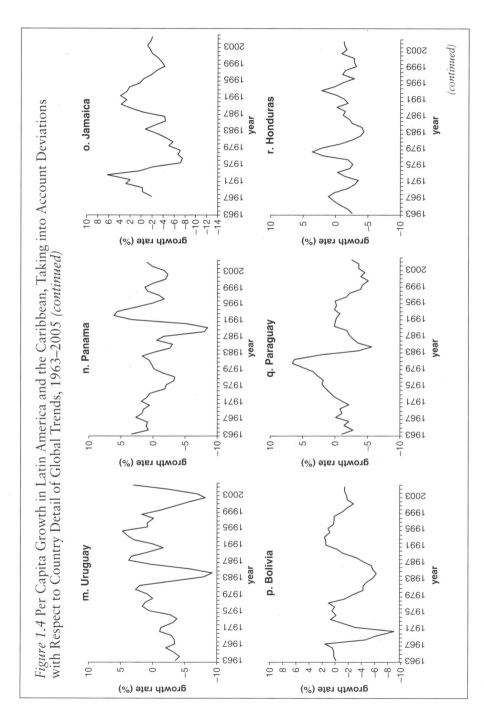

Figure 1.4 Per Capita Growth in Latin America and the Caribbean, Taking into Account Deviations with Respect to Country Detail of Global Trends, 1963–2005 *(continued)*

(continued)

9

Figure 1.4 Per Capita Growth in Latin America and the Caribbean, Taking into Account Deviations with Respect to Country Detail of Global Trends, 1963–2005 *(continued)*

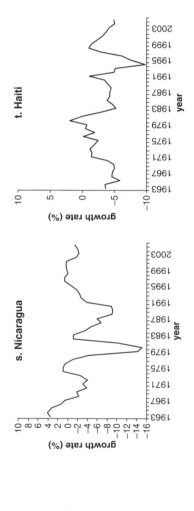

Source: Authors' calculations based on data from World Bank 2007b.

Note: Countries have been ordered by overall size of the economy. The figure shows the annual median growth rate of the region minus annual median growth rate of the reference group. The series have been smoothed with a backward looking three-year moving average.

trend or be clearly below it. Second, and focusing on the most recent years, one can see that in 2005 almost two-thirds of Latin American countries had growth rates lower than global trends. That is, the disappointing performance on the growth front in relative terms extends well beyond the median country and would reach a significant majority of countries in the region. Third, the problem is less marked in the larger economies. For example, among the seven largest economies, four had positive deviations during recent years: Argentina, Chile, Peru, and the República Bolivariana de Venezuela. In two of these cases (Argentina and the República Bolivariana de Venezuela), however, the relatively high growth rates observed recently have come after an especially profound crisis in the early years of the present decade, with drops in per capita GDP of about 20 percent.[6] In contrast, among the 13 smallest economies, only three countries (Ecuador, Panama, and Uruguay) had recent positive deviations with respect to global trends.

On the whole, the previous discussion indicates that the track record of the region on the growth front during the past 40 years has been quite poor. Moreover, while one must recognize the marked economic improvement in per capita GDP growth rates experienced by the region since 2003, one must also recognize that when these rates are compared with the experience in a variety of countries (developed, middle-income, East Asian, and natural resource–abundant countries), there is still plenty of room for improvement in the region. Thus, even though the region is going through reasonably good times on the growth front, understanding the factors that may help tackle and secure the so far elusive long-term sustainability of economic growth is still a priority for most Latin American countries.

Where to Go from Here?

What leads to poor performance on the (per capita) growth front? From an accounting perspective, two main reasons may explain differences in per capita growth rates across countries. One is differences in capital accumulation (that is, investment). When savings (either domestic or foreign) are converted into domestic investment, output per worker typically expands. For example the neoclassical growth models of Cass (1965), Koopmans (1965), and Solow (1956) and the "AK" models of Frankel (1962) and Romer (1986) all emphasized capital accumulation as the source of economic growth. True, in the short run, the relationship between investment and growth tends to be weak at best, and a number of papers have found even negative correlations (Attanasio, Picci, and Scorcu 2000; Blomstrom, Lipsey, and Zejan 1996; Loayza, Fajnzylber and Calderón 2005). Yet over the long run, investment appears to be one of the few robust correlates of economic growth (Levine and Renelt 1992).

The second reason that may explain differences in growth rates is differences in factor productivity. This source is particularly important because a number of recent papers have argued that cross-country variations in GDP growth are mostly driven by cross-country differences in total factor productivity (TFP) (see Easterly and Levine 2001; Loayza, Fajnzylber and Calderón 2005). Whereas TFP—being calculated as a residual after subtracting from observed GDP growth the contributions attributable to the expansion of labor and capital stocks—has been fairly described as "a measure of our ignorance," economists have often interpreted it as an indicator of technological change. In other words, TFP growth is often thought to be the result of product or production process innovations that increase the value that can be produced using the same amount of factor inputs (that is, capital and labor). Models emphasizing technological progress as the main engine of economic growth include those of Aghion and Howitt (1992, 1998) and Romer (1990), among others.[7] As will be discussed, however, several caveats should be kept in mind when relating TFP growth exclusively to innovation and technological change, including the fact that TFP could reflect unobserved improvements in the quality of factors of production, related for instance to human capital accumulation or the upgrading of physical infrastructure.

Investment in Latin America

How does Latin America score in each of these two different areas? To start with investment, the rates of capital accumulation found in the Latin American region seem to be relatively low. As can be seen in figure 1.5, which plots gross capital formation for different geographic regions and for countries in different income groups, the only geographic region with investment rates lower than those of Latin America in 2004 is Sub-Saharan Africa, which, like Latin America, exhibits investment rates that hover around 20 percent. At the other extreme is East Asia and the Pacific, with investment rates close to 35 percent of GDP, followed by the Middle East and North Africa, where gross capital formation represents between 25 and 30 percent of GDP. Latin America's investment levels are also lower than those found in both low- and middle-income countries, whereas they are comparable to those of high-income countries.

The low investment rates in Latin America suggested by figure 1.5 are in part a reflection of the situation found in countries such as Bolivia, Uruguay, and El Salvador, which in 2004 had investment rates of 12, 13, and 16 percent of GDP, respectively. True, the evidence of a single year is likely to offer a somewhat distorted view of the situation. Yet as seen in figure 1.6, when one considers the average investment rate of the median Latin American country over the period from 2000 to 2005 or over the longer time span from 1970 to 2005, the value is still around 21 percent of GDP.[8]

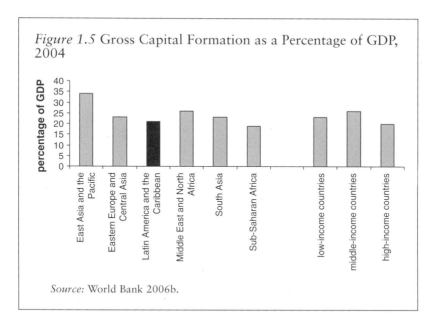

Figure 1.5 Gross Capital Formation as a Percentage of GDP, 2004

Source: World Bank 2006b.

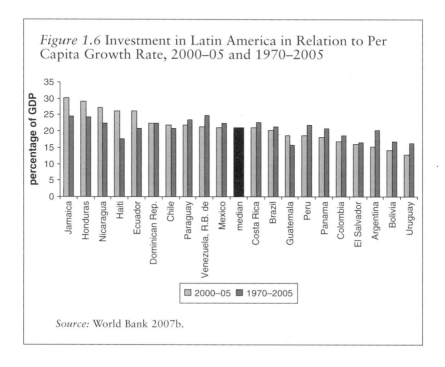

Figure 1.6 Investment in Latin America in Relation to Per Capita Growth Rate, 2000–05 and 1970–2005

Source: World Bank 2007b.

What does change when a longer time horizon is used is the dispersion found across countries, which becomes much smaller. For example, from 1970 to 2005, investment rates ranged from 16 percent of GDP (Guatemala) to 25 percent of GDP (the República Bolivariana de Venezuela), whereas from 2000 to 2005, they ranged from 13 percent of GDP (Uruguay) to 30 percent of GDP (Jamaica). Another interesting regularity that emerges from the data in figure 1.6 is that there is considerable "inertia" in investment rates. Regardless of whether one looks at the most recent history or at the past three and one-half decades, some countries exhibit relatively high investment rates (such as the Dominican Republic, Honduras, and Jamaica), while others appear to have persistently low investment rates (such as Bolivia, El Salvador, and Uruguay). This finding is confirmed and illustrated in table 1.2, which reports the results of estimating a simple autoregressive model for the investment rate using annual pooled data. Indeed, the autoregressive parameter in this regression varies from 0.72, when one allows for heterogeneous parameters across countries, to 0.80, when all countries are pooled together.

Another interesting finding that emerges from inspecting figure 1.6 in conjunction with information on countries' growth performance is that investment and per capita growth rates do not appear to have a high correlation. For example, among the countries with high investment rates is not only the best growth performer over the 1970 to 2005 period (the Dominican Republic), but also countries with below-average growth performances such as Honduras and Jamaica. Similarly, among the countries with low investment rates is not only Bolivia, which has a poor growth record, but also Uruguay, which has performed above average. Finally, countries like Brazil and Chile, with investment rates around the average, have had growth records that are among the best in the region.

Table 1.2 The Persistence of Investment Rates in Latin America

Variable	Pooled ordinary least squares	Fixed effects	Heterogeneous
Investment rate (−1)	0.8	0.74	0.72
Standard error	0.02	0.02	0.03
R-squared	0.66	0.66	
Number of observations	860	860	860
Number of countries	20	20	20

Source: Authors' calculations.
Note: The dependent variable is the investment rate. The table reports the results of regressing gross fixed capital formation as a share of GDP on the lagged dependent variable. All the regressions include a constant. The column "Heterogeneous" reports the average autoregressive parameter of estimating individual country regressions.

Figure 1.7 further explores the relationship between investment and growth. The figure plots investment (gross capital formation as a percentage of GDP) against per capita growth in the region for the 20 Latin American countries under consideration. It also breaks the sample into different time periods (1970s, 1980s, 1990s, and 2000s, as well as the

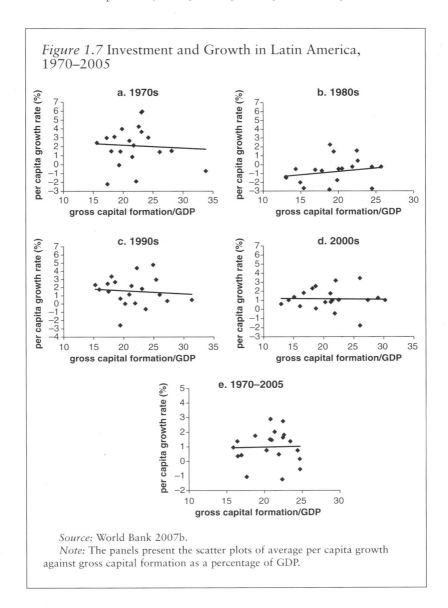

Figure 1.7 Investment and Growth in Latin America, 1970–2005

Source: World Bank 2007b.
Note: The panels present the scatter plots of average per capita growth against gross capital formation as a percentage of GDP.

period from 1970 to 2005) to explore whether the relationship between investment and growth rates varies over time.

Inspection of figure 1.7 indicates that in the 1980s there was a modest positive (but statistically insignificant) correlation; however, during the other periods under consideration, Latin America's investment and GDP growth rates do not show any significant positive correlation. In fact, the point estimates of the slopes are negative in a number of cases.

This picture is in contrast to what is observed when the exercise is repeated using the rest of the world (figure 1.8),[9] where investment and growth appear to be positively correlated. The point estimates of the slopes of the regression lines in this global sample (a) are always positive, (b) would range from around 0.07 in the 1980s to about 0.20 in the 1970s and 2000s, and (c) would be statistically significant in all cases. For the period from 1970 to 2005, the point estimate of the slope of the regression line is 0.12, which would roughly correspond with an incremental capital output ratio (ICOR) of about 8.[10]

Thus, it seems not only that Latin America's investment rate is low but also that the existing investment has had a low return in terms of its growth payoff. This last element is particularly important, because if the problem were lack of capital, growth strategies aimed at shifting spending from consumption to capital accumulation might lead to rapid growth accelerations. However, the dispersion in growth outcomes that emerges from figure 1.7 also suggests that growth strategies that rely solely on raising investment levels without addressing possible constraints to the productivity of capital may be doomed to fail. In other words, policy makers should be concerned not only with promoting a larger *quantity* of investment, but also with creating conditions that are conducive to investments of a better *quality*, which pay off by increasing the productivity and competitiveness of firms and generating sustained growth.

Factor Productivity

As discussed previously, in an accounting approach, the second factor affecting growth performance is factor productivity. The tradition in the economics literature of factor productivity dates back to Robert Solow, who in the late 1950s first decomposed output growth in a weighted average of the rate of growth of labor and capital and of a residual that became known as *total factor productivity growth*.

More specifically, consider a simple neoclassical production function that relates output Y to physical capital K, labor L, and the level of total factor productivity A through a Cobb-Douglas production function:

$$Y = AK^{\alpha} L^{1-\alpha}. \tag{1.1}$$

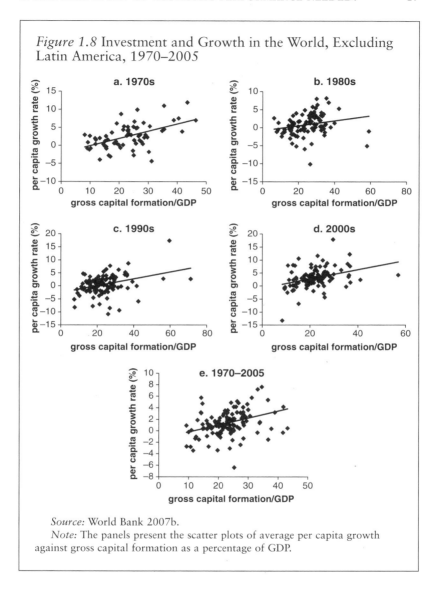

Figure 1.8 Investment and Growth in the World, Excluding Latin America, 1970–2005

Source: World Bank 2007b.
Note: The panels present the scatter plots of average per capita growth against gross capital formation as a percentage of GDP.

If one takes logs and time derivatives in equation 1.1 and rearranges, it follows that:

$$\text{TFP growth} = \text{GDP growth} - S_K * K \text{ growth} - (1 - S_K) * L \text{ growth}, \quad (1.2)$$

where S_K is the share of capital in income.[11] In this decomposition, capital growth consists simply of investment net of depreciation, and labor growth comprises only the expansion of the working-age population. TFP growth is therefore the part of GDP growth that cannot be explained by capital growth (K growth) and labor growth (L growth), and this component is typically interpreted by the economics profession as a measure of technological change.

True, this measure of technological change has a number of important limitations. First, the TFP component can have significant noise. By construction, the TFP component is a residual and, as such, any measurement errors present in the variables used to measure labor and capital are automatically passed to TFP. In other words, measurement error in the factors of production will be interpreted as productivity changes. Second, as noted by Loayza, Fajnzylber, and Calderón (2005), even if there is no measurement error in the production factors, estimates of TFP can capture forces other than technological change. For example, TFP can also reflect the role played by economies of scale and externalities included in many growth models or even the occurrence of changes in the sectoral composition of output. Finally, the TFP estimates are based on the assumption of independence among employment growth, capital accumulation, and productivity growth—an assumption that is unlikely to be very realistic. As argued by a number of authors (Klenow and Rodríguez-Clare 1997; Maloney and Rodríguez-Clare 2006), (a) TFP growth can help materialize previously unprofitable investment projects, so that the rate of capital accumulation will depend on productivity growth, and (b) many technological innovations are embodied in capital goods and, thus, associated with investment, which makes TFP growth dependent on the rate and factors that determine capital accumulation.

With those caveats in mind, one may now explore differences in TFP growth between Latin America and other regions. Figure 1.9 presents the results of such an exercise for the median country of each region or group of reference. Inspection of this figure suggests that Latin America's TFP growth has not been particularly high. In fact, except for the periods from 1971 to 1975 and from 1991 to 1995, Latin America's TFP growth rates have been lower than those of most of the other regions.

For example, between 2001 and 2005, the only group that had lower TFP growth than Latin America (1.1 percent per year on average) was the OECD (0.77 percent per year). This finding is in contrast to the productivity performance of East Asia and the Pacific, the Middle East and North Africa, South Asia, and even Sub-Saharan Africa, where the TFP growth rate was around 2 percent per year on average. Similarly, from 1976 to 1980, TFP growth was around 2 percent per year for Latin America, but during that same period, East Asia had TFP growth rates above 4 percent and the Middle East and North Africa, South Asia, and the OECD had TFP growth rates of around 3 percent. More dramatically, from 1981 to 1985 and from 1996 to 2000, Latin America is clearly the

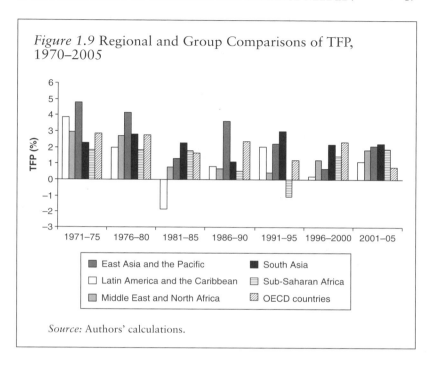

Figure 1.9 Regional and Group Comparisons of TFP, 1970–2005

Source: Authors' calculations.

worst performer, with TFP growth rates of –1.83 percent and 0.20 percent, respectively.

From 1971 to 2005, Latin America experienced an average productivity growth of 1.6 percent per year. This rate would be similar to the one for Sub-Saharan African and well below the one for East Asia and the Pacific (3.8 percent) and the OECD (2.8 percent).

There is, however, significant country heterogeneity within the Latin American region (figure 1.10 and table 1.3).[12] For example, over the 2001 to 2005 period, one can find countries such as Trinidad and Tobago, where TFP growth was greater than 6 percent, and countries such as El Salvador and Mexico, where it was negative. Beyond those extreme cases, during the first five years of the 21st century, the Latin American countries in the sample display TFP growth rates that generally lie between 1 and 2 percent. Alternatively, during the 1970 to 2005 period, the country displaying higher TFP growth would have been Chile (above 2 percent per year on average), followed by Uruguay (1.9 percent per year on average) and Brazil (1.7 percent per year on average). At the other extreme, it is possible to find Jamaica, which had negative TFP growth over the past three and one-half decades, and the República Bolivariana de Venezuela, which had an average estimated annual TFP growth of less than 0.1 percent.

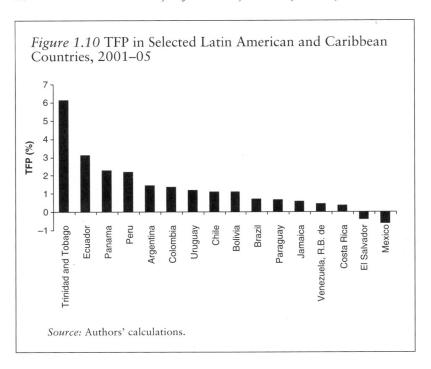

Figure 1.10 TFP in Selected Latin American and Caribbean Countries, 2001–05

Source: Authors' calculations.

As for the relevance of TFP in explaining growth fluctuations, the last row of table 1.3 indicates that the share of cross-country growth fluctuations explained by TFP would have ranged between 56 percent in the 1981 to 1985 period and 91 percent in 1991 to 1995 period. For the whole period being considered here, the average would be 75 percent. In other words, for the Latin American sample under consideration, differences in factor productivity may explain almost three-fourths of cross-country differences in growth rates.

In summary, Latin America performs rather poorly on the two factors that may explain differences in per capita growth rates across countries. First, not only has the region had relatively low levels of investments, but the effect of those investments appears to have been rather low in a number of countries. And second, the region also scores rather low on its capacity to efficiently use and improve the inputs of production.

A First Pass at the Investment Climate

So far, this chapter has shown that even with the significant improvements in the growth performance since 2003, Latin America can and

Table 1.3 Total Factor Productivity in Latin America: Selected Countries

Country and growth component	Growth (%)						
	1970–75	1975–80	1981–85	1985–90	1991–95	1996–2000	2001–05
Argentina							
GDP	3.10	2.81	−2.53577	−0.47	6.55	2.58	1.99
Capital	1.53	0.93	1.24	1.40	1.70	1.40	1.39
Labor	−0.84	0.72	−1.30	−1.66	0.70	2.09	−0.73
TFP	2.51	1.97	−2.76	−0.65	5.25	0.90	1.45
Bolivia							
GDP	5.79	2.05	−1.93	2.21	4.10	3.44	3.01
Capital	−3.10	−1.29	−3.18	−1.83	0.93	4.26	0.88
Labor	2.43	2.54	2.40	2.56	2.35	2.40	2.45
TFP	5.18	0.77	−2.49	1.10	2.21	0.42	1.08
Brazil							
GDP	10.27	6.67	1.09	2.01	3.13	2.24	2.19
Capital	1.95	3.96	1.08	1.73	0.77	1.68	1.06
Labor	3.09	3.11	2.66	2.37	2.30	2.25	1.74
TFP	7.58	3.27	−1.02	−0.14	1.36	0.19	0.68
Chile							
GDP	−1.36	7.26	0.89	6.73	8.69	4.16	4.39
Capital	−2.63	−1.92	−1.07	2.09	6.58	7.26	5.46

(continued)

Table 1.3 Total Factor Productivity in Latin America: Selected Countries (continued)

Country and growth component	Growth (%)						
	1970–75	1975–80	1981–85	1985–90	1991–95	1996–2000	2001–05
Labor	2.59	2.69	2.23	1.94	1.71	1.75	1.75
TFP	-1.81	6.46	0.01	4.73	4.98	0.15	1.11
Colombia							
GDP	5.65	5.37	2.24	4.94	4.13	0.92	3.42
Capital	-1.39	0.29	2.12	2.60	4.35	2.44	2.07
Labor	3.23	3.27	3.12	2.53	2.44	2.25	2.07
TFP	4.04	3.15	-0.52	2.39	1.03	-1.40	1.36
Costa Rica							
GDP	6.04	5.24	0.28	4.59	5.47	4.93	3.71
Capital	-1.07	2.41	-0.62	2.25	4.05	4.72	4.56
Labor	3.74	4.05	3.39	2.69	2.89	3.30	2.89
TFP	3.60	1.64	-2.03	2.02	2.27	1.24	0.37
Ecuador							
GDP	8.71	5.27	1.37	2.73	2.67	0.94	4.95
Capital	3.21	6.19	2.43	1.06	1.51	0.58	1.72
Labor	3.26	3.29	3.34	3.21	2.89	1.99	1.91
TFP	5.47	0.96	-1.65	0.27	0.27	-0.55	3.11

(continued)

Table 1.3 Total Factor Productivity in Latin America: Selected Countries *(continued)*

Country and growth component	Growth (%)							
	1970–75	1975–80	1981–85	1985–90	1991–95.	1996–2000	2001–05
El Salvador							
GDP	4.61	-0.02	-2.78	2.06	6.18	3.06	2.19
Capital	-2.74	-0.41	-3.13	-1.52	2.33	3.26	3.03
Labor	2.95	2.36	1.12	2.26	3.19	2.56	2.28
TFP	4.05	-1.22	-2.11	1.39	3.35	0.21	-0.41
Jamaica							
GDP	1.77	-3.26	0.40	4.99	2.39	-0.08	1.52
Capital	0.047	-3.06	-0.99	0.66	3.12	1.91	0.60
Labor	2.13	2.79	2.85	1.08	1.20	1.05	1.15
TFP	0.47	-3.71	-0.91	4.08	0.42	-1.47	0.59
Mexico							
GDP	6.26	7.11	1.94	1.68	1.53	5.45	1.82
Capital	-0.01	2.33	2.18	0.65	2.42	3.28	3.35
Labor	3.19	3.27	3.33	3.26	2.78	2.13	1.71
TFP	4.51	4.26	-0.87	-0.41	-1.09	2.81	-0.63
Panama							
GDP			3.44	-0.67	5.49	4.63	4.16
Capital			-3.21	-4.20	0.38	3.09	1.03

(continued)

Table 1.3 Total Factor Productivity in Latin America: Selected Countries *(continued)*

Country and growth component	Growth (%)						
	1970–75	1975–80	1981–85	1985–90	1991–95	1996–2000	2001–05
Labor			3.19	2.85	2.61	2.37	2.18
TFP			1.98	-1.62	3.48	2.07	2.29
Paraguay							
GDP	6.72	11.07	1.67	3.89	3.24	0.72	1.90
Capital	-0.60	6.79	5.32	3.31	3.66	2.21	-0.53
Labor	3.17	4.00	3.17	3.38	2.93	3.27	3.04
TFP	5.48	5.65	-2.60	0.55	-0.07	-2.01	0.68
Peru							
GDP	4.99	2.28	0.32	-1.90	5.481	2.46	4.09
Capital	-1.39	-0.63	0.09	0.04	1.59	3.67	1.63
Labor	3.09	3.18	3.05	2.79	2.37	2.18	2.10
TFP	3.87	0.78	-1.43	-3.49	3.45	-0.38	2.20
Trinidad and Tobago							
GDP	2.74	7.88	-2.25	-2.24	1.39	4.95	7.68
Capital	-0.42	2.37	1.85	-2.08	2.72	2.83	2.38
Labor	2.15	2.44	1.92	0.47	1.67	1.93	1.16
TFP	1.38	5.46	-4.14	-1.92	-0.61	2.74	6.14

(continued)

Table 1.3 Total Factor Productivity in Latin America: Selected Countries (continued)

Country and growth component	Growth (%)						
	1970–75	1975–80	1981–85	1985–90	1991–95	1996–2000	2001–05
Uruguay							
GDP	1.50	4.55	-3.78	3.87	3.94	2.11	0.99
Capital	-3.85	0.75	-1.75	-2.34	0.74	2.05	-1.62
Labor	-0.03	0.57	0.54	0.69	0.79	0.61	0.81
TFP	3.14	3.90	-3.36	4.46	3.17	0.89	1.20
Venezuela, R.B. de							
GDP	2.95	2.45	-0.93	2.59	3.45	0.75	2.30
Capital	-2.05	1.92	-1.14	-1.36	0.19	3.15	1.17
Labor	4.34	4.41	3.50	2.75	2.77	2.61	2.45
TFP	1.61	-0.79	-2.24	1.77	1.89	-2.11	0.46
Percentage of growth fluctuations explained by TFP	61.55	63.91	55.70	84.00	90.68	77.57	86.32

Source: Authors' calculations using data from World Bank (2007b) for GDP and labor growth. Capital is computed using an inventory rule assuming a 7 percent depreciation of the capital stock and an initial capital to output ratio of 5. Gross investment is also from the World Bank (2007b). The share of capital is from Loayza, Fajnzylber, and Calderón (2005).

should do even better. Those gains may, in principle, be a reflection of improvements on the macroeconomic front.[13] For example, as it emerges from figure 1.11,[14] the primary fiscal balance has increased from 0.1 percent of GDP in 2002 to 1.5 percent of GDP in 2006. Similarly, public debt

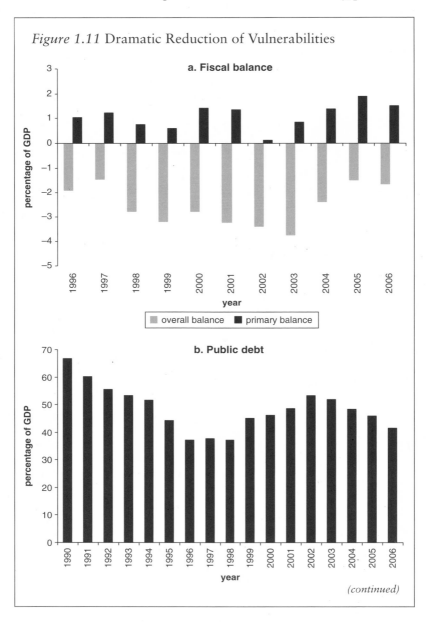

Figure 1.11 Dramatic Reduction of Vulnerabilities

(continued)

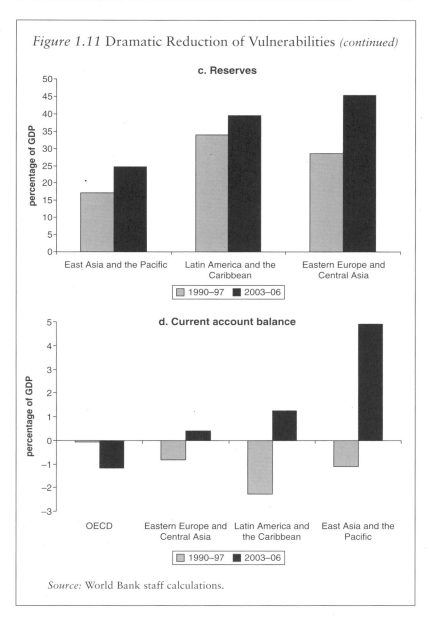

Figure 1.11 Dramatic Reduction of Vulnerabilities *(continued)*

c. Reserves

(bar chart — percentage of GDP; categories: East Asia and the Pacific, Latin America and the Caribbean, Eastern Europe and Central Asia; series: 1990–97, 2003–06)

d. Current account balance

(bar chart — percentage of GDP; categories: OECD, Eastern Europe and Central Asia, Latin America and the Caribbean, East Asia and the Pacific; series: 1990–97, 2003–06)

Source: World Bank staff calculations.

has been declining since 2002 and is now around 40 percent of GDP. On the external front, reserves have increased from 35 percent to 40 percent of the monetary base (M2), whereas the current account balance has moved from a 2 percent deficit during 1990 to 1997 to a 1 percent surplus during

2003 to 2006. Compared with the situation in the early and mid 1990s, Latin American countries today have better macroeconomic frameworks, are more open to trade, and have more developed financial sectors. Moreover, in virtually all countries, public spending in health has increased and education coverage has expanded. Although progress can still be made in these areas (openness to trade in Latin America is still very low by any standard, and financial markets are very shallow), those significant improvements in the macroeconomic framework have, in all likelihood, contributed positively to GDP growth.

But a strong macroeconomic framework is not sufficient to predict sustained high growth. It needs to be complemented by a good microeconomic environment driven by reforms in the investment climate arena. Unfortunately, however, those themes have not received the attention devoted to macroeconomic stability issues, and the corresponding policy agenda has developed very unevenly in the region. Only recently have countries begun to focus on microeconomic reforms and improvement of the investment climate in their pursuit of that elusive sustained growth. All of the usual estimations and rankings show the Latin American region lagging in microeconomic reforms and well below the average (WEF 2006; World Bank 2006a). Given the large development impact of those reforms (World Bank 2005), it can be argued that the poor investment climate in Latin America could be responsible for its weak overall economic performance and, in particular, its investment and TFP performance.

But what is the investment climate? This chapter defines *investment climate* in line with the *World Development Report 2005*, as the "factors that shape the opportunities and incentives for firms to invest productively, create jobs, and expand" (World Bank 2005: 1). After all, a country's GDP growth rate is just the result of aggregating the growth experienced by the different firms operating in the economy. In this regard, if firms find it difficult to invest and operate, one may reasonably assume that the country as a whole will experience low growth rates.

Paying attention to the investment climate is rather trivial if the main culprit behind low growth is the presence of low rates of capital accumulation. Yet even if the main reason behind a country's poor growth performance is related to low TFP growth, there may be good reasons to focus on the investment climate. As discussed previously, one of the shortcomings of TFP estimates is that they are computed under the assumption of independence between factor productivity and capital accumulation, something that is probably not very realistic, because, in practice, technological progress is likely to be embedded in capital accumulation. The likelihood is even greater in the case in developing countries, where technological progress usually takes the form of technology adoption rather than creation of new technologies and where most capital goods are imported from countries that are more advanced technologically.

Although, in principle, a wide range of factors, including both public policies and private sector characteristics, may affect productivity and investment, it might be helpful to organize the discussion about the investment climate around four broad areas that have received significant attention in the economics literature as key determinants of success: (a) the quality of governance, institutions, and regulations; (b) the availability and quality of physical infrastructure; (c) the development of the financial sector and firms' access to financial services; and (d) education, training, and the national innovation system. The subsections that follow discuss the rationale for focusing on those areas, paying special attention to the Latin American context.

The Quality of Governance and Institutions

The quality of governance and institutions can be addressed from several perspectives. One of them focuses on the prevalence of corruption and its impact on economic performance. In fact, a number of theories now link corruption to slower economic growth (see Svensson 2005 for a review on the issue). In some cases, the problem is related to entrepreneurs who choose not to start or expand an activity because of the risk that potential profits will be taken away by corruption or who select inefficient technologies that allow firms to "fly by night" in response to excessive future demands from corrupt officials (Svensson 2003). In other theories (Murphy, Shleifer, and Vishny 1991, 1993), the problem is related to the inefficient allocation of investment, technology, and human capital, because corruption may allocate resources away from their most productive uses. Finally, corruption may also affect entrepreneurial skills, with firms devoting more time to securing preferential treatments from government officials and surmounting regulatory barriers to market access (for example, because of the red tape associated with obtaining mandatory licenses and permits) than to improving productivity (Murphy, Shleifer, and Vishny 1991).

Those predictions of the theoretical literature have found empirical support in a number of microstudies. For example, Svensson (2003) argues that bribe payments faced by Ugandan firms are positively correlated with the reversibility of the installed capital. Bates (1981) argues that peasant farmers in Sub-Saharan Africa may avoid corruption by moving to (inefficient) subsistence agriculture. Finally, Fisman (2001) notes that the growth strategy of some Indonesian firms is based mainly on political connectedness. Other empirical works have focused on how corruption negatively affects human capital accumulation (Reinikka and Svensson 2005) and firm growth (Fisman and Svensson 2000), thus having a damaging impact on long-run economic growth. At the macrolevel, Mauro (1995) presents evidence indicating that countries with higher levels of corruption tend to grow less than corruption-free countries.

Beyond corruption, there are also issues related to the country's regulatory and institutional quality. Ease of entry and exit, mandatory compliance with time-consuming norms and regulations, excessive red tape and bureaucracy, unclear rules of the game, and weak rule of law, among other governance-related factors, increase significantly the cost of doing business, dissuade investments, and harm overall competitiveness and growth. The strong impact of an inefficient and burdensome regulatory environment has been extensively documented (Guasch and Hahn 1999; World Bank 2005). Mauro (1995) also finds evidence that bureaucratic inefficiency correlates negatively with growth. Djankov, McLiesh, and Ramalho (2006), using objective measures of business regulations in 135 countries, conclude that countries with better regulations grow faster: improving from the worst quartile of business regulations to the best implies a 2.3 percentage point increase in annual growth. The point of institutional quality is also made by Loayza, Oviedo, and Servén (2004), who argue that it is important to focus not only on the quantity of regulation (discussed later) but also on its quality: better institutions help mitigate and even eliminate the negative impact of regulation on growth.

Similarly, Demirgüç-Kunt, Love, and Maksimovic (2006) argue that businesses are more likely to choose the corporate form in countries with efficient legal systems, strong shareholder and creditor rights, low regulatory burdens and corporate taxes, and efficient bankruptcy processes. Their observation is important in this context because evidence also suggests that incorporated firms tend to grow faster than unincorporated firms (Harhoff, Stahl, and Woywode 1998), because corporations typically report fewer financing, legal, and regulatory obstacles than do unincorporated firms (see also chapter 2).

That Latin America has substantial room for making progress on the regulatory front is illustrated in figure 1.12, which plots the average for the six indexes contained in the Kaufmann, Kraay, and Mastruzzi (2004) database of institutional quality measured against the log per capita income level of each country. Two main messages emerge from figure 1.12. First, there is a very close association between income levels and institutional quality.[15] Second, a majority of Latin American countries (about two-thirds) are below the regression line (that is, they have indexes of institutional quality that are below what one would expect for their level of development).

Latin America also performs poorly with regard to the "ease of doing business" indicators produced by the World Bank. Indeed, Latin America is the region with the largest number of both procedures (12) and days (66) required to start a new business (figure 1.13). Those numbers compare with 9 procedures and 56 days in East Asia or 7 procedures and 24 days in high-income countries. Even Sub-Saharan Africa performs better than Latin America with respect to the number of days (64) and procedures (11) required to start a business. Latin America also scores poorly

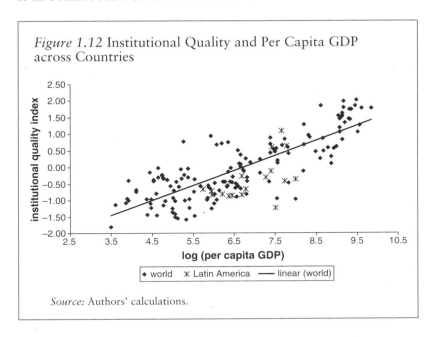

Figure 1.12 Institutional Quality and Per Capita GDP across Countries

Source: Authors' calculations.

regarding the time required to enforce contracts—470 days, compared with 423 in East Asia and 282 in high-income countries—and the financial and ownership information that companies are mandated to disclose to the public (a measure of investment protection). Indeed, the average Latin American country obtains a score of 4 in the World Bank's Doing Business Disclosure Index, compared with a score of 5 for other low- and middle-income countries and 6 for high-income countries.

Similarly, according to statistics presented in González and Lamanna (2007), Latin America is the region with the highest (a) total number of taxes paid by businesses (49); (b) number of hours per year needed to prepare, file, and pay taxes (549); and (c) taxes paid as a percentage of profit (54.5 percent). Those figures compare with 40 taxes, 398 hours, and 48.5 percent of profits in an average low- or middle-income country and 18 taxes, 181 hours, and 38.8 percent of profits in an average high-income country.

The Availability and Quality of Infrastructure

As documented by Calderón, Easterly, and Servén (2003), the 1980s and 1990s saw a widening of the infrastructure gap (both in terms of quantity and quality) between Latin America and successful East Asian countries. To some extent, this widening would have been the result of declines in

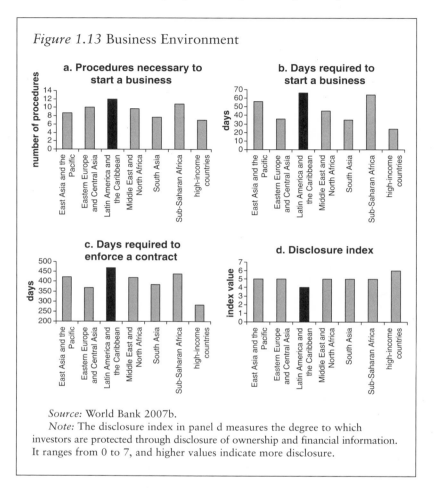

Figure 1.13 Business Environment

Source: World Bank 2007b.
Note: The disclosure index in panel d measures the degree to which
investors are protected through disclosure of ownership and financial information.
It ranges from 0 to 7, and higher values indicate more disclosure.

public infrastructure spending during the late 1980s and 1990s, which
were not offset by comparable increases in private spending (figure 1.14).
Given that infrastructure spending appears to be a good predictor of
growth in infrastructure stocks, one could infer that Latin America's infrastructure gap is not likely to close unless spending increases substantially.

This observation is particularly important in this context because several studies have estimated a possible cross-country association between
economic growth and infrastructure growth (Easterly and Rebelo 1993;
Esfahani and Ramírez 2003). In addition, infrastructure has been found to
contribute significantly to output, with rates of return that are sometimes
found to be larger than those of noninfrastructure capital (Calderón and
Servén 2003; Gramlich 1994). Similarly, Guasch (2005) has shown that
poor infrastructure and limited transport and trade services tend to increase

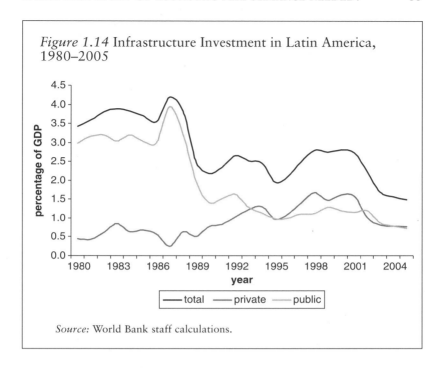

Figure 1.14 Infrastructure Investment in Latin America, 1980–2005

Source: World Bank staff calculations.

logistics costs—which are about 25 percent of product value in Latin America versus 9 percent in OECD countries (figure 1.15, panel a)—as well as to render otherwise competitive products uncompetitive and limit rural production and people's access to markets, which, in turn, adversely affects poverty and economic activity. Poor electrical infrastructure also appears to have negative impact on the bottom lines of Latin American firms. In fact, in countries such as Ecuador, Honduras, and Nicaragua, more than 3 percent of annual sales are lost to power outages (figure 1.15, panel b).

According to estimates by Calderón and Servén (2003), the slowdown in infrastructure investments in Latin America relative to East Asia could account for about one-third of the widening output gap between the average Latin American and Asian countries. True, there is significant country heterogeneity, and in some countries, such as Uruguay, infrastructure may account for a mere 12 percent of the widening gap. Yet in other countries, such as Chile (the best performer in the region), lags on the infrastructure front may account for two-thirds of the output gap.

The Development of the Financial Sector

Well-functioning financial systems ameliorate the problems created by information and transaction costs and help to allocate resources across space and time. Not surprisingly, a large number of studies have found a

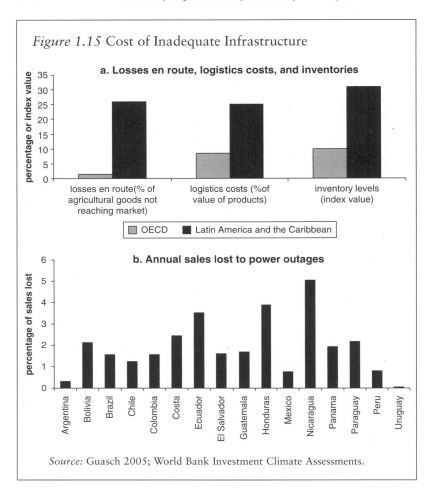

Figure 1.15 Cost of Inadequate Infrastructure

a. Losses en route, logistics costs, and inventories

Source: Guasch 2005; World Bank Investment Climate Assessments.

robust relationship between the level of financial development and long-run growth (Beck, Levine, and Loayza 2000; Loayza, Fajnzylber, and Calderón 2005). Financial development affects capital accumulation and technological innovation through at least five channels: (a) by facilitating risk management, (b) by reducing the costs of acquiring information about new investment opportunities, (c) by simplifying corporate control over managers, (d) by mobilizing savings, and (e) by facilitating exchanges and thus promoting specialization and innovation (Levine 1997).

How does the Latin American region fare in this area? Figure 1.16 presents the ratio of domestic credit to the private sector as a percentage of GDP for several regions in 1990 and 2004. Credit is an important link in the monetary transmission process because it finances production, consumption,

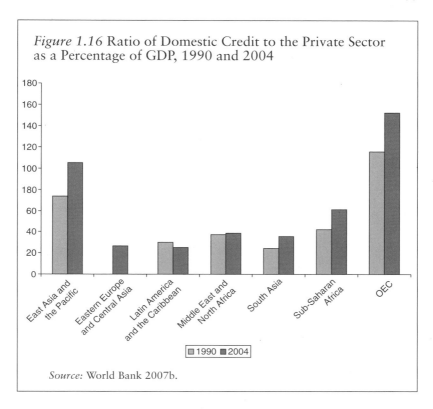

Figure 1.16 Ratio of Domestic Credit to the Private Sector as a Percentage of GDP, 1990 and 2004

Source: World Bank 2007b.

and capital formation, which, in turn, affect the overall level of economic activity. Figure 1.16 indicates (a) that Latin America is well behind not only the high-income countries but also most of the other regions of the developing world and (b) that over the past one and one-half decades credit to the private sector (as a percentage of GDP) has remained basically constant in Latin America, while it has significantly increased in other regions.

A related concern is whether access to financial services at the household and firm level—an issue that is often denominated *financial breadth*—is also comparatively low in the Latin American region, as the relatively low levels of financial depth would lead one to expect. Indeed, a booming literature now argues that imperfect capital markets coupled with fixed investment costs imply that important segments of the population may get excluded from investment or education opportunities. For example, Banerjee and Newman (1994) stress the effect that an individual's initial wealth has on the level of physical investment when there are credit constraints. Thus, for a given income level, countries with high inequality (that is, most countries in Latin America) and limited access to the financial sector can be expected to have lower investment rates and hence also lower growth. Similarly, Aghion, Caroli, and García-Penalosa (1999) show that if (a) there are decreasing returns with respect to individual capital investments and (b) credit imperfections mean that individual investments are an increasing function of initial endowments, then the concentration of investment in fewer richer people (that is, high inequality) will negatively affect growth.

Although international comparative data on the extent to which firms and households use financial services remain limited, figure 1.17 reports a summary financial system breadth index constructed by the World Bank on the basis of indicators of demographic and geographic penetration of physical bank outlets and on the basis of the number and average size of bank loans and deposits. Figure 1.17 suggests that access to financial services in Latin America is considerably behind that found in high-income countries. However, it is very close to the level of financial breadth observed in other middle-income countries, and it is above the level observed in low-income countries. In terms of this summary financial access index, Latin America is also ahead of East Asia and the Pacific and South Asia, as well as Sub-Saharan Africa, whereas it is behind Eastern Europe and Central Asia and the Middle East and North Africa.

Table 1.4 (adapted from Beck, Demirgüç-Kunt, and Martínez Pería 2005) shows some of the physical penetration variables on which the index reported in figure 1.17 is based. These data show that Latin America exhibits the lowest indexes of geographic penetration of bank branches and automated teller machines (ATMs) of the developing world. When measured per capita, however, the penetration of physical banking services outlets appears to be higher in Latin America than in most other regions. Moreover, the costs of maintaining a bank account and the fees associated with loans are

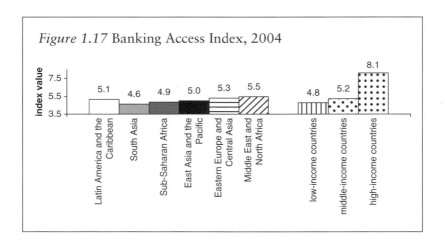

Figure 1.17 Banking Access Index, 2004

Table 1.4 Factors That Might Affect Access to the Financial Sector

Factor	Latin America	Eastern Europe and Central Asia	East Asia and the Pacific	South Asia	Middle East and North Africa	Sub-Saharan Africa
Physical bank presence						
Branches per 1,000 square kilometers	4.8	7.5	15.5	20.0	33.8	6.3
Branches per 100,000 people	9.3	8.6	6.8	4.5	9.5	2.9
ATMs per 1,000 square kilometers	10.3	16.1	71.6	3.2	50.8	14.3
ATMs per 100,000 people	19	19.9	21.4	1.1	12.5	6.7
Cost of using banking services						
Fees associated with checking accounts (as a % of GDP per capita)	0.9	0.2	0.0	5.5	0.5	10.4
Fees associated with savings accounts (as a % of GDP per capita)	0.6	0.1	0.1	3.0	0	1.8
Average fees on loans (as a % of GDP per capita)	1.6	1.2	1.3	4.5	0.8	1.3

Source: Beck, Demirgüç-Kunt, and Martínez Pería 2005.

higher in Latin America than in most of the other regions of the developing world, with the exception of South Asia and Sub-Saharan Africa.

Education, Training, and the National Innovation System

Innovation and human capital are major drivers of growth and productivity. Roughly half of cross-country differences in per capita income are driven by differences in TFP, generally attributed to technological development and innovative capacity (Dollar and Wolff 1998; Hall and Jones 1999). According to Prescott (1998), one of the main candidates to explain large international income and productivity (TFP) differences is resistance to the adoption of new technologies and to the efficient use of current operating technologies, which, in turn, are conditioned by the institutional and policy arrangements of each society. Moreover, productivity growth is intrinsically related to the availability of a skilled workforce and to the extent to which countries invest in research and development (R&D), whether to generate new technologies, to absorb innovations generated by others (de Ferranti and others 2003; Lederman and Maloney 2003), or to counteract the forces of diminishing returns in other accumulable factors such as physical capital (Lucas 1988).

Could it thus be the case that the region's poor showing on the TFP front is related to lack of a sufficiently skilled labor force or to R&D investment that is too low by international standards? In that case, would making progress on the educational and R&D fronts be a key part of the solution for raising Latin America's growth rates? With regard to human capital, according to de Ferranti and others (2003), during the 1990s many of the countries in Latin America exhibited secondary school enrollment rates that were significantly lower than those of other developing regions of the world, including East Asia and the Pacific as well as Eastern Europe and Central Asia. During the following decade, however, the region has made significant progress, reaching secondary school enrollment rates that are now higher than those found in East Asia and close to the levels of Eastern Europe and Central Asia (figure 1.18, panel a). This development has to be welcomed. Yet the extent to which the population is prepared to participate productively in the economy will depend not only on the number of years that people stay in school but also on the quality of the education they receive. And here things are less positive. Even if most Latin American countries do not participate regularly in international tests, the few that do (Argentina, Brazil, Mexico, Peru, and Uruguay) seem to perform poorly even after controlling for per capita income levels. For example, panel b of figure 1.18 reports the scores for a selected number of countries of the OECD's Programme for International Student Assessment (PISA) tests. It shows that all the Latin American countries are below the regression line, with scores that in some cases (such as Peru) are considerably lower than what countries' levels of per capita income would lead one to expect.

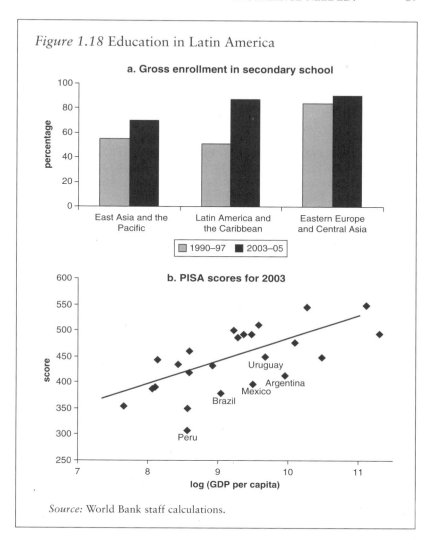

Figure 1.18 Education in Latin America

a. Gross enrollment in secondary school

b. PISA scores for 2003

Source: World Bank staff calculations.

As for the region's standing with respect to innovation expenditures, Latin American countries invest less than 0.5 percent of GDP on R&D, whereas most OECD countries have R&D investment rates of around 2.0 percent. Moreover, as shown in figure 1.19, Latin American countries such as Argentina and Mexico invest in R&D a percentage of GDP that is lower than what their levels of income would lead one to expect, whereas the opposite is found for fast-growing countries such as China, India, and the Republic of Korea. In a recent paper, Maloney and Rodríguez-Clare

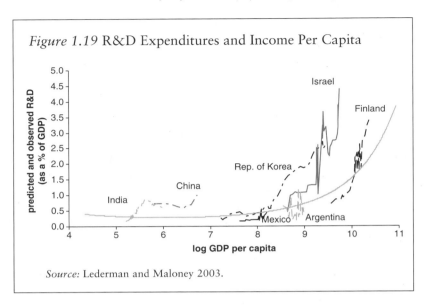

Figure 1.19 R&D Expenditures and Income Per Capita

Source: Lederman and Maloney 2003.

(2006) have argued that before concluding that additional R&D investment is really needed, one has to consider the pattern of specialization of the economy. As those authors put it, natural resource–abundant economies like those in Latin America cannot be expected to invest in R&D as much as the East Asian countries that focus mainly on manufacturing activities. To address this concern, Maloney and Rodríguez-Clare (2006) estimate the shortfall of actual R&D investment relative to predicted R&D investment, after taking into consideration the effect that output composition has on the latter. Yet their results continue to suggest that one cannot rule out the possibility that Latin American countries exhibit a considerable innovation shortfall.

Though expenditures in R&D are the most common proxy of firms' and countries' innovation efforts, other non-R&D activities aimed at adopting rather than generating new technologies may be of equal or larger importance for increasing TFP growth, especially in developing countries. Despite an extensive literature on the importance of R&D to the learning process, the distinction between adoption and invention suggests that R&D may be less central to developing countries than to more advanced countries. Other relevant types of innovation inputs include quality enhancements and certification, technology licensing and joint venture agreements, worker training, and investments in machinery and equipment. Even within the OECD, observers argue that the role of R&D is small compared to the introduction of new organizational and managerial practices. The Italian and Spanish experiences, in particular, suggest that large potential exists in non-R&D sources of TFP growth such as those related to technology adoption and organizational and management innovation.

On the quality front, evidence suggests that Latin American countries are lagging in the adoption and use of internationally accepted standards and in the implementation of coherent national quality systems. National quality systems are critical for increasing access to markets and for better facing external competition. Moreover, quality upgrades are often the entry point into innovation. Figure 1.20 shows the number of Latin American and OECD firms with ISO (International Organization for Standardization) 9000 and 14000 certification, per million workers. Using that figure as a proxy for quality adoption, one sees that Latin American countries are way behind, with about one-tenth of the number of certified firms in the OECD (after normalizing by the size of the labor force). Brazil is the leading country in the region, with 8,500 firms with ISO 9000 certification in 2005. It is followed by Argentina with 5,500 certified firms, Colombia with 4,900 firms, and Mexico with 2,900. After one normalizes by the size

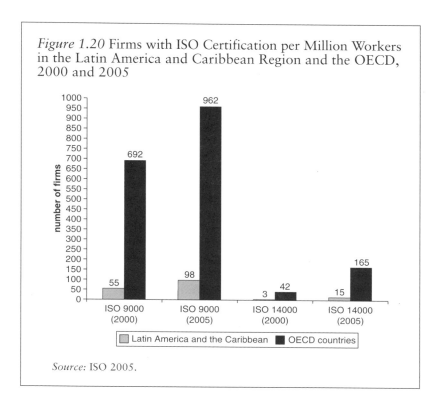

Figure 1.20 Firms with ISO Certification per Million Workers in the Latin America and Caribbean Region and the OECD, 2000 and 2005

Source: ISO 2005.

of the countries' labor force, however, Argentina and Colombia exhibit the highest rates of ISO 9000 certification in Latin America, with 303 and 221 firms per million workers, respectively, compared with 93 firms for Brazil and 67 firms for Mexico. In comparison, in 2005, the average high-income OECD country had 962 ISO 9000–certified firms per million workers (almost 450,000 firms), while China had 185 certified firms per million workers (almost 144,000 firms).

Conclusions

This chapter began by asking whether, in the present favorable growth environment, there would be sufficient motivation for yet another growth study. The answer is clearly yes. Indeed, even though Latin America's growth rates are at a three-decade high, the region is losing ground not only with respect to the world at large, but also in comparison with various other reference groups—including middle-income countries, East Asia, and natural resource–abundant countries. Moreover, this phenomenon is not new: Latin America's growth has been historically disappointing in relative terms.[16] A second motivation for the present study is that, as shown in this chapter, growth in Latin America has been hampered not only by relatively low investment rates, but also by low rates of return of that investment in terms of GDP growth, as well as by low rates of TFP growth.

This negative performance cannot be dissociated from the microeconomic environment in which Latin American firms operate or, in other words, from the region's investment climate. Indeed, evidence from various secondary sources suggests that Latin America is lagging significantly in issues related to the quality of governance and institutions, the availability of physical infrastructure, the development of the financial sector, and the levels of education of the labor force and innovative capacity of the private sector. Those shortcomings in the region's investment climate can arguably create obstacles not only for increasing the region's investment levels, but also for raising firm and aggregate productivity. Thus, to secure that elusive sustained high growth, policy makers may need to complement the necessary focus on macroeconomic stability with increased efforts in the microeconomic reforms agenda. There is, however, little empirical evidence to inform that agenda—or to link actual firm performance to the various shortcomings of Latin America's investment climate. The rest of this report aims at helping to fill that gap, by using recently collected firm-level data. In addition, it seeks to gain a better understanding of the policies that could have a larger influence on firm productivity by means of improving the environment in which firms invest and operate.

Notes

1. When one is interested in country performance, the sample median growth rate appears to be the natural measure. However, problems can arise when comparisons are performed across regions and over time. First, medians give the same weight to small economies such as Haiti and to large economies such as Brazil, which may not be fair in all circumstances. Second, if the best-performing countries improve their performance and the worst-performing countries do not, the median will not capture the improvement at the regional level. In those cases, the mean, rather than the median, may be more appropriate. However, means may be influenced by a handful of extreme observations and may also present a biased picture.

2. The results remain basically unchanged when comparisons are based on the means of the respective groups rather than on the medians.

3. Natural resource–abundant countries are selected on the basis of the Leamer index and, more specifically, on the basis of the average index over 1990 to 1999 for each country. Whenever this index is positive, it implies that net exports of natural resources are positive, and therefore, the country is classified as resource abundant.

4. Between the early 1960s and the late 1990s, figure 1.3 is to a large extent consistent with figure 1.2. Except for the natural resource–abundant countries in the 1960s and 1970s and in a few years in the early 1990s, Latin America has been consistently losing ground with respect to almost any reference group.

5. The authors have also computed correlation coefficients using three-year lag periods but have found them to be always insignificant.

6. GDP projections for Argentina and the República Bolivariana de Venezuela suggest a deceleration in per capita growth rates in 2007 and 2008 to about 4 percent from 7.6 and 9.9 percent, respectively, over the period from 2004 to 2006.

7. In the case of Aghion and Howitt (1992) and Romer (1990), capital accumulation is ignored. In the case of Aghion and Howitt (1998), what is emphasized is the complementarity between capital accumulation and innovation.

8. Those low rates do not account for the quality of investments. A number of studies have shown not only that the investment amounts have been low but that the quality of those investments has also been low (Birdsall and Nellis 2002; Fay and Morrison 2006).

9. It is important to note that the scale of the y axis in figures 1.7 and 1.8 is different. If the scale of the axis were adjusted to be the same, the differences would appear even more marked.

10. To the extent that investment rates are constrained by national saving rates, their lower levels in the case of Latin America could be linked to low levels of financial development, as well as to demographic factors (such as higher age dependency ratios) and, in the case of public savings, higher levels of political instability (Edwards 1996). Moreover, the lack of correlation between growth and the cyclical component of saving (and investment) rates in the case of Latin America—in contrast with the strong procyclicality of savings observed in the OECD—could be explained, as argued by Lane and Tornell (1998), by the presence of weak institutional environments in which powerful groups have an incentive to respond to positive productivity shocks by increasing their levels of appropriation and consumption—a factor that dominates consumption smoothing considerations.

11. Alternative Solow decompositions adjust for the quality of labor, for the actual use of the stocks of labor and capital, or both. See Loayza, Fajnzylber, and Calderón (2005) for TFP estimates using these types of adjustments. Such decompositions are likely to provide a better measure of TFP. Yet even with such adjustments,

these more refined TFP calculations still have many of the limitations that apply to the simple measure resulting from equation 1.1. An additional caveat is that the measure of TFP used here is based on the assumptions of constant returns to scale and perfect competition.

12. The results in table 1.3 are mostly consistent with in the findings of Loayza, Fajnzylber, and Calderón (2005), who present TFP growth estimates for 10-year intervals.

13. See Loayza, Fajnzylber, and Calderón (2005) for an analysis of the recent growth performance of the region and for how growth may be related to an important number of macropolicy variables.

14. The authors thank Cesar Calderón for providing the data underlying the charts in figures 1.11, 1.12, and 1.13.

15. It must be noted that causality can run in both directions here. Thus, for instance, although good institutional quality can help increase per capita income by means of facilitating technology adoption (as in Parente and Prescott 1994), richer countries also have more resources to make improvements in the various components of the institutional quality index used in figure 1.12.

16. Beyond the data on the past three and one-half decades examined in this chapter, Perry and others (2006) argue that the decline of Latin America goes back to at least the end of the 19th century, when GDP per capita was about 50 percent of that in the OECD countries.

References

Aghion, P., and P. Howitt. 1992. "A Model of Growth through Creative Destruction." *Econometrica* 60 (2): 323–51.

———. 1998. *Endogenous Growth Theory*. Cambridge, MA: MIT Press.

Aghion, P., E. Caroli, and C. García-Penalosa. 1999. "Inequality and Economic Growth: The Perspective of the New Growth Theories." *Journal of Economic Literature* 37 (4): 1615–60.

Attanasio, O. P., L. Picci, and A. E. Scorcu. 2000. "Saving, Growth, and Investment: A Macroeconomic Analysis Using a Panel of Countries." *Review of Economics and Statistics* 82 (20): 182–211.

Banerjee, A., and A. Newman. 1994. "Poverty, Incentives, and Development," *American Economic Review* 84 (2): 211–15.

Bates, R. 1981. *Markets and States in Tropical Africa: The Political Basis of Agricultural Policies*. Berkeley: University of California Press.

Beck, T., A. Demirgüç-Kunt, and M. Martínez Pería. 2005. "Reaching Out: Access to and Use of Banking Services across Countries." Policy Research Working Paper 3754, World Bank, Washington, DC.

Beck, T., R. Levine, and N. Loayza. 2000. "Finance and the Sources of Growth." *Journal of Financial Economics* 58 (1–2): 261–300.

Birdsall, N., and J. Nellis. 2002. "Winners and Losers: Assessing the Distributional Impact of Privatization," CGD Working Paper 6, Center for Global Development, Washington, DC.

Blomstrom, M., R. E. Lipsey and M. Zejan. 1996. "Is Fixed Investment the Key to Economic Growth?" *Quarterly Journal of Economics* 111 (1): 269–76.

Calderón, C., W. Easterly, and L. Servén. 2003. "Infrastructure Compression and Public Sector Solvency in Latin America." In *The Limits of Stabilization:*

Infrastructure, Public Deficits, and Growth in Latin America, ed. W. Easterly and L. Servén, 119–38. Washington, DC: World Bank.

Calderón, C., and L. Servén. 2003. "The Output Cost of Latin American's Infrastructure Gap." In *The Limits of Stabilization: Infrastructure, Public Deficits, and Growth in Latin America*, ed. W. Easterly and L. Servén, 95–118. Washington, DC: World Bank.

Cass, D. 1965. "Optimum Growth in an Aggregate Model of Capital Accumulation." *Review of Economic Studies* 32 (3): 233–40.

de Ferranti, D., G. Perry, I. Gill, J. Guasch, W. Maloney, C. Sánchez-Páramo, and N. Schady. 2003. *Closing the Gap in Education and Technology*. Washington, DC: World Bank.

Demirgüç-Kunt, A., I. Love, and V. Maksimovic. 2006. "Business Environment and the Incorporation Decision." *Journal of Banking and Finance* 30 (11): 2967–93.

Djankov, S., C. McLiesh, and R. Ramalho. 2006. "Regulation and Growth." *Economics Letters* 92 (3): 395–401.

Dollar, D., and E. N. Wolff. 1998. "Convergence of Industry Labor Productivity among Advanced Economies, 1963–1982." *Review of Economics and Statistics* 20 (40): 549–58.

Easterly, W., and R. Levine. 2001. "It's Not Factor Accumulation: Stylized Facts and Growth Models." *World Bank Economic Review* 15 (2): 177–219.

Easterly, W., and S. Rebelo. 1993. "Fiscal Policy and Economic Growth: An Empirical Investigation." *Journal of Monetary Economics* 32 (3): 417–458.

Edwards, S. 1996. "Why Are Latin America's Savings Rates So Low? An International Comparative Analysis." *Journal of Development Economics* 51 (1): 5–44.

Esfahani, H., and M. Ramírez. 2003. "Institutions, Infrastructure, and Economic Growth." *Journal of Development Economics* 70 (2): 443–77.

Fay, M., and M. Morrison. 2006. *Infrastructure in Latin America and the Caribbean: Recent Development and Key Challenges*. Washington, DC: World Bank.

Fisman, R. 2001. "Estimating the Value of Political Connections." *American Economic Review* 91 (4): 1095–102.

Fisman, R., and J. Svensson. 2000. "Are Corruption and Taxation Really Harmful to Growth? Firm-Level Evidence." Policy Research Working Paper 2485, World Bank, Washington, DC.

Frankel, M. 1962. "The Production Function in Allocation and Growth: A Synthesis." *American Economic Review* 52 (5): 996–1022.

Gasparini, L., F. Gutiérrez, and L. Tornarolli. 2007. "Growth and Income Poverty in Latin America and the Caribbean: Evidence from Household Surveys." *Review of Income and Wealth* 53 (2): 209–45.

González, A., and F. Lamanna. 2007. "Who Fears Competition from Informal Firms?" Policy Research Working Paper 4316, World Bank, Washington, DC.

Gramlich, E. 1994. "Infrastructure Investment: A Review Essay." *Journal of Economic Literature* 32 (3): 1176–96.

Guasch, J. L. 2005. *Granting and Renegotiating Infrastructure Concessions: Doing It Right*. Washington, DC: World Bank.

Guasch, J. L., and R. Hahn. 1999. "The Costs and Benefits of Regulation: Implications for Developing Countries." *World Bank Research Observer* 14 (1): 137–58.

Hall, R., and C. Jones. 1999. "Why Do Some Countries Produce So Much More Output per Worker Than Others?" *Quarterly Journal of Economics* 114 (1): 83–116.

Harhoff, D., K. Stahl, and M. Woywode. 1998. "Legal Form, Growth, and Exit of West German Firms: Empirical Results for Manufacturing, Construction, Trade, and Service Industries." *Journal of Industrial Economics* 46 (4): 453–88.

ISO (International Organization for Standardization). 2005. *The ISO Survey of Certifications 2004.* Geneva: ISO.

Kaufmann, D., A. Kraay, and M. Mastruzzi. 2004. "Governance Matters III: Governance Indicators for 1996, 1998, 2000, and 2002." *World Bank Economic Review* 18 (2): 253–87.

Klenow, P., and A. Rodríguez-Clare. 1997. "Economic Growth: A Review Essay." *Journal of Monetary Economics* 40 (3): 597–617.

Koopmans, T. C. 1965. "On the Concept of Optimal Economic Growth." In *The Econometric Approach to Development Planning,* 225–87. Amsterdam: North-Holland.

Lane, P. R., and A. Tornell. 1998. "Why Aren't Savings Rates in Latin America Procyclical?" *Journal of Development Economics* 57 (1): 185–99.

Lederman, D., and W. Maloney. 2003. "Research and Development (R&D) and Development." Policy Research Working Paper 3024, World Bank, Washington, DC.

Levine, R. 1997. "Financial Development and Economic Growth: Views and Agenda." *Journal of Economic Literature* 35 (2): 688–726.

Levine, R., and D. Renelt. 1992. "A Sensitivity Analysis of Cross-Country Growth Regressions." *American Economic Review* 82 (4): 942–63.

Loayza, N., P. Fajnzylber, and C. Calderón. 2005. *Economic Growth in Latin America and the Caribbean: Stylized Facts, Explanations, and Forecasts.* Washington, DC: World Bank.

Loayza, N., A. M. Oviedo, and L. Servén. 2004. "Regulation and Macroeconomic Performance." Policy Research Working Paper 3469, World Bank, Washington, DC.

Lucas, R. 1988. "On the Mechanics of Economic Development." *Journal of Monetary Economics* 22 (1): 3–22.

Maloney, W., and A. Rodríguez-Clare. 2006. "Innovation Shortfalls." Inter-American Development Bank, Washington, DC. http://www.iadb.org/res/publications/pubfiles/pubWP-543.pdf.

Mauro, P. 1995. "Corruption and Growth." *Quarterly Journal of Economics* 110 (3): 681–712.

Murphy, K., A. Shleifer, and R. Vishny. 1991. "The Allocation of Talent: Implications for Growth." *Quarterly Journal of Economics* 106 (2): 503–30.

———. 1993. "Why Is Rent-Seeking So Costly to Growth?" *American Economic Review* 83 (2): 409–14.

Parente, S. L., and E. C. Prescott. 1994. "Barriers to Technology Adoption and Development." *Journal of Political Economy* 102 (2): 298–321.

Perry, G., O. Arias, H. López, W. Maloney, and L. Servén. 2006. *Poverty Reduction and Growth: Virtuous and Vicious Circles.* Washington, DC: World Bank.

Perry, G., W. Maloney, O. Arias, P. Fajnzylber, A. Mason, and J. Saavedra. 2007. *Informality: Exit and Exclusion.* Washington, DC: World Bank.

Prescott, E. 1998. "Needed: A Theory of Total Factor Productivity." *International Economic Review* 39 (3): 525–51.

Reinikka, R., and J. Svensson. 2005. "Fighting Corruption to Improve Schooling: Evidence from a Newspaper Campaign in Uganda." *Journal of the European Economic Association* 3 (2–3): 259–67.

Romer, P. M. 1986. "Increasing Returns and Long-Run Growth." *Journal of Political Economy* 94 (5): 1002–37.

———. 1990. "Endogenous Technological Change." *Journal of Political Economy* 98 (5): S71–102.

Solow, R. M. 1956. "A Contribution to the Theory of Economic Growth." *Quarterly Journal of Economics* 70 (1): 65–94.

Svensson, J. 2003. "Who Must Pay Bribes and How Much? Evidence from a Cross-Section of Firms." *Quarterly Journal of Economics* 118 (1): 207–30.

———. 2005. "Eight Questions about Corruption." *Journal of Economic Perspectives* 19 (3): 19–42.

WEF (World Economic Forum). 2006. *The Latin America Competitiveness Review 2006: Paving the Way for Regional Prosperity*. Geneva: WEF.

World Bank. 2005. *World Development Report: A Better Investment Climate for Everyone*. Washington, DC: World Bank.

———. 2006a. *Doing Business in 2006: Creating Jobs*. Washington, DC: World Bank.

———. 2006b. *World Development Indicators 2006*. Washington, DC: World Bank.

———. 2007a. *Global Economic Prospects 2007: Managing the Next Wave of Globalization*. Washington, DC: World Bank.

———. 2007b. *World Development Indicators 2007*. Washington, DC: World Bank.

2

The Investment Climate in Latin America

Verónica Alaimo, Pablo Fajnzylber,
J. Luis Guasch, J. Humberto López, and
Ana María Oviedo

Latin America can significantly improve its investment climate. However, what can be realistically expected from progress in each of the main areas of the investment climate? Do all investment climate attributes play a similar role, or are some more important than others? If so, which areas of reform should be prioritized? Are the benefits of a better investment climate felt only by firms, or do workers also share some of the benefits? Similarly, do all firms benefit from the investment climate in a similar fashion, or do differences exist across firms of varying sizes, industries, and regions?

The previous chapter argued that Latin America could benefit from improvements to the region's investment climate. To a large extent, that assessment was based on the picture emerging from a number of aggregate indicators (showing that Latin America lags other regions) that the cross-country econometrics literature has found to affect economic growth significantly. This chapter argues that the analysis of microeconomic survey data can provide a number of further insights into the relationship between the investment climate and growth, especially when the focus is placed on objective rather than subjective business environment indicators.

First, firm-level data allow measurement of some dimensions of the investment climate for which limited, if any, data sources exist at the aggregate level—notably for indicators of the quality of governance and institutions and, in particular, for measures of the incidence of corruption or regulatory burdens. Second, firm-level data allow researchers to take into account how investment climate conditions can vary significantly within countries, across firms of different sizes, or in different industries or regions. Ignoring the presence of this within-country heterogeneity (for instance, in the context of aggregate cross-country analysis) can make identifying the growth effects of some aspects of the business environment harder. Third, not only can investment climate conditions vary within countries, but also they can have different effects on firms of different types, a possibility that can be explored only by using microeconomic data.

It is thus not surprising that some of the most popular attempts to benchmark investment conditions across countries have been based on microeconomic surveys of firms or business executives. Examples include the competitiveness indicators of the World Economic Forum (WEF) as well as the governance measures collected by ADBI Institute's *International Country Risk Guide* (ICRG) or Transparency International.[1] In fact, the idea of directly asking firms about the various aspects of the business environment that affect their performance is the underlying premise of the Enterprise Surveys prepared by the International Finance Corporation of the World Bank.[2] These surveys, which are the main data source for the various analyses conducted in this report, were launched in 2001 under the name Investment Climate Surveys.[3] Enterprise Surveys now cover 105 countries and more than 76,000 firms. Like some of the other surveys mentioned, such as those by the WEF and the ICRG, these World Bank surveys capture business perceptions about various business environment obstacles to firm competitiveness.

In contrast to existing data sources on the subject, however, the World Bank surveys also collect information on objective indicators of the seriousness of investment climate constraints as well as objective data on firm performance—for example, sales, employment, and productivity. The availability of perception-based as well as objective information about the obstacles faced by firms, together with hard data on their actual performance, is an important advantage for two reasons.

First, the presence in the Enterprise Surveys of information on firm performance allows researchers to analyze statistically the extent to which investment climate shortcomings are correlated with—or even have a causal effect on—firm productivity and, indirectly, growth. That question is precisely the main objective of this chapter.

Second, the extensive use in the literature of subjective indicators of the quality of the business environment has revealed their shortcomings, particularly when the purpose is to perform international comparisons. Indeed, perceptions may be biased by recent events reported in the media, and they may reflect the interviewees' specific cultural and socioeconomic background. Managers of firms that concentrate on local rather than national or international markets may lack the necessary benchmarks to judge the severity of the problems existing in their cities or provinces in the light of national or international best practices. Conversely, although opinion surveys conducted on business executives with international experience may be better suited for international comparisons, they are unlikely to provide a representative picture of the constraints faced by most local businesses.

Hence, having both objective and subjective indicators of obstacles to businesses allows researchers to gauge the quality of subjective indicators with respect to cross-country comparisons and to rely on objective measures to explore the actual channels through which these obstacles affect firm performance. Given the caveats related to subjective indicators, this study tends to prefer objective measures; however, on several occasions, particularly for examining the role of the legal system, this study resorts to subjective measures. In most cases, the results obtained from those indicators are contrasted with those from alternative objective measures.

This chapter uses a pooled sample of more than 10,000 firms from 16 Latin American countries to analyze the extent to which various investment climate indicators in the four areas highlighted in chapter 1—governance and institutional quality, infrastructure, access to finance, and skills and technology—have a significant and robust effect on labor productivity, total factor productivity, and wages. As a preamble to this analysis, this chapter describes the data and methodologies and presents the main econometric results, followed by a series of robustness checks. The latter consist of examining whether the basic results are maintained when the estimation is performed controlling for the effect of outliers, as well as when the sample is restricted to specific groups of firms or countries or expanded to include firms surveyed in other regions of the world. Finally, this chapter's results are compared to those of existing studies.

In line with previous studies on growth in the region (see, among others, Loayza, Fajnzylber, and Calderón 2005), this chapter finds that Latin American countries should reduce their shortcomings in the areas of human capital and innovation, infrastructure, and financial development. Yet it also finds that the rule of law and the regulatory framework are among the most relevant determinants of firm performance in the region. Because addressing shortcomings in these areas appears to be a prerequisite for making significant progress on other potential growth determinants, one conclusion is that they should be put at the top of the region's policy agenda.

Another important message drawn from the results of this chapter is that the benefits of a better investment climate are not limited to firms and that wages also tend to rise with improvements in governance, institutions, and other investment climate attributes. Similarly, to the extent that a better investment climate leads to productivity increases, it can also indirectly foster job creation through its effects on firm competitiveness and growth. Finally, considering that labor income is the poor's main source of income, poverty reduction and development strategies should promote improvements to the investment climate.

How Do Firms Perceive the Key Investment Climate Constraints to Growth?

Before moving to the proposed econometric approach, one may find it useful to examine what Latin American entrepreneurs perceive to be the main obstacles to their productivity and growth. This information allows the results on the statistical links between objective investment climate indicators and firm performance to be compared with the entrepreneurs' perceptions. Table 2.1 presents the top five constraints revealed by Enterprise Surveys performed in 16 Latin American countries. In each of the 16 countries for which data are available, the five constraints listed are mentioned most frequently as being "major" or "very severe."

Table 2.1 Top Five Constraints to Productivity and Growth

Country	Year	Firms' perceptions: Major obstacles to growth
Argentina	2006	• Tax rates • Corruption • Macroeconomic instability • Education • Labor regulations
Bolivia	2006	• Corruption • Practices of informal competitors • Macroeconomic instability • Transportation • Electricity
Brazil	2003	• Access to finance (availability and cost) • Tax rates • Macroeconomic instability • Corruption • Tax administration
Chile	2004	• Access to finance (availability and cost) • Labor regulations • Macroeconomic instability • Education • Practices of informal competitors
Colombia	2006	• Practices of informal competitors • Corruption • Electricity • Macroeconomic instability • Tax rates

(continued)

Table 2.1 Top Five Constraints to Productivity and Growth
(continued)

Country	Year	Firms' perceptions: Major obstacles to growth
Costa Rica	2005	• Access to finance (availability and cost) • Macroeconomic instability • Practices of informal competitors • Corruption • Tax rates
Ecuador	2003	• Access to finance (availability and cost) • Macroeconomic instability • Corruption • Practices of informal competitors • Tax rates
El Salvador	2003	• Crime • Practices of informal competitors • Access to finance (availability and cost) • Corruption • Macroeconomic instability
Guatemala	2006	• Corruption • Electricity • Macroeconomic instability • Practices of informal competitors • Crime
Honduras	2003	• Access to finance (availability and cost) • Corruption • Crime • Macroeconomic instability • Practices of informal competitors
Mexico	2006	• Corruption • Macroeconomic instability • Tax rates • Practices of informal competitors • Electricity
Nicaragua	2003	• Access to finance (availability and cost) • Corruption • Macroeconomic instability • Practices of informal competitors • Crime
Panama	2006	• Electricity • Corruption • Crime • Tax rates • Macroeconomic instability

(continued)

Table 2.1 Top Five Constraints to Productivity and Growth
(continued)

Country	Year	Firms' perceptions: Major obstacles to growth
Paraguay	2006	• Corruption • Practices of informal competitors • Macroeconomic instability • Education • Access to finance (availability and cost)
Peru	2006	• Corruption • Practices of informal competitors • Macroeconomic instability • Tax administration • Education
Uruguay	2006	• Tax rates • Practices of informal competitors • Macroeconomic instability • Corruption • Electricity

Source: Constructed by the authors using the Enterprise Surveys database.

As illustrated in table 2.1, some notable commonalities arise across countries of Latin America. Indeed, three constraints appear in the top five list in almost all countries: macroeconomic instability (all 16 countries), corruption (15 countries), and practices of informal competitors (13 countries). Also very frequent are issues related to taxes (nine countries) and access to finance (eight countries).

Also mentioned, although less frequently, are issues related to infrastructure (electricity) and crime—each variable appearing among the top issues in six and five countries, respectively. Finally, note that workforce education is seen as one of the major constraints to firms' operations in only four countries (Argentina, Chile, Paraguay, and Peru), and labor regulations are a major obstacle in just two (Argentina and Chile). This finding is particularly striking, given the ample evidence, at least at the aggregate level, of the effect of human capital on productivity and growth. As seen later in this chapter, human capital issues do appear to significantly affect firm performance in the econometric analysis, which serves as a good illustration of the possible limitations of analyses that are based solely on the perceptions of entrepreneurs.

Data and Econometric Methodology

The sample used in the empirical analysis in this chapter covers eight countries for which a wave of Enterprise Surveys was concluded in 2007

(Argentina, Bolivia, Colombia, Mexico, Panama, Paraguay, Peru, and Uruguay) and another group of eight countries for which least one survey was concluded between 2003 and 2006 (Brazil, Chile, Costa Rica, Ecuador, El Salvador, Guatemala, Honduras, and Nicaragua).[4] Roughly speaking, these countries account for more than 90 percent of the region's gross domestic product (GDP), gross investment, and population.

Fieldwork for the Enterprise Surveys is conducted by private contractors, who collect data from managing directors, human resources officials, and other relevant staff members of a sample of companies. Data cover more than 200 firm aspects (some of which are assessments of constraints facing firms and some of which are objective data related to the firm) on topics such as bureaucracy and corruption, use of the courts and crime, access to finance, informality, infrastructure, innovation, taxes, and trade. Box 2.1 provides some details regarding the Enterprise Surveys.

Enterprise Surveys are complementary but different from the Doing Business project, a collaboration of the World Bank and the International Finance Corporation.[5] Briefly, the Doing Business project measures for 175 economies the cost of doing business for a hypothetical firm on an annual basis.[6] Frequent observations based on a constant firm description can be extremely useful for monitoring progress in the areas covered (which include the costs of starting and closing a business, employing workers, trading across borders, registering property and getting credit, dealing with licenses, and paying taxes; investor protection issues; and contract enforcement) as well as for making cross-country comparisons. However, the Doing Business data do not allow the productivity effects of the cross-firm, within-country variation in investment climate conditions to be studied, which explains this report's focus on Enterprise Survey data.

With regard to estimation methodology, one important problem that emerges when one faces 200-plus potential explanatory variables is difficulty in deciding which indicators are the most important. This issue is critical because in many countries a large number of areas may require attention. In other words, the problem is not identifying areas that are keeping countries behind, but rather identifying those where policy reform is likely to have a larger influence on development. This choice involves combining information on how far behind a country is in each area with estimates of the expected effect that gains in each different area will have on firm performance.

The econometric methodology used in this report builds on and refines the work of Escribano and Guasch (2005) for Guatemala, Honduras, and Nicaragua and Escribano, Guasch, and de Orte (2006) for Chile. In particular, the methodology minimizes possible concerns about the endogeneity of firm-level investment climate indicators by holding basic firm characteristics constant and using instrumental variables measured for strata defined on the basis of firm size, industry, and state. As a result, this

Box 2.1 Enterprise Surveys at a Glance

Source of Data

Surveys that use stratified sampling are taken of hundreds of entrepreneurs per country, who describe the effect of their country's investment climate on their firm. Responses reflect managers' actual experiences, allowing analysts to see what happens to firms in actual practice. Typical sample sizes vary from 250 to 1,500 businesses, following simple random sample or stratified sampling.

Use

Breadth and depth of data allow analysis across country geography and firm attributes (size, ownership, industry) and can probe the relationship between investment climate characteristics and firm productivity.

Type of Issues Covered

Enterprise Surveys span all major investment climate topics, albeit in less depth than Doing Business case studies, ranging from infrastructure to crime. Detailed productivity information includes firm finances, costs such as labor and materials, sales, and investment.

Country Coverage

Currently, 105 countries are covered; 15 to 20 Enterprise Surveys per year are implemented, with updates planned for each country approximately every three to five years. This schedule reflects the intense nature of administering firm surveys and the difficulty for the firms of responding to the many, detailed questions (survey fatigue).

Source: Enterprise Surveys database.

report argues that its estimated coefficients can be interpreted as reflecting causality from the investment climate to firm performance. Methodological issues apart, however, the main difference between the analysis in this study and that in the individual Investment Climate Assessments performed at the World Bank is that this study pools the data of the different countries. This difference is relevant because if investment climate conditions affect all the firms in a country in a similar fashion, then analyses of individual countries likely will not be able to capture the effect on firm performance of the corresponding investment climate attributes.[7]

To deal with the problem of choosing the set of relevant explanatory variables, this study follows Escribano and Guasch (2005) in using a general-to-specific strategy in which an initial model with a large number of variables is simplified to achieve a parsimonious specification. In principle, this strategy enables the study to avoid the omitted variables problem (that is, biases and inconsistent parameter estimates) likely to arise when starting from too simple a model.

The approach departs from Escribano and Guasch (2005) in that the full set of variables in the database is not used. There are two reasons for this difference. First, following the previous discussion on subjective compared with objective indicators of investment climate constraints, this study focuses only on objective ones.[8] Second, this study does not include all questions in the questionnaire indiscriminately as potential investment climate indicators. Instead, it concentrates on only the four areas previously highlighted: governance, infrastructure, access to finance, and technology. Within each area, the study restricts the set of explanatory variables to indicators that are straightforward to interpret and that have a significant and robust effect on firm performance, as measured by the productivity of labor.

Table 2.2 summarizes the 10 investment climate variables that this analysis shows to be strong determinants of labor productivity at the firm level across the sample of 16 Latin American countries. Of the 10 investment climate attributes in this table, 6 may measure several dimensions of governance and institutional quality. For example, there is a variable that captures the extent to which firms pay *bribes* to access government services or public contracts, which would measure the degree of corruption;

Table 2.2 Main Investment Climate Determinants of Labor Productivity, by Theme

Governance	Regulatory framework	Infrastructure	Finance	Human capital and technology
Bribes	Sales declared for tax purposes	Losses caused by power outages	Access to credit	Worker training
Crime losses	External audits			Internet use
Security costs	Incorporation			

Source: Authors' estimates using the Enterprise Surveys database.

two variables (expenses on *security* and losses from theft and *crime*) measure the safety of the firm's environment in a physical sense; three variables are likely to capture the effect of regulation and institutional quality (namely, the extent of *regulatory compliance* as measured by the share of sales declared for tax purposes, which is interpreted as being a reflection of excessive or arbitrarily enforced rules and regulations).[9] In addition, this study includes variables measuring whether firms have their financial statements externally *audited* and whether they choose the *corporate* form. As in the case of regulatory compliance, a high prevalence of incorporated and externally audited firms is interpreted as reflecting an efficient legal system, strong shareholder and creditors' rights, and low regulatory burdens.[10]

The remaining variables are related to the other three broad areas of the investment climate. Firms' losses caused by power outages would capture the effect that *infrastructure* quality has on firm productivity; *access to the financial sector* looks at the extent to which firms are credit constrained in financing their operations; finally, the use of the Internet to communicate with clients and suppliers and the offering of training to employees can be interpreted as indicators of firms' investments in *human capital* and new *technologies*. Table 2A.1 provides country and overall average values for each of the variables used in the regression analysis. In a robustness exercise described later, the average years of schooling of workers employed in the corresponding countries, industries, and regions are also included; they are calculated using household survey data.

As noted, the set of variables described in table 2.2 is the result of using significance and robustness to reduce a more general model that initially included a larger number of variables. Variables that are not significant in an initial very general model are dropped to reach a more parsimonious model.[11] Some examples of variables that were included in the estimation but discarded because of their lack of significance are (a) the time needed to clear exports or imports in customs, (b) the losses suffered during merchandise transportation, (c) the average wait (in days) to obtain electrical or telephone connections, (d) whether firms are certified by the International Organization for Standardization (ISO), and (e) whether they have invested in research and development (R&D) during the previous year.

The failure to find a significant effect for the preceding variables does not imply, however, that they are irrelevant or that they do not affect firm performance. For instance, one could argue that different types of data and estimation methodologies would be needed for capturing the effects of some of those variables. As an example, delays at customs could have direct effects on only the subset of firms that either export or rely substantially on imported inputs, and transportation losses could directly affect only firms that cater to national or international markets rather than those that concentrate on local markets. Similarly, the ease of accessing infrastructure services (for example, new electricity connections) could have a greater effect on the entry of new firms and less effect on those that are already established. Finally, the finding that investments in R&D or ISO certification appear not to affect productivity in this study's sample could simply reflect the fact that the magnitude of those effects varies considerably across industries and may actually be restricted to only some of them. Thus, the effect of those variables on firm performance could be dissipated—that is, "averaged out"—when considering economywide samples such as those used in this report.[12]

In summary, a much larger weight should be given to the report's positive findings (that is, the results concerning the significance of the set of variables described in table 2.2) than to the negative ones (the fact that the variables excluded from the basic specification do not appear to be relevant for understanding firm performance, at least when using this study's estimation approach). That said, the investment climate attributes retained in this analysis do cover most of the top microeconomic constraints to firm performance subjectively identified by the region's entrepreneurs (see table 2.1 and the discussion in the previous section): namely, aspects related to corruption or law and order; regulatory compliance; access to finance; and provision of electricity. However, although the variables in this study's model cover the four investment climate areas highlighted in this report—governance and institutional quality; access to finance; infrastructure; and education, innovation, and technology—not all areas seem to be represented with the same number of variables. In the view of the authors, this unequal distribution reflects the fact that the Enterprise Survey data and the preferred estimation methodology of this study are better suited to capturing the effect of issues related to governance and institutional quality than to measuring the effects of issues in other investment climate areas.

Because the preliminary examination of the data indicated that the correlation between the different variables in each area was relatively low, this analysis does not attempt to construct summary indicators for each area. Rather, it looks at how each individual investment climate variable correlates with the selected measures of firm performance.[13] The following is the study's basic econometric specification:

$$\log(Y_i / L_i) = \sum_j \beta_{1j} IC_{ij} + \sum_j \delta_{1j} C_{ij} + \upsilon_{1i}, \qquad (2.1)$$

where Y is output as measured by the firm sales, and L is labor (so that the dependent variable can be interpreted as labor productivity). IC refers to investment climate variables, C to other firm control variables, and υ is a random error term.

The set of control variables, C_i, includes sector, region, and country dummies, which are aimed at capturing unobservable firm characteristics that are not directly related to the investment climate but can be expected to affect firm performance. In addition, the following are included as controls: (a) log of firm age, (b) dummies for firm size of 20 to 99 employees and of 100 or more employees, (c) a dummy for single-establishment firms, (d) a dummy for partially or entirely foreign-owned firms, and (e) an exporter dummy. Note that the dependent variable in equation 2.1 can be interpreted as the productivity of labor, which the variables in IC and C could influence through effects either on total factor productivity (TFP) or on capital intensity. In fact, to investigate the effect of investment climate attributes on TFP, a different specification is estimated, which is based on the following simple production function:

$$Y_i = M_i + P_i K_i^{\alpha} L_i^{1-\alpha} \tag{2.2a}$$

$$P_i = P(IC_{pi}, C_{pi}) \exp(v_{2i}), \tag{2.2b}$$

where K is capital, M is intermediate inputs, P is total factor productivity, and v is a random error term. Rearranging equation 2.2a and taking logs, one can rewrite as follows:

$$\log(Y_i / L_i - M_i / L_i) = \log(VA_i / L_i) = \log(P_i) + \alpha \log(K_i / L_i). \tag{2.3}$$

Then, if one substitutes equation 2.2b into equation 2.3, and assumes a linear specification for $log(P(.))$, such as

$$\log(P_i) = \sum_j \beta_{2j} IC_{ij} + \sum_j \delta_{2j} C_{ij} + u_i, \tag{2.4}$$

equation 2.3 can be rewritten as

$$\log(VA_i / L_i) = \sum_j \beta_{2j} IC_{ij} + \sum_j \delta_{2j} C_{ij} + \alpha \log(K_i / L_i) + v_{2i}. \tag{2.5}$$

It follows from equations 2.4 and 2.5 that in this second specification the estimated parameters of the investment climate attributes can be interpreted as representing the effect of these variables on total factor productivity.

Clearly, if improving the investment climate is seen as an engine of development, then how the different attributes affect variables beyond labor and total factor productivity might also be worth exploring. For example, one could focus on whether the IC and C variables affect workers' conditions. To explore this particular issue, one may estimate a variation of equation 2.1 where the dependent variable has been substituted by the average wage per worker paid by the firm: that is,

$$\log(Wage_i / L_i) = \sum_j \beta_{3j} IC_{ij} + \sum_j \delta_{3j} C_{ij} + v_{3i}. \tag{2.6}$$

Estimation of equations 2.1, 2.5, and 2.6 presents a number of challenges. To start with, it assumes homogeneity across sectors, countries, regions, and firms, which is unrealistic unless there is a common production function. To some extent, this issue has been addressed by including sector, country, and regional dummies in the different econometric specifications to capture as much heterogeneity as possible. Later, the analysis also explores whether the study's investment climate attributes affect different firms differently, therefore allowing for some heterogeneity in the system.

An additional challenge in this context is related to the potential endogeneity of some of the observed attributes in the right-hand side of equations 2.1, 2.5, and 2.6, driven by reverse causality from firm performance to the quality of government- and market-provided services to which individual firms have access. Thus, for instance, better-performing firms could be targeted by tax inspectors, as well as by corrupt officials and criminals; they could also be better placed to gain access to bank credit and better infrastructure services; and they could have better incentives to train their workers and use state-of-the-art technologies. Because most of the Enterprise Surveys provide only a single year's data, the analysis cannot rely on instruments such as lagged values of the explanatory variables. Thus, the study follows standard practice and instruments the firm-specific *IC* variables with their corresponding group means. The intuition behind this approach is that the performance of individual firms may affect firm-level measures of the quality of the investment climate, but it is likely to have a much smaller effect on the environment in which all the other firms of the same size, sector, and region operate (provided that there is a sufficiently large number of such firms in the corresponding group). In other words, the idea is to identify the effect of the investment climate on firm performance, after purging the firm-level measures of investment climate from the effect of individual firm characteristics.

A *group* is defined as a region–industry–firm size and a minimum of 10 observations is imposed to compute the group average. Whenever there are fewer than 10 observations in a group, the average of the corresponding region-industry is used, regardless of firm size. If the observations are still below the threshold of 10, then the industry average, or else the region average, is used. Beyond that, the corresponding data point is treated as a missing observation.[14]

One question that still has to be solved in this context regards whether one should use instrument sample averages or weighted averages of each investment climate attribute.[15] Underlying the use of averages as valid instruments is the idea that each investment climate attribute j of a firm i belonging to a group s can be expressed as

$$IC_{ij} = IC_{sj} + w_{ij}, \qquad (2.7)$$

where IC_{sj} is the average value of the variable for group s. In particular, if interest centers, for instance, on equation 2.1, one needs to make the following assumption for group averages to be valid instruments: $E(IC_{sj}\,v_i) = 0$.[16] In particular, if one sees the group averages as the result of a first-stage regression of the explanatory variables on a set of instruments (a set of dummies in this case), then using the sample average would be justified. This choice would also be a natural one, considering that sample weights are not used in the second-stage regression either.[17] In such a case, the resulting two-stage least squares (2SLS) estimator would be identical to the ordinary least squares (OLS) estimator obtained by replacing the explanatory variables with their group means.

In contrast, even if in the second-stage regression weighted least squares are not used, good reasons exist to use weights to compute the mean. In particular, it is well known that when the probability of selection into the sample varies by group, the sample average $I\hat{C}_{sj} = S^{-1} \sum_{i=1}^{S} IC_{ij}$ would in principle be an inconsistent estimator of the population mean: that is,

$$\text{plim}(I\hat{C}_{sj}) \neq IC_{sj}. \qquad (2.8)$$

Thus, one could also argue that an estimate of the mean based on a weighted average would be more appropriate as an instrument for the second-stage regression.[18] On the basis of the preceding, and because none of the main findings hinge on whether weighted or simple averages are used to compute the instruments, this analysis focuses on the 2SLS results obtained using weighted averages and reports those based on the sample averages approach in annex 2A.

A third challenge faced in this context is related to the effect of missing observations at the firm level, which as the number of explanatory variables increases may dramatically affect sample size. Here the analysis follows Escribano and Guasch (2005) and substitutes the missing values with region–industry–firm size means, both for investment climate attributes and for firm controls.[19] Replacing the missing values in the sample with the same variable used to instrument nonmissing observations adds limited information to the sample, but the authors believe that the gains from proceeding in this way far exceed the costs of substantially reducing sample sizes when all observations with at least some missing values are dropped.

Estimation Results

This section presents the results of estimating equations 2.1, 2.5, and 2.6 using different samples and econometric assumptions. Whereas it focuses on results obtained using the full sample and a two-stage least-squares estimator, it also reports, for the sake of testing the robustness of the main estimates, results obtained using subsamples of firms defined by size or location as well as on the basis of other estimation methods.

Labor Productivity

Table 2.3 presents the results of estimating the basic specification (2.1) concerning the effect of investment climate indicators on labor productivity—specifically sales per worker. To assess the robustness of

Table 2.3 Investment Climate Effect on Labor Productivity

	Dependent variable: Log of sales per worker		
	(1) OLS	*(2)* 2SLS	*(3)* 2SLS
Substitution	No	No	Yes
Instruments		Weighted averages	Weighted averages
Investment climate attributes			
Bribes	−0.016 [0.044]	−0.467** [0.199]	−0.454*** [0.114]
Security	−1.116*** [0.338]	−2.222 [1.637]	−3.616*** [1.175]
Crime	−2.969*** [0.736]	−11.746*** [3.294]	−6.164*** [1.930]
Regulatory compliance	0.335*** [0.060]	1.702*** [0.293]	1.048*** [0.160]
Audited	0.272*** [0.043]	0.483** [0.208]	0.377*** [0.131]
Incorporated	0.290*** [0.051]	0.376** [0.172]	0.415*** [0.109]
Infrastructure quality	0.899** [0.397]	2.770* [1.600]	2.079** [0.930]
Access to finance	0.204*** [0.047]	0.048 [0.257]	0.275* [0.161]
Technology	0.169*** [0.046]	0.229 [0.243]	0.314** [0.135]
Training	0.102*** [0.038]	−0.004 [0.202]	0.234** [0.108]

(continued)

Table 2.3 Investment Climate Effect on Labor Productivity
(continued)

	Dependent variable: Log of sales per worker		
	(1) OLS	*(2)* 2SLS	*(3)* 2SLS
Substitution	No	No	Yes
Instruments		Weighted averages	Weighted averages
Firm controls			
Unique establishment	−0.339*** [0.051]	−0.302*** [0.060]	−0.237*** [0.039]
Log of firm's age	0.121*** [0.026]	0.091*** [0.029]	0.089*** [0.016]
Foreign owned	0.356*** [0.078]	0.247*** [0.086]	0.386*** [0.050]
Exporter	0.255*** [0.045]	0.222*** [0.068]	0.165*** [0.039]
20–99 employees	0.032 [0.044]	−0.054 [0.090]	−0.064 [0.051]
100+ employees	−0.098 [0.070]	−0.298* [0.156]	−0.278*** [0.086]
Observations	4,207	4,207	10,535

Source: Authors' calculations.

Note: * = significant at the 10 percent level; ** = significant at the 5 percent level; *** = significant at the 1 percent level. Robust standard errors are in brackets. The table reports the results of regressing the log of sales per worker on the investment climate attributes and firm controls in the first column. Annex A describes in detail the different variables used in the regression. Column 1 uses OLS; column 2 uses 2SLS with region–industry–firm size weighted averages as instruments; column 3 uses 2SLS with region–industry–firm size weighted averages as instruments and replaces missing observations with the instrumental variable. 2SLS instruments are constructed using a minimum threshold of 10 observations. All regressions include country, industry, and region dummies.

the results, the table presents estimates obtained under several alternative econometric assumptions. The first estimates, presented in column 1, are obtained using OLS without correcting for potential endogeneity issues. The results in this column are based on the original sample of 4,207 firms for which all variables are available, without substituting missing observations for group means. The results presented in the remaining columns are 2SLS estimates, with all investment climate variables instrumented with their corresponding group averages. In the case of column 2, the sample is also the original one, without substituting for missing observations, whereas in column 3, the missing observations are replaced with group means (weighted averages). As a result, the number of observations increases dramatically to 10,535 firms.[20] All reported standard errors are robust to the presence of heteroskedasticity. Note that the significance of the variables remains basically unchanged when inference is based on clustered standard errors.

Comparing the OLS results in column 1 with 2SLS estimates obtained with the same sample in column 2 reveals that controlling for reverse causality affects parameter estimates markedly, which suggests that endogeneity should be an important concern in this context. In the case of finance and also for the measure of technology adoption, the estimated effect on labor productivity is significant only when the larger sample, resulting from substituting missing values with group means, is used. Overall, the replacement of missing values with group means has some effect in terms of increasing efficiency (the standard errors associated to the parameter estimates become lower) but less so on the magnitude of the parameters themselves, which continue to be of the same order. This finding suggests that the replacement of missing values with group averages may be a welcome step after all.[21]

With respect to the economic significance of the study's econometric results, in almost all cases the selected investment climate variables carry the expected signs.[22] Thus, the results suggest that firms operating in areas where prevalence of the rule of law is low—as captured by firms' losses derived from *crime*, firms' expenditures on *security*, and the incidence of *bribes* (that is, corruption)—tend to have lower levels of labor productivity. In contrast, improvements in the quality of institutions and regulations, as reflected in increases in firms' *regulatory compliance* and in higher incidences of *audited* and *incorporated* firms, positively affect firm performance. The result is also positive for improvements in the quality of *infrastructure* and in *financial system breadth*, which are respectively proxied through reductions in firm losses associated with power outages and reductions in the incidence of credit-constrained firms. Finally, the results confirm previous evidence regarding the positive productivity effects of firms' investments in *skills* and *technology*, as measured by worker training and firms' Internet use.

As for the study's control variables, exporters, firms with foreign ownership, older firms, and firms that operate more than one establishment exhibit higher levels of labor productivity.[23] Interestingly, after controlling for all of the preceding, the study found that smaller firms generate more output per worker. Nevertheless, because the study focuses on how the investment climate affects firm performance, corrections are not performed to account for the potential endogeneity of the mentioned control variables, meaning that the results should be interpreted as correlations, subject to possible reverse causality effects. In results not reported here, however, the models of tables 2.3 and 2A.2 (found in the annex) have been estimated without firm-level controls; in those results, the sign and significance of the investment climate attributes remain unchanged in every specification. In addition, although the magnitude of the coefficients does change slightly, the relative importance of each variable with respect to the others remains basically the same.

To provide an idea of the economic significance of the coefficients reported in table 2.3, figure 2.1 provides the relative magnitudes of the coefficients in column 3 of table 2.3. Specifically, each coefficient is multiplied times one standard deviation of the corresponding variable within the regression sample. The figure reveals that the strongest effects come from *regulatory compliance* and *crime*, followed by *bribes*, *audited*, and *incorporated*.

In addition, table 2.4 reports the same exercise at the country level. Similarly to the exercise reported in table 2.1, the strongest effects vary across countries; however, *regulatory compliance*, *crime*, *bribes*, *audited*, and *incorporated* appear consistently to have larger magnitudes relative to other areas.

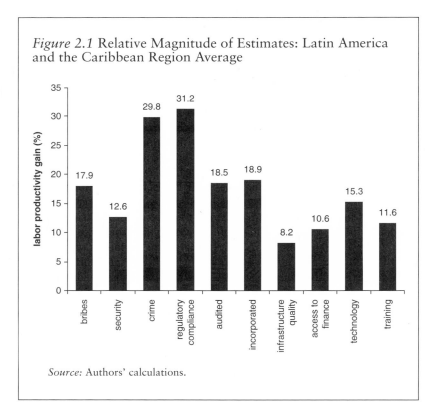

Figure 2.1 Relative Magnitude of Estimates: Latin America and the Caribbean Region Average

Source: Authors' calculations.

Table 2.4 Relative Magnitude of Estimates, by Country

Log of sales per worker

	Coefficient	Argentina	Bolivia	Brazil	Chile	Colombia	Costa Rica	Ecuador	El Salvador
		Estimated coefficient multiplied by standard deviation of each variable							
Bribes	−0.454	0.213	0.224	0.194	0.109	0.145	0.186	0.215	0.217
Security	−3.616	0.172	0.087	0.139	0.159	0.075	0.109	0.614	0.268
Crime	−6.164	0.423	0.288	0.133	0.251	0.160	0.165	0.194	0.234
Regulatory compliance	1.048	0.251	0.280	0.260	0.113	0.301	0.278	0.322	0.328
Audited	0.377	0.180	0.168	0.148	0.186	0.187	0.188	0.188	0.151
Incorporated	0.415	0.133	0.201	0.102	0.112	0.190	0.150	0.077	0.198
Infrastructure quality	2.079	0.033	0.152	0.138	0.094	0.135	0.140	0.169	0.106
Access to finance	0.275	0.096	0.104	0.099	0.067	0.099	0.101	0.116	0.092
Technology	0.314	0.140	0.155	0.140	0.132	0.144	0.138	0.156	0.145
Training	0.234	0.117	0.115	0.110	0.106	0.109	0.117	0.106	0.117

(continued)

Table 2.4 Relative Magnitude of Estimates, by Country (continued)

Log of sales per worker

	Coefficient	Estimated coefficient multiplied by standard deviation of each variable							
		Guatemala	Honduras	Mexico	Nicaragua	Panama	Paraguay	Peru	Uruguay
Bribes	−0.454	0.208	0.220	0.153	0.219	0.155	0.227	0.209	0.131
Security	−3.616	0.141	0.286	0.095	0.274	0.236	0.246	0.107	0.129
Crime	−6.164	0.504	0.207	0.293	0.242	0.139	0.297	0.152	0.189
Regulatory compliance	1.048	0.354	0.355	0.332	0.364	0.419	0.297	0.235	0.200
Audited	0.377	0.189	0.186	0.171	0.168	0.136	0.146	0.178	0.153
Incorporated	0.415	0.202	0.040	0.203	0.058	0.115	0.139	0.088	0.114
Infrastructure quality	2.079	0.114	0.141	0.057	0.172	0.163	0.130	0.085	0.012
Access to finance	0.275	0.079	0.107	0.114	0.123	0.048	0.080	0.078	0.104
Technology	0.314	0.155	0.127	0.138	0.116	0.152	0.150	0.156	0.150
Training	0.234	0.116	0.116	0.101	0.116	0.117	0.117	0.116	0.106

Source: Authors' calculations.

Note: Each estimate from column 3 of table 2.3 is multiplied by the standard deviation (within country) of the corresponding variable. The total number of observations corresponds to those in the regression.

Controlling for Self-Selection: Results for Domestic Small and Medium Enterprises

A possible concern with this study's approach to correcting for the endogeneity of investment climate attributes using group means of the corresponding variables is that better-performing firms and entrepreneurs could self-select into—that is, choose to locate in—regions with better investment climate conditions. To the extent that the study cannot control for the determinants of self-selection, even the 2SLS estimators would yield inconsistent estimates. This issue has been highlighted in a similar context by Dollar, Hallward-Driemeier, and Mengistae (2005), who address it by restricting their sample to small and medium firms and excluding those with some degree of foreign ownership. The idea is that smaller, domestically owned firms are typically less mobile and tend to be based where the founder was living at the time of starting up. Thus, with the exception of entrepreneurs who have migrated to their present location motivated by the search for a better environment for starting new businesses, self-selection would be less of an issue within this type of sample. Table 2.5 reports the results of reestimating the basic model using this approach.

Table 2.5 Investment Climate Effect on Labor Productivity: Domestic Firms with Fewer than 100 Employees

Dependent variable	Log of sales per worker	
	Small and medium firms (<100 employees)	
	(1)	(2)
	2SLS	2SLS
Substitution	No	Yes
Instruments	Weighted averages	Weighted averages
Investment climate attributes		
Bribes	−0.206	−0.463***
	[0.242]	[0.130]
Security	−1.426	−2.896**
	[1.683]	[1.226]
Crime	−11.383***	−6.449***
	[3.122]	[1.878]
Regulatory compliance	1.276***	0.778***
	[0.341]	[0.180]

(continued)

Table 2.5 Investment Climate Effect on Labor Productivity:
Domestic Firms with Fewer Than 100 Employees *(continued)*

Dependent variable	Log of sales per worker	
	Small and medium firms (<100 employees)	
	(1)	(2)
	2SLS	2SLS
Substitution	No	Yes
Instruments	Weighted averages	Weighted averages
Audited	0.396*	0.279**
	[0.210]	[0.130]
Incorporated	0.521***	0.483***
	[0.175]	[0.106]
Infrastructure quality	3.776**	2.674***
	[1.705]	[0.997]
Access to finance	−0.05	0.340**
	[0.262]	[0.173]
Technology	0.455**	0.353***
	[0.222]	[0.130]
Training	0.01	0.259**
	[0.181]	[0.116]
Firm controls		
Unique establishment	−0.295***	−0.193***
	[0.075]	[0.046]
Log of firm's age	0.043	0.047**
	[0.033]	[0.019]
Exporter	0.234***	0.155***
	[0.073]	[0.041]
Observations	3,141	7,906

Source: Authors' calculations.

Note: * = significant at the 10 percent level; ** = significant at the 5 percent
level; *** = significant at the 1 percent level. Robust standard errors are in
brackets. The table reports the results of regressing the log of sales per worker on
the investment climate attributes and firm controls in the first column, restricting
the sample to domestic small and medium firms. Column 1 uses 2SLS with region–
industry–firm size weighted averages as instruments; column 2 uses 2SLS with
region–industry–firm size weighted averages as instruments and replaces missing
observations with the instrumental variable. 2SLS instruments are constructed using
a minimum threshold of 10 observations. All regressions include country, industry,
and region dummies.

Inspection of table 2.5 suggests that, unlike in the case of Dollar, Hallward-Driemeier, and Mengistae (2005), self-selection is not an important issue in this report's context. Indeed, there are only small differences in parameter estimates when a sample restricted to domestic small and medium enterprises (SMEs) is used rather than the full sample.[24] One possible explanation for not finding evidence of selectivity problems is that this model includes a significantly larger number of explanatory variables than does that of Dollar, Hallward-Driemeier, and Mengistae (2005), including location and sectoral dummies.

Robustness to the Presence of Outliers

An additional issue to consider in this context is whether the previous results are affected by the presence of outliers in the sample. To address this concern, table 2.6 reports 2SLS robust regression estimates using the sample group average instrument. More specifically, the reported results are based on a robust regression that uses an iterative procedure with Huber and Tukey biweights to control for outliers. This procedure is relatively straightforward in the case of the sample average because, as discussed previously, the 2SLS estimator can be expressed in the form of an OLS regression on which the algorithm for the robust regression estimator is based. However, the procedure presents a number of significant challenges when weighting is involved in the computation of the instrumental variables.

Comparison of these specifications with their noncorrected counterparts indicates that in the case of the variables *bribes, crime, regulatory compliance, incorporation,* and *training,* the previous findings appear to be robust to the use of estimation methods that correct for the influence of outliers. With regard to the remaining five variables, the results are sensitive to the sample being considered. With the full sample, *infrastructure* also appears as a relevant investment climate determinant, although *access to finance* and *technology* do not. On the contrary, with the sample that includes only small and medium domestic firms, the parameter of *infrastructure* is not significantly different from zero, whereas *access to finance* and *technology* now appear to belong to the equation. Finally, *security* and *audit* are not significant in either case.

Thus, to some extent, these results indicate that whereas the findings for most variables in the governance and institutional quality group appear to be robust to controlling for outliers, the same cannot be claimed for some of the other groups.

Total Factor Productivity Effects

As previously discussed, the investment climate potentially matters for aspects related to both physical capital accumulation and factor

Table 2.6 Investment Climate Effect on Labor Productivity:
Robust Regression Estimates

	(1)	*(2)*
	2SLS-R	*2SLS-R*
Substitution	Yes	Yes
Sample	*Full*	*Small and medium firms*
Investment climate attributes		
Bribes	−0.434***	−0.420***
	[0.094]	[0.109]
Security	−0.779	−0.621
	[0.719]	[0.773]
Crime	−6.536***	−7.285***
	[1.328]	[1.441]
Regulatory compliance	0.949***	0.724***
	[0.137]	[0.156]
Audited	0.041	−0.047
	[0.080]	[0.097]
Incorporated	0.256***	0.381***
	[0.082]	[0.088]
Infrastructure quality	1.465*	1.47
	[0.860]	[0.947]
Access to finance	0.092	0.412***
	[0.128]	[0.141]
Technology	0.016	0.217**
	[0.082]	[0.093]
Training	0.196**	0.332***
	[0.086]	[0.101]
Firm controls		
Unique establishment	−0.292***	−0.220***
	[0.026]	[0.034]
Log of firm's age	0.114***	0.081***
	[0.013]	[0.014]
Foreign owned	0.523***	
	[0.034]	
Exporter	0.287***	0.274***
	[0.024]	[0.028]

(continued)

Table 2.6 Investment Climate Effect on Labor Productivity:
Robust Regression Estimates *(continued)*

	(1)	(2)
	2SLS-R	2SLS-R
Substitution	Yes	Yes
Sample	Full	Small and medium firms
20–99 employees	0.083*** [0.026]	
100+ employees	0.127*** [0.038]	
Observations	10,535	7,906
R-squared	0.39	0.35

Source: Authors' calculations.
Note: * = significant at the 10 percent level; ** = significant at the 5 percent level;
*** = significant at the 1 percent level. Robust standard errors are in brackets.
The table reports the results of a robust regression for the log of sales per worker
on the investment climate attributes and firm controls in the first column. Both
columns report 2SLS estimates using sample group averages as instruments. Column
1 uses the full sample; column (2) restricts the sample to domestic SMEs. Both
regressions include country, industry, and region dummies.

productivity (beyond labor productivity).[25] Yet the coefficient estimates
reported in tables 2.3 to 2.5 are weighted averages of the effects of investment climate attributes on labor productivity that operate through increases
in TFP and of those that act through increases in investment. Comparing
those coefficients with the corresponding parameters estimated on the
basis of model 2.5 allows assessment of the relative importance of these
two types of potential effects of investment climate improvements. In particular, if the magnitude of the coefficients in columns 1 to 3 of table 2.7 is
larger (smaller) than that of the corresponding estimates in table 2.3, then
one could argue that the TFP effects of improvements in the investment
climate are larger (smaller) than the corresponding effects on investment.

There is, however, a practical problem in performing these comparisons, related to the fact that the capital stock and intermediate inputs costs
variables, which are needed to estimate model 2.5, have a relatively large
number of missing values. The samples used in table 2.7 are thus smaller
and probably less representative than the samples used in table 2.4. As a
result, differences between the parameter estimates reported in both tables
may reflect these sample changes rather than differences between the effect
of investment climate variables on TFP and capital accumulation. To deal
with this problem, table 2.7, column 4, reports estimates of model 2.1
using the same sample and estimation methods employed to estimate
model 2.5 in column 3.

Table 2.7 Investment Climate Effect on Total Factor Productivity

Dependent variable	Log of value added per worker			Log sales per worker
	(1)	*(2)*	*(3)*	*(4)*
	OLS	2SLS	2SLS	2SLS
Substitution	No	No	Yes	Yes
Instruments		Weighted averages	Weighted averages	Weighted averages
Investment climate attributes				
Bribes	0.001 [0.047]	–0.484** [0.213]	–0.489*** [0.134]	–0.487*** [0.130]
Security	–1.478*** [0.375]	–3.932** [1.923]	–2.588** [1.311]	–1.829 [1.211]
Crime	–2.689*** [0.770]	–9.596*** [3.572]	–5.076** [2.300]	–6.051*** [2.251]
Regulatory compliance	0.318*** [0.064]	1.662*** [0.313]	1.404*** [0.212]	1.575*** [0.203]
Audited	0.281*** [0.046]	0.338* [0.200]	0.299* [0.155]	0.374** [0.151]
Incorporated	0.262*** [0.060]	0.196 [0.200]	0.123 [0.140]	0.125 [0.135]
Infrastructure	0.688* [0.377]	2.428 [1.687]	1.242 [1.084]	1.461 [1.058]
Access to finance	0.185*** [0.055]	–0.015 [0.280]	0.091 [0.193]	0.015 [0.188]
Technology	0.131*** [0.050]	–0.007 [0.259]	–0.142 [0.172]	0.073 [0.170]
Training	0.094** [0.041]	0.167 [0.218]	0.209 [0.152]	0.004 [0.146]
Firm controls				
Unique establishment	–0.249*** [0.054]	–0.237*** [0.063]	–0.252*** [0.048]	–0.292*** [0.047]
Log of firm's age	0.133*** [0.028]	0.122*** [0.031]	0.110*** [0.021]	0.078*** [0.021]
Foreign owned	0.402*** [0.081]	0.333*** [0.088]	0.293*** [0.062]	0.331*** [0.061]
Exporter	0.281*** [0.049]	0.272*** [0.067]	0.273*** [0.049]	0.261*** [0.048]

(continued)

Table 2.7 Investment Climate Effect on Total Factor Productivity *(continued)*

Dependent variable	Log of value added per worker			Log sales per worker
	(1)	(2)	(3)	(4)
	OLS	2SLS	2SLS	2SLS
Substitution	No	No	Yes	Yes
Instruments		Weighted averages	Weighted averages	Weighted averages
20–99 employees	−0.024 [0.048]	−0.067 [0.094]	−0.003 [0.068]	0.037 [0.068]
100+ employees	−0.122 [0.074]	−0.262* [0.158]	−0.049 [0.110]	−0.02 [0.110]
Log capital per worker	0.027*** [0.004]	0.024*** [0.005]	0.026*** [0.003]	
Observations	3,654	3,653	6,880	6,880

Source: Authors' calculations.

Note: * = significant at the 10 percent level; ** = significant at the 5 percent level; *** = significant at the 1 percent level. Robust standard errors are in brackets. Columns 1 to 3 report the results of regressing the log of value added per worker on the investment climate attributes and firm controls in the first column. Column 1 uses OLS; column 2 uses 2SLS with region–industry–firm size weighted averages as instruments; column 3 uses 2SLS with region–industry–firm size weighted averages as instruments and replaces missing observations with the instrumental variable. 2SLS instruments are constructed using a minimum threshold of 10 observations. Column 4 is as column 3 in table 2.3 but restricting the sample to the one used in column 3. All regressions include country, industry, and region dummies.

Comparing the results of columns 1 in tables 2.3 and 2.7 suggests very small differences between TFP and investment effects. Nevertheless, after controlling for endogeneity, only five variables, all from the governance and institutional group—associated with *corruption, crime, regulatory compliance*, and the incidence of firms with externally *audited* financial statements—retain their significance. Comparing column 3 of table 2.3 with column 4 of table 2.7, however, indicates that the lack of significance of the *incorporated* dummy and the *infrastructure, access to credit, skills*, and *technology* variables applies, in this smaller sample, not only to TFP effects but also to the effects of those variables on labor productivity, without controlling for materials costs and capital stocks. Thus, given the sample limitations, this empirical exercise does not allow for determining whether the significant effects obtained for these variables in table 2.3, using larger samples than in table 2.7, are driven by the effects of the variables on TFP or on investment.

For the previously mentioned set of five variables from the governance and institutional quality group, however, the relative importance of investment and TFP effects can be assessed. The main findings are as follows. First, the impact of high losses derived directly from *crime* is larger on investment than on TFP. Second, the reverse is true for the effect of high *security* expenditures, which is larger in absolute value for TFP than for investment. Finally, in the case of *corruption*, *regulatory compliance*, and *audited* firms, both types of effects are of similar magnitude.

Wage Effects

The results so far indicate that improvements in a number of investment climate attributes would lead to higher labor productivity, something that in turn may positively affect profitability, capital accumulation, and growth. Would these improvements also translate to a better standard of living for the workers of the corresponding firms? In other words, does a better investment climate also contribute to higher wages and salaries?

Table 2.8 explores this question. It reports the results for regression models similar to those in tables 2.3 and 2.7 but now using wages as the dependent variable. An additional difference is that the model also controls for the educational attainment of the typical production worker in the firm in question. More specifically, two dummy variables are introduced that are activated for firms where the typical production worker has between 7 and 12 years of schooling and for those where that worker has 13 years or more, respectively. Group weighted averages are used as instruments. In addition, in column 1 the effect of outliers is controlled for, and in column 3 education is instrumented to control for the possibility that in each firm the workers' levels of education are determined, at least in part, by the prevailing wages. In annex 2A, the results are reported using simple averages as instruments (table 2A.5).

Table 2.8 indicates that improvements in 7 of the 10 investment climate variables have a positive effect not only on firms' productivity but also on the average wages that they pay. Thus, companies that face higher levels of *corruption* or *crime*, or where governance and institutional quality issues lead to high levels of *regulatory noncompliance*, tend to pay lower wages per worker. In contrast, *audited* and *incorporated* firms, those with *access to the financial sector*, and companies with better *technology* appear to pay higher wages. Somewhat surprisingly, firms that offer more *training* do not pay more. As for the role of firm controls, table 2.8 indicates that exporters as well as older and foreign-owned firms tend to pay higher wages.[26] After controlling for all of the above, one finds that larger firms and firms with a unique establishment tend to pay lower wages.

Finally, regarding the role played by education, in the first and the second specification in table 2.8, where education is not instrumented, education affects wages. However, when the education variable is instrumented,

Table 2.8 Investment Climate Effect on Wages

	Dependent variable: Log of wage		
	(1)	*(2)*	*(3)*
	2SLS-R	*2SLS*	*2SLS*
		Education not instrumented	*Education instrumented*
Substitution	*Yes*	*Yes*	*Yes*
Instruments	*Weighted averages*	*Weighted averages*	*Weighted averages*
Investment climate attributes			
Bribes	−0.276***	−0.211**	−0.213**
	[0.064]	[0.099]	[0.099]
Security	0.401	−0.847	−0.857
	[0.557]	[0.823]	[0.824]
Crime	−1.580*	−3.551*	−3.505*
	[0.888]	[2.041]	[2.033]
Regulatory compliance	0.447***	0.652***	0.640***
	[0.098]	[0.134]	[0.137]
Audited	0.255***	0.397***	0.398***
	[0.057]	[0.117]	[0.117]
Incorporated	0.179***	0.174*	0.177*
	[0.058]	[0.091]	[0.091]
Infrastructure quality	−0.133	0.191	0.162
	[0.604]	[0.774]	[0.786]
Access to finance	0.281***	0.278*	0.284*
	[0.090]	[0.146]	[0.146]
Technology	0.002	0.218*	0.224*
	[0.059]	[0.120]	[0.121]
Training	−0.081	0.007	−0.006
	[0.063]	[0.098]	[0.099]
Firm controls			
Unique establishment	−0.136***	−0.082**	−0.079**
	[0.020]	[0.034]	[0.034]
Log of firm's age	0.063	0.090***	0.092***
	[0.042]	[0.014]	[0.014]
Foreign owned	0.371***	0.228***	0.224***
	[0.025]	[0.045]	[0.045]

(continued)

Table 2.8 Investment Climate Effect on Wages *(continued)*

	Dependent variable: Log of wage		
	(1)	*(2)*	*(3)*
	2SLS-R	2SLS	2SLS
		Education not instrumented	Education instrumented
Substitution	Yes	Yes	Yes
Instruments	Weighted averages	Weighted averages	Weighted averages
Exporter	0.174*** [0.018]	0.129*** [0.035]	0.128*** [0.035]
20–99 employees	0.027 [0.019]	–0.111** [0.047]	–0.107** [0.047]
100+ employees	0.070** [0.027]	–0.235*** [0.076]	–0.232*** [0.077]
Education of the average worker 7–12 years	0.325*** [0.068]	0.087*** [0.033]	0.121 [0.115]
Education of the average worker 13+ years	0.493*** [0.124]	0.124** [0.057]	0.301 [0.215]
Observations	10,205	10,205	10,205

Source: Authors' calculations.

Note: * = significant at the 10 percent level; ** = significant at the 5 percent level; *** = significant at the 1 percent level. Robust standard errors are in brackets. The table reports the results of regressing the log of wages per worker on the investment climate attributes and firm controls in the first column. Columns 1 to 3 use 2SLS with region–industry–firm size weighted averages as instruments. Education is instrumented in column 3. All regressions include country, industry, and region dummies.

its coefficient is not significantly different from zero (although perhaps this result is caused by the dramatic increase in the standard errors of the different estimates). Taken at face value, these results indicate that causality seems to run from wages to education (that is, better-paid jobs attract people with more years of education rather than the other way around). Nevertheless, using or not using instrumental variables for education seems to have an almost negligible effect on the coefficients of the rest of the variables.

Differential Productivity Effects for Small Firms

Some evidence (Hallward-Driemeier and Stewart 2004; World Bank 2005) now indicates that smaller firms would benefit more than proportionally from improvements in the investment climate. So that these issues can be explored, a small variation is introduced in equation 2.1 and the following model estimated:

$$\log(Y_i / L_i) = \sum_j \beta_{4j} IC_{ij} + \sum_j \beta_{5j} IC_{ij}^* A_i + \sum_j \delta_{4j} C_{ij} + v_{4i}, \qquad (2.9)$$

where A_i is a dummy variable that takes a value of 1 when firm i is a small firm (with fewer than 20 workers) so that the effect of changes in the investment climate on small firms is given by

$$\frac{\partial \log(Y_i / L_i)}{\partial IC_{ij}} = \beta_{4j} + \beta_{5j} A_i. \qquad (2.10)$$

That is, β_{5j} is the differential effect of the investment climate variable j on small firms.

The results of this exercise are reported in table 2.9.[27] Note that the productivity of small firms tends to be more affected by *corruption* and by the need to invest more in *security*. Similarly, smaller firms seem to be more negatively affected by the quality of *infrastructure* and to benefit more from the use of new *technology* than do larger firms. Somewhat surprisingly, though, increases in *regulatory compliance* lead to smaller productivity increases for firms with fewer than 20 workers.

Subregional Differences

Pooling data from several country surveys has the benefit of dramatically increasing the sample size and also introducing variability into the system that can be useful to isolate how a particular investment climate attribute affects firm performance. Yet it has the well-known problem of imposing parameter homogeneity across countries and, as is well known, this factor can be problematic if firms react to changes in investment climate conditions in different manners in different countries. In fact, when the full sample is broken into three subregional samples (Mercosur, Andes, and Central America) and two income groups (upper-middle-income and lower-middle-income countries) and the models are reestimated, the results indicate that parameter heterogeneity can be an important issue.[28] As can be seen in table 2.10, the number of investment climate attributes that enter in the different subregional samples is much smaller than in the full sample. Although the results vary by subsample, only about half of the 10 investment climate attributes are now significantly different from zero.

Columns 1 to 3 present the results for geographic subregions. Although the governance variables appear to be relevant in all the subregional groups, different variables have a different effect in different regional groups. For example, whereas *security* appears to be particularly relevant in the Andes and Central American groups, *crime* and *bribes* appear to

Table 2.9 Investment Climate Effect on Labor Productivity, by Firm Size

	Dependent variable: Log of sales per worker	
	(1)	(2)
	2SLS	2SLS
Substitution	No	Yes
Instruments	Weighted averages	Weighted averages
Investment climate attributes		
Bribes	−0.205	−0.292**
	[0.223]	[0.127]
Security	−3.313*	−3.400***
	[1.800]	[1.170]
Crime	−15.653**	−7.629**
	[6.148]	[3.604]
Regulatory compliance	2.199***	1.059***
	[0.381]	[0.213]
Audited	0.540**	0.419***
	[0.229]	[0.144]
Incorporated	0.583***	0.605***
	[0.219]	[0.139]
Infrastructure quality	1.857	0.386
	[2.399]	[1.287]
Access to finance	0.107	0.313
	[0.404]	[0.255]
Technology	0.14	0.105
	[0.263]	[0.160]
Training	0.014	0.333***
	[0.254]	[0.124]
Investment climate attributes interacted with small firm size (< 20 employees)		
Bribes	−0.881***	−0.392***
	[0.282]	[0.143]
Security	−1.142	−3.952*
	[2.325]	[2.162]

(continued)

Table 2.9 Investment Climate Effect on Labor Productivity, by Firm Size *(continued)*

	Dependent variable: Log of sales per worker	
	(1)	(2)
	2SLS	2SLS
Substitution	No	Yes
Instruments	Weighted averages	Weighted averages
Crime	9.867	2.385
	[7.261]	[4.181]
Regulatory compliance	−1.338***	−0.119
	[0.491]	[0.262]
Audited	−0.305	−0.033
	[0.248]	[0.131]
Incorporated	0.086	−0.056
	[0.197]	[0.124]
Infrastructure quality	2.409	3.488**
	[2.770]	[1.675]
Access to finance	−0.366	−0.054
	[0.450]	[0.291]
Technology	0.488*	0.404***
	[0.280]	[0.156]
Training	−0.043	−0.271
	[0.338]	[0.186]

Source: Authors' calculations.

Note: * = significant at the 10 percent level; ** = significant at the 5 percent level; *** = significant at the 1 percent level. Robust standard errors are in brackets. The table reports the results of regressing the log of sales per worker on the investment climate attributes in the first column. All columns use 2SLS and instrument region–industry–firm size weighted averages. Column 2 replaces missing observations with the instrumental variable. Instruments are constructed using a minimum threshold of 10 observations. All regressions include country, industry, and region dummies and the set of controls used in table 2.3.

be particularly relevant in the Mercosur group. *Infrastructure* and *training* appear to be more significant for the Andes group, whereas *access to finance* is positively related to labor productivity in the Mercosur group, and better *technology* is associated with better firm performance in both the Mercosur and the Andes groups.

Table 2.10 Investment Climate Effect on Labor Productivity, by Latin American and Caribbean Subregions and Income Levels

	Dependent variable: Log of sales per worker				
	(1)	*(2)*	*(3)*	*(4)*	*(5)*
	Mercosur	Andes	Central American	Upper middle income	Lower middle income
	2SLS	2SLS	2SLS	2SLS	2SLS
Substitution	Yes	Yes	Yes	Yes	Yes
Instruments	Weighted averages	Weighted averages	Weighted averages	Weighted averages	Weighted averages
Investment climate attributes					
Bribes	-0.537**	-0.343	-0.280	-0.802***	0.002
	[0.214]	[0.268]	[0.182]	[0.170]	[0.165]
Security	-7.836	-5.076**	-3.593**	-6.711***	-2.740**
	[4.848]	[2.242]	[1.683]	[2.055]	[1.363]
Crime	-11.958**	-2.313	-2.823	-7.091*	-2.763
	[4.734]	[4.738]	[2.957]	[4.209]	[1.845]
Regulatory compliance	1.323***	0.065	0.982***	1.558***	0.152
	[0.380]	[0.451]	[0.217]	[0.242]	[0.245]
Audited	0.52	0.536**	0.389*	0.510**	0.264
	[0.351]	[0.218]	[0.207]	[0.206]	[0.167]
Incorporated	0.345	0.745**	0.143	0.557**	0.183
	[0.283]	[0.294]	[0.140]	[0.227]	[0.124]
Infrastructure quality	1.008	10.116***	0.103	3.498**	0.162
	[1.808]	[2.774]	[1.414]	[1.422]	[1.303]
Access to finance	0.546*	0.009	0.036	0.079	0.567**
	[0.331]	[0.465]	[0.239]	[0.242]	[0.255]
Technology	0.528*	0.466*	-0.201	0.178	0.425**
	[0.271]	[0.275]	[0.238]	[0.204]	[0.202]
Training	0.27	0.437*	0.212	0.128	0.393**
	[0.180]	[0.243]	[0.197]	[0.154]	[0.156]
Firm controls					
Unique establishment	-0.215***	-0.174**	-0.267***	-0.277***	-0.135**
	[0.071]	[0.087]	[0.067]	[0.054]	[0.064]
Log of firm's age	0.054*	0.118***	0.086***	0.098***	0.076***
	[0.030]	[0.032]	[0.029]	[0.024]	[0.023]

(continued)

Table 2.10 Investment Climate Effect on Labor Productivity, by Latin American and Caribbean Subregions and Income Levels *(continued)*

	Dependent variable: Log of sales per worker				
	(1)	*(2)*	*(3)*	*(4)*	*(5)*
	Mercosur	*Andes*	*Central American*	*Upper middle income*	*Lower middle income*
	2SLS	*2SLS*	*2SLS*	*2SLS*	*2SLS*
Substitution	Yes	Yes	Yes	Yes	Yes
Instruments	*Weighted averages*	*Weighted averages*	*Weighted averages*	*Weighted averages*	*Weighted averages*
Foreign owned	0.398*** [0.125]	0.399*** [0.099]	0.267*** [0.076]	0.327*** [0.070]	0.493*** [0.076]
Exporter	0.215*** [0.081]	0.033 [0.081]	0.158** [0.064]	0.198*** [0.058]	0.117** [0.057]
20–99 employees	−0.165* [0.099]	−0.190* [0.107]	0.192** [0.085]	−0.127 [0.083]	0.014 [0.072]
100+ employees	−0.415** [0.194]	−0.545*** [0.154]	0.085 [0.155]	−0.359*** [0.135]	−0.211* [0.125]
Observations	3,577	3,296	3,662	5,922	4,613

Source: Authors' calculations.

Note: * = significant at the 10 percent level; ** = significant at the 5 percent level; *** = significant at the 1 percent level. Robust standard errors are in brackets. The table reports the results of regressing the log of wages per worker on the investment climate attributes and firm controls in the first column. All columns use 2SLS with region–industry–firm size weighted averages as instruments. Column 1 covers Argentina, Brazil, Paraguay, and Uruguay; column 2 Bolivia, Chile, Colombia, Ecuador, and Peru; column 3 Costa Rica, El Salvador, Guatemala, Honduras, Mexico, Nicaragua, and Panama; column 4 Argentina, Brazil, Chile, Costa Rica, Mexico, Panama, and Uruguay; and column 5 Bolivia, Colombia, Ecuador, El Salvador, Honduras, Guatemala, Nicaragua, Paraguay, and Peru. All regressions include country, industry, and region dummies.

One may argue that significant differences exist between neighboring countries—for example, between Chile and the rest of Andean countries, or between Mexico and the Central American countries. To address this issue, columns 4 and 5 break the sample into two income groups, upper-middle-income countries, and lower-middle-income countries. All governance variables and the *infrastructure* variable appear to be significantly associated with labor productivity in upper-middle-income countries, while this relationship is true only for *security* expenses in lower-middle-income countries. In contrast, *access to finance, technology,* and *training* appear as key constraints for lower-middle-income countries.

Global Effects

Are the findings presented for this Latin American sample specific to that sample, or would they apply similarly to other regions? To address this question, table 2.11 reports the results of estimating model 2.1 with a global sample that pools all existing Enterprise Surveys, from Latin America and elsewhere, and covers approximately 21,000 firms. As seen in this table, the global results show limited sensitivity to the use of different instruments or to the replacement of missing values by group averages (beyond clearly obtaining more efficient estimates when missing values are replaced). Moreover, apart from bribes and access to finance, which in the global sample do not appear to belong to the estimated equation, the remaining findings obtained for Latin America appear to hold in the global sample, with even the magnitude of the estimated coefficients being statistically the same in most cases.

Merging Enterprise Surveys and Household Data

The introduction to this chapter stressed the strengths of Enterprise Surveys to measure aspects related to the quality of governance and institutions. Nevertheless, because some other aspects, such as human capital levels, are probably captured less well in these surveys, bringing additional data sources to this exercise could enrich the analysis. The study explores this issue further by merging the Enterprise Surveys data with human capital data from household surveys, a source that in principle is likely to have more reliable information on that variable than Enterprise Surveys.

Before looking at the results of this exercise, one may want to review the econometrics behind it, especially because the information in the household data does not allow matching an individual with a particular firm in the Enterprise Survey. However, under fairly general conditions, this disparity does not prevent the estimation of the parameters of interest of the underlying econometric model.

To facilitate the exposition as much as possible, consider the following simplified version of model 2.1:

$$y_{ijs} = \gamma h_{ijs} + v_{ijs},\qquad\qquad(2.11)$$

where y is the log of sales per worker; h is, for example, a measure of the human capital of the labor force working for the firm; and v is the error term. The subscript indicates that the data refer to firm i in industry j and region s. The parameter of interest in this case is γ.

Table 2.11 Investment Climate Effect on Labor Productivity: Global Sample

	Dependent variable: Log of sales per worker		
	(1)	*(2)*	*(3)*
	OLS	2SLS	2SLS
Substitution	No	No	Yes
Instruments		Weighted averages	Weighted averages
Investment climate attributes			
Bribes	0.059**	−0.087	−0.096
	[0.025]	[0.118]	[0.080]
Security	−1.179***	−1.013	−1.828*
	[0.396]	[1.459]	[0.935]
Crime	−1.638***	−8.129***	−7.100***
	[0.481]	[2.362]	[1.446]
Regulatory compliance	0.279***	1.398***	1.160***
	[0.046]	[0.227]	[0.141]
Audited	0.233***	0.633***	0.563***
	[0.026]	[0.118]·	[0.085]
Incorporated	0.139***	0.166*	0.181**
	[0.025]	[0.100]	[0.072]
Infrastructure quality	0.651***	2.241**	1.226**
	[0.231]	[1.142]	[0.610]
Access to finance	0.155***	−0.118	0.049
	[0.025]	[0.141]	[0.102]
Technology	0.217***	0.565***	0.513***
	[0.027]	[0.136]	[0.092]
Training	0.105***	0.293**	0.315***
	[0.023]	[0.116]	[0.077]
Firm controls			
Unique establishment	−0.170***	−0.106***	−0.115***
	[0.029]	[0.036]	[0.025]
Log of firm's age	0.025	−0.003	0.011
	[0.016]	[0.018]	[0.012]
Foreign owned	0.341***	0.217***	0.281***
	[0.043]	[0.047]	[0.032]
Exporter	0.178***	0.086**	0.071***
	[0.028]	[0.038]	[0.027]

(continued)

Table 2.11 Investment Climate Effect on Labor Productivity:
Global Sample *(continued)*

	Dependent variable: Log of sales per worker		
	(1)	*(2)*	*(3)*
	OLS	2SLS	2SLS
Substitution	No	No	Yes
Instruments		Weighted averages	Weighted averages
20–99 employees	–0.032	–0.220***	–0.169***
	[0.027]	[0.056]	[0.037]
100+ employees	–0.124***	–0.494***	–0.372***
	[0.040]	[0.090]	[0.058]
Observations	9,761	9,760	20,990
Region dummies	Yes	Yes	Yes

Source: Authors' calculations.

Note: * = significant at the 10 percent level; ** = significant at the 5 percent level; *** = significant at the 1 percent level. Robust standard errors are in brackets. The table reports the results of regressing the log of sales per worker on the investment climate attributes in the first column. All columns use 2SLS and region–industry–firm size weighted averages as instruments. Column 3 replaces missing observations with the instrumental variable. Instruments are constructed using a minimum threshold of 10 observations. All regressions include country, industry, and region dummies and the set of controls used in table 2.3.

Assume now that reasons exist to believe that there is reverse causality in equation 2.11 but that $h._{js}$ (the average value of h in industry j and region s) is a valid instrument. In these circumstances, as already discussed, the OLS estimator of γ in

$$y_{ijs} = \gamma h._{js} + v_{ijs} \qquad (2.12)$$

will be identical to the instrumental variable (IV) estimator of γ in equation 2.11 when h_{ijs} is instrumented with $h._j$. Thus, it follows that to obtain the IV estimator of γ in equation 2.11, one need not match the data of the two surveys. It is enough to be able to identify the industry and region (and any other attribute used to compute group averages, such as firm size) to which the firm and individual belong—for which, in general, the information is available.

Against this background, the basic model is reestimated but augmented with an education variable from the household survey: the average years of education of the adult population. Table 2.12 presents the results. They indicate that when education is brought into the empirical model from the

Table 2.12 Education and the Investment Climate

	Dependent variable: Log of sales per worker		
	(1)	*(2)*	*(3)*
	OLS	2SLS	2SLS
Substitution	No	No	Yes
Instruments		Weighted averages	Weighted averages
Investment climate attributes			
Bribes	0.009	0.163	−0.288
	[0.069]	[0.419]	[0.191]
Security	−4.512***	−9.331*	−9.268**
	[1.438]	[5.130]	[3.788]
Crime	−3.244**	−19.553**	−7.081**
	[1.335]	[9.609]	[2.943]
Regulatory compliance	0.337***	1.346**	0.317
	[0.102]	[0.611]	[0.256]
Audited	0.092	0.438	0.241
	[0.059]	[0.309]	[0.167]
Incorporated	0.411***	0.912**	0.998***
	[0.079]	[0.393]	[0.190]
Infrastructure quality	1.948**	2.787	1.622
	[0.965]	[4.978]	[2.282]
Access to finance	0.201**	0.345	0.444*
	[0.081]	[0.463]	[0.251]
Technology	0.258***	0.686	0.462**
	[0.063]	[0.452]	[0.207]
Training	−0.034	0.269	0.377**
	[0.057]	[0.388]	[0.156]
Firm controls			
Unique establishment	−0.192**	0.011	−0.085
	[0.090]	[0.146]	[0.059]
Log of firm's age	0.109***	0.074*	0.094***
	[0.034]	[0.045]	[0.023]
Foreign owned	0.250**	0.029	0.453***
	[0.119]	[0.161]	[0.070]
Exporter	0.07	−0.055	0.035
	[0.068]	[0.160]	[0.065]

(continued)

Table 2.12 Education and the Investment Climate *(continued)*

	Dependent variable: Log of sales per worker		
	(1)	*(2)*	*(3)*
	OLS	2SLS	2SLS
Substitution	No	No	Yes
Instruments		Weighted averages	Weighted averages
20–99 employees	−0.004	−0.305	−0.240***
	[0.061]	[0.191]	[0.071]
100+ employees	−0.04	−0.662*	−0.522***
	[0.099]	[0.344]	[0.121]
Average education	0.005	−0.003	0.018*
	[0.015]	[0.019]	[0.010]
Observations	1,513	1,513	5,212

Source: Authors' calculations.

Note: * = significant at the 10 percent level; ** = significant at the 5 percent level; *** = significant at the 1 percent level. Robust standard errors are in brackets. The table reports the results of regressing the log of sales/wages per worker on the investment climate attributes and firm controls in the first column. Columns 2 and 3 use 2SLS with region–industry–firm size weighted averages as instruments. All regressions include country, industry, and region dummies.

household surveys, it appears to belong to both the productivity and the wage equations.

Taking Stock of Previous Studies

How do these results compare to those in the literature? Over the past few years, a large number of (typically cross-national) studies have focused on understanding the determinants of economic growth in Latin America. Here the last and perhaps the most complete of these studies is reviewed: a recent study of the World Bank's Latin American region by Loayza, Fajnzylber, and Calderón (2005). A summary of their main results follows. First, they show that structural factors such as human capital, financial depth, trade openness, public infrastructure, and low government burden have a positive and robust relationship with growth. Second, they find evidence that growth is discouraged by high inflation rates, by the volatility of the cyclical component of GDP, by real exchange rate misalignment, and by the frequency of systemic banking crises, thus indicating a link between macroeconomic stability and long-run growth. Third, their results confirm that external shocks significantly affect economic growth.

These results are broadly supported by a vast empirical literature on endogenous growth, including Barro (1991) on the role of education, trade, and government burden, among other variables; Dollar (1992) on trade openness; Canning, Fay, and Perotti (1994) on public infrastructure; and Beck, Levine, and Loayza (2000) on financial depth.

Somewhat surprisingly, however, Loayza, Fajnzylber, and Calderón (2005) find that their governance variable does not have a statistically significant effect on economic growth, and the corresponding coefficient even presents a negative sign.[29] Interestingly, among the variables they use, the governance variable has the second-largest positive correlation with the growth rate of GDP per capita.[30] They interpret their results on governance by saying that its effect on economic growth works through the actual economic policies that governments implement. This hypothesis also finds support in the background study for this report by Loayza and Sugawara (2007), who argue that governance appears to have significant beneficial effects on the (long-run) levels and (medium-term) changes of a large number of growth determinants. In a sense, their results contrast with those in Easterly and Levine (2001), who find that governance, not specific policies, matters for explaining cross-country differences in income levels.

The results of Loayza, Fajnzylber, and Calderón (2005) can also be used to estimate the contribution of each driver of growth to the explanation of changes in countries' growth performance over a given period. This exercise is illustrated in figure 2.2, which confirms that to understand the recent Latin American growth experience—for example, the factors that explain growth changes between the first and the second half of the 1990s—one has to pay attention to at least four areas of policy reform: infrastructure, education, international trade, and financial development.

On the whole, the analysis in this study seems to complement the existing literature. On the one hand, the econometric estimates on the determinants of firm performance suggest an important role for areas that previous studies have found to be critical in the region: human capital and innovation, infrastructure, and financial development. Similarly, this study finds that exporters perform better (see chapter 7 for more on this issue) than firms focusing on domestic markets.

On the other hand, this analysis stresses the role played by governance and institutional quality factors. In fact, the prevalence of the rule of law (as reflected in corruption and crime levels) and the quality of the regulatory framework (as illustrated by the extent of regulatory compliance and corporate governance–related aspects) are found to be among the most relevant determinants of firm performance in the region. Given that addressing shortcomings in these two areas is likely to be a prerequisite for making significant progress with other potential growth determinants, they should be put at the top of the policy agenda in the region.

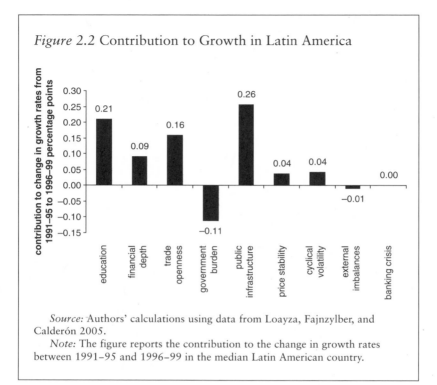

Figure 2.2 Contribution to Growth in Latin America

Source: Authors' calculations using data from Loayza, Fajnzylber, and Calderón 2005.

Note: The figure reports the contribution to the change in growth rates between 1991–95 and 1996–99 in the median Latin American country.

Summary and Conclusions

The main results of this econometric analysis show that the four broad areas of the investment climate previously discussed affect the performance of Latin American firms. More specifically, the results suggest that the prevalence of the rule of law is a critical element of the investment climate, in that it has a robust effect on firm productivity. In the econometric models, three variables point in that direction. One is *corruption*, measured through firms' payment of bribes to secure public contracts and to obtain public services (electricity, telephone, and so on). The two others are the share of sales lost to *crime* and the preventive *security* expenditures made by firms. In the three cases, these variables are associated with lower levels of labor productivity, both through reductions in investment rates and through lower levels of TFP. However, whereas the effects of *corruption* on investment and TFP are similar in magnitude, *crime* appears to have a larger impact on investment and *security* expenditures have a large effect on TFP. In addition, both *corruption* and *crime* have a significant negative effect on average wages.

Evidence is also found of the role played by a good regulatory framework in shaping firm performance. For example, the level of *regulatory compliance* (as measured by the share of sales declared for tax purposes) has a positive effect on both labor and total factor productivity, as well as on average wages. High levels of tax evasion—and for that matter a high incidence of firm informality—can be considered a symptom of excessive or arbitrarily enforced rules and regulations. Thus, it is not that high tax evasion—or informality, for that matter—necessarily negatively affect productivity, but rather that the factors that lead to low regulatory compliance also lead to lower levels of firm productivity.[31] Similarly, the results of this study indicate that wages and firm productivity tend to be higher in areas where a high proportion of firms have their financial statements externally *audited* and where a high fraction of firms choose the *corporate* form, which again is interpreted as evidence that regulatory reforms that generate stronger investor protection mechanisms and reduce regulatory burdens have the potential for boosting firm productivity, which is reflected in average wages.

Beyond the findings for governance and institutional quality, the results suggest that deficiencies in the quality of *infrastructure*, as measured by firms' losses because of power outages, are negatively and significantly related to labor productivity. Moreover, on the finance front, firms that are not credit constrained exhibit higher levels of labor productivity and wages. Finally, in the area of *skills* and *technology*, the study finds that where workers have more years of schooling, employers offer *training* to their workers, and more firms use the Internet to communicate with clients and suppliers, labor productivity tends to be significantly greater and, with the exception of *training,* wages also tend to be higher. On a related matter, the results also indicate that, after one controls for other factors, exporters tend to pay higher wages and exhibit higher labor and total factor productivity than nonexporters, as do foreign-owned firms in comparison with their domestic counterparts. As argued later in this report, these results could be partially driven by the fact that access to foreign product and capital markets could allow the transfer of more modern technologies than those available to companies that are restricted to local markets.

Most of these findings are robust to the exclusion of firms with 100-plus workers and firms with foreign capital from the samples, which, following Dollar, Hallward-Driemeier, and Mengistae (2005), is interpreted as evidence that these results are not driven by the self-selection of better-performing firms into good investment climate areas—smaller domestic firms being considerably less mobile than the excluded group of firms. In addition, these results are in most cases robust to the use of estimation methods that control for the influence of outliers; the only exceptions are the effect of *security expenditures* and *audits.*

Another important finding is that improvements in the investment climate have the potential to improve the relative performance of SMEs. In particular, this study finds that the labor productivity of firms with fewer than 20 workers is more adversely affected, compared with that of larger firms, by a high incidence of *corruption* and the need for higher *security* expenditures. Moreover, smaller firms would benefit to a larger extent from improvements in the areas of *infrastructure* quality and *technology* adoption.

Incidentally, these results on the larger effect of the investment climate on SMEs are consistent with previous findings obtained for other regions (see World Bank 2005). In fact, the basic model is also estimated using a global sample that includes about 10,000 firms from the surveys performed by the World Bank in other regions of the world. Most results are maintained, with the exception of *corruption* and *access to finance*, which cease to be significant in the global sample. This result may indicate that imposing homogeneity in parameter values across different regions may be too strong an assumption. In fact, evidence is found of considerable heterogeneity across geographically defined subsets of Latin American countries.

Noteworthy is the fact that 6 of the 10 variables that are found to be significant drivers of firm productivity can be thought of as belonging to the governance–regulatory quality group, whereas variables from the infrastructure, technology, and finance groups are represented more meagerly in the study's set. In other words, whereas these results do lend credence to the hypothesis that all four main investment climate areas of focus are relevant for improving firm performance, reforms associated with the regulatory and governance frameworks appear to be a particularly important potential avenue for boosting growth in the region. A question that emerges in this context is whether this finding can be interpreted as evidence that in the Latin American region those issues are more important than other investment climate aspects or, alternatively, it is a reflection of the nature of the data or empirical methodology.

Both factors are likely to play a role. Thus, on one hand, Latin America's poor international standing in various indicators of the quality of governance and institutions is consistent with the finding that those aspects have a relatively large effect on the performance of firms operating in the region. On the other hand, the selection of the set of critical investment climate variables described in table 2.2 may also be driven by the nature of the data and estimation methodology that is employed in the study. In particular, the nature of the survey questionnaire is such that it is harder to find good infrastructure, finance, human capital, and technology indicators that meet the criteria of being measured objectively, being comparable across firms, and being easy to interpret. Moreover, some of the *infrastructure* and *technology* variables could arguably have direct effects on only some subset of firms—for example, those that are more knowledge or transportation intensive or those that are deciding whether to enter the market.

As a result, a much larger weight should be given to the study's positive findings than to its negative ones—that is, the fact that the variables excluded from the basic specification do not appear to be relevant for understanding firm performance, at least when using the study's data and estimation approach. Thus, the results are interpreted as being complementary to those of previous cross-country studies, which have emphasized the need to focus mainly on education, infrastructure, and financial development but have failed to uncover robust links between growth and the quality of governance and institutions, perhaps because of the aggregate nature of their data. In particular, one of the main messages of this report is that the improvement of governance and institutional factors should be added to the set of policy priorities to promote growth in the region.

Comment is necessary on a final issue: improvements to the investment climate are likely to require cooperation among many actors. In particular, although the actions needed to improve regulatory frameworks and the rule of law are direct responsibilities of the public sector, in these and other microeconomic reform areas a combination of public intervention and private action is likely to be needed for achieving greater effect. Thus, for instance, the participation of the private sector is crucial in programs as varied as those aimed at reducing corruption, fighting crime by creating economic opportunities for at-risk youth, improving regulatory frameworks, reducing red tape, increasing regulatory compliance, upgrading private corporate governance standards, developing financial markets, increasing the adoption of modern technologies, and improving worker training systems.

True, in many of these areas coordination and other types of market failures make government interventions critical. Thus, for instance, it is a government responsibility to ensure that good basic education is available to all and that property rights are well protected—and even to create monetary incentives that allow for the development of missing markets (as in the case of SMEs' finance) or to compensate for the inability of private firms to capture all the social benefits of their investments (as in the case of worker training and innovation). However, unless competitive pressures are such that achieving faster productivity growth is an integral component of the business strategies of private companies, achieving any meaningful result would be difficult on the basis of public sector reforms only.

Annex 2A Statistical Tables

Table 2A.1 Descriptive Statistics of Variables Used in Econometric Analyses, Average by Country

	Latin America and the Caribbean		Argentina	Bolivia	Brazil	Chile	Colombia	Costa Rica	Ecuador
	Observations	Mean							
Investment climate attributes									
Bribes	7,452	0.19	0.31	0.43	0.76	0.06	0.11	0.19	0.68
Security	11,101	0.01	0.01	0.01	0.02	0.01	0.01	0.01	0.09
Crime	11,289	0.01	0.01	0.01	0.01	0.01	0.01	0.01	0.01
Regulatory compliance	10,336	0.76	0.83	0.79	0.67	0.97	0.80	0.72	0.80
Audited	11,644	0.40	0.63	0.71	0.19	0.60	0.47	0.56	0.47
Incorporated	11,781	0.72	0.88	0.61	0.93	0.92	0.67	0.86	0.97
Infrastructure quality	10,958	0.99	1.00	0.98	0.98	0.99	0.98	0.98	0.96
Access to finance	11,649	0.83	0.85	0.82	0.85	0.93	0.85	0.85	0.77
Technology	11,479	0.39	0.72	0.43	0.73	0.77	0.29	0.77	0.55
Training	9,091	0.43	0.52	0.54	0.67	0.72	0.39	0.46	0.70
Firm controls									
Unique establishment	11,787	0.83	0.75	0.84	0.74	0.58	0.97	0.76	0.72
Log of firm's age	11,672	2.60	3.03	2.60	2.86	3.05	2.30	2.82	2.99
Foreign owned	11,787	0.08	0.14	0.14	0.05	0.16	0.01	0.09	0.13
Exporter	11,769	0.16	0.44	0.19	0.31	0.39	0.15	0.39	0.30
Fewer than 20 employees	11,787	0.63	0.47	0.55	0.18	0.34	0.64	0.63	0.30

(continued)

Table 2A.1 Descriptive Statistics of Variables Used in Econometric Analyses, Average by Country (*continued*)

	Latin America and the Caribbean									
	Observations	Mean	Argentina	Bolivia	Brazil	Chile	Colombia	Costa Rica	Ecuador
20–99 employees	11,787	0.28	0.37	0.39	0.54	0.36	0.31	0.25	0.47
100+ employees	11,787	0.08	0.16	0.06	0.28	0.30	0.04	0.12	0.18
Firm controls									
Food	11,787	0.06	0.10	0.07	0.08	0.23	0.03	0.12	0.25
Garments	11,716	0.03	0.02	0.12	0.27	0.00	0.04	0.09	0.08
Textile	11,716	0.03	0.02	0.00	0.06	0.00	0.05	0.06	0.08
Metals and machinery	11,716	0.04	0.16	0.00	0.11	0.20	0.01	0.15	0.17
Chemicals	11,716	0.05	0.17	0.02	0.05	0.15	0.02	0.00	0.20
Electronics	11,716	0.00	0.00	0.00	0.05	0.00	0.00	0.01	0.00
Nonmetallic	11,716	0.02	0.01	0.01	0.00	0.00	0.00	0.24	0.09
Other manufacturing	11,716	0.21	0.25	0.31	0.38	0.18	0.25	0.34	0.13
Retail	11,716	0.25	0.15	0.17	0.00	0.00	0.26	0.00	0.00
Information technology	11,716	0.01	0.01	0.00	0.00	0.22	0.03	0.00	0.00
Other services	11,716	0.22	0.11	0.10	0.00	0.00	0.16	0.00	0.00
Construction and transportation	11,716	0.09	0.02	0.19	0.00	0.00	0.16	0.00	0.00
Wholesale (Panama)	11,716	0.00	0.00	0.00	0.00	0.00	0.00	0.00	0.00

(*continued*)

Table 2A.1 Descriptive Statistics of Variables Used in Econometric Analyses, Average by Country *(continued)*

	El Salvador	Guatemala	Honduras	Mexico	Nicaragua	Panama	Paraguay	Peru	Uruguay
Investment climate attributes									
Bribes	0.35	0.30	0.36	0.13	0.37	0.14	0.50	0.31	0.09
Security	0.04	0.02	0.04	0.01	0.03	0.02	0.02	0.01	0.01
Crime	0.01	0.02	0.01	0.01	0.01	0.01	0.01	0.00	0.01
Regulatory compliance	0.77	0.78	0.68	0.72	0.66	0.60	0.81	0.89	0.87
Audited	0.79	0.52	0.43	0.28	0.27	0.86	0.19	0.33	0.21
Incorporated	0.35	0.63	0.01	0.65	0.02	0.92	0.86	0.95	0.91
Infrastructure quality	0.98	0.98	0.96	0.99	0.95	0.98	0.98	0.99	1.00
Access to finance	0.87	0.91	0.82	0.80	0.72	0.97	0.89	0.92	0.83
Technology	0.30	0.42	0.22	0.28	0.16	0.39	0.34	0.55	0.33
Training	0.52	0.43	0.57	0.25	0.44	0.44	0.47	0.58	0.25
Firm controls									
Unique establishment	0.82	0.88	0.72	0.82	0.83	0.80	0.92	0.89	0.88
Log of firm's age	2.91	2.76	2.62	2.45	2.89	2.94	2.74	2.64	2.91
Foreign owned	0.09	0.10	0.16	0.07	0.10	0.11	0.11	0.10	0.08
Exporter	0.45	0.33	0.38	0.03	0.26	0.26	0.19	0.30	0.28
Fewer than 20 employees	0.41	0.40	0.51	0.72	0.64	0.62	0.52	0.35	0.68

(continued)

Table 2A.1 Descriptive Statistics of Variables Used in Econometric Analyses, Average by Country (continued)

	El Salvador	Guatemala	Honduras	Mexico	Nicaragua	Panama	Paraguay	Peru	Uruguay
20–99 employees	0.38	0.38	0.25	0.22	0.28	0.27	0.37	0.46	0.27
100+ employees	0.21	0.22	0.24	0.06	0.08	0.10	0.10	0.20	0.05
Firm controls									
Food	0.25	0.16	0.26	0.05	0.19	0.06	0.19	0.04	0.09
Garments	0.23	0.07	0.18	0.02	0.12	0.01	0.10	0.10	0.05
Textile	0.03	0.07	0.04	0.01	0.03	0.01	0.01	0.12	0.13
Metals and machinery	0.16	0.00	0.07	0.02	0.10	0.02	0.03	0.00	0.00
Chemicals	0.10	0.03	0.04	0.01	0.08	0.01	0.11	0.04	0.04
Electronics	0.00	0.00	0.00	0.00	0.00	0.00	0.02	0.00	0.00
Nonmetallic	0.19	0.02	0.14	0.01	0.15	0.02	0.06	0.00	0.18
Other manufacturing	0.04	0.30	0.28	0.20	0.34	0.11	0.15	0.00	0.12
Retail	0.00	0.14	0.00	0.31	0.00	0.23	0.25	0.12	0.21
Information technology	0.00	0.01	0.00	0.01	0.00	0.00	0.01	0.00	0.01
Other services	0.00	0.13	0.00	0.28	0.00	0.13	0.03	0.47	0.10
Construction and transportation	0.00	0.08	0.00	0.08	0.00	0.32	0.06	0.11	0.07
Wholesale (Panama)	0.00	0.00	0.00	0.00	0.00	0.07	0.00	0.00	0.00

Source: Authors' calculations.

Table 2A.2 Investment Climate Effect on Labor Productivity

	Dependent variable: Log of sales per worker		
	(1)	(2)	(3)
	OLS	2SLS	2SLS
Substitution	No	No	Yes
Instruments		Sample averages	Sample averages
Investment climate attributes			
Bribes	−0.016 [0.044]	−0.515** [0.201]	−0.469*** [0.117]
Security	−1.116*** [0.338]	−2.002 [1.631]	−3.556*** [1.168]
Crime	−2.969*** [0.736]	−10.644*** [3.032]	−7.476*** [1.764]
Regulatory compliance	0.335*** [0.060]	1.687*** [0.282]	1.136*** [0.157]
Audited	0.272*** [0.043]	0.486** [0.205]	0.273** [0.128]
Incorporated	0.290*** [0.051]	0.351** [0.172]	0.338*** [0.105]
Infrastructure quality	0.899** [0.397]	3.030* [1.573]	1.880** [0.906]
Access to finance	0.204*** [0.047]	0.002 [0.253]	0.209 [0.166]
Technology	0.169*** [0.046]	0.213 [0.237]	0.194 [0.126]
Training	0.102*** [0.038]	−0.012 [0.199]	0.306*** [0.112]
Firm controls			
Unique establishment	−0.339*** [0.051]	−0.305*** [0.059]	−0.253*** [0.038]
Log of firm's age	0.121*** [0.026]	0.092*** [0.029]	0.095*** [0.016]
Foreign owned	0.356*** [0.078]	0.244*** [0.085]	0.400*** [0.050]
Exporter	0.255*** [0.045]	0.224*** [0.067]	0.181*** [0.038]

(continued)

Table 2A.2 Investment Climate Effect on Labor Productivity *(continued)*

	Dependent variable: Log of sales per worker		
	(1)	*(2)*	*(3)*
	OLS	2SLS	2SLS
Substitution	No	No	Yes
Instruments		Sample averages	Sample averages
20–99 employees	0.032	−0.044	−0.031
	[0.044]	[0.088]	[0.050]
100+ employees	−0.098	−0.282*	−0.222***
	[0.070]	[0.152]	[0.085]
Observations	4,207	4,207	10,535

Source: Authors' calculations.

Note: * = significant at the 10 percent level; ** = significant at the 5 percent level; *** = significant at the 1 percent level. Robust standard errors are in brackets. The table reports the results of regressing the log of sales per worker on the investment climate attributes and firm controls in the first column. Column 1 uses OLS; column 2 uses 2SLS with region–industry–firm size sample averages as instruments; column 3 uses 2SLS with region–industry–firm size sample averages as instruments and replaces missing observations with the instrumental variable. 2SLS instruments are constructed using a minimum threshold of 10 observations. All regressions include country, industry, and region dummies.

Table 2A.3 Investment Climate Effect on Labor Productivity:
Domestic Firms with Fewer than 100 Employees

	Dependent variable: Log of sales per worker	
	Small and medium firms (<100 employees)	
	(1)	(2)
	2SLS	2SLS
Substitution	No	Yes
Instruments	Sample averages	Sample averages
Investment climate attributes		
Bribes	–0.396**	–0.470***
	[0.177]	[0.139]
Security	–1.556	–2.828**
	[1.223]	[1.220]
Crime	–8.282***	–7.385***
	[2.164]	[1.769]
Regulatory compliance	0.954***	0.870***
	[0.247]	[0.180]
Audited	0.026	0.189
	[0.151]	[0.130]
Incorporated	0.556***	0.431***
	[0.140]	[0.103]
Infrastructure quality	4.803***	2.398**
	[1.485]	[1.000]
Access to finance	0.155	0.330*
	[0.231]	[0.170]
Technology	0.255	0.246*
	[0.158]	[0.129]
Training	0.183	0.372***
	[0.167]	[0.121]

(continued)

Table 2A.3 Investment Climate Effect on Labor Productivity: Domestic Firms with Fewer Than 100 Employees *(continued)*

	Dependent variable: Log of sales per worker	
	Small and medium firms (<100 employees)	
	(1)	(2)
	2SLS	2SLS
Substitution	No	Yes
Instruments	Sample averages	Sample averages
Firm controls		
Unique establishment	−0.332***	−0.207***
	[0.061]	[0.046]
Log of firm's age	0.074***	0.052***
	[0.025]	[0.019]
Exporter	0.316***	0.169***
	[0.050]	[0.041]
Observations	3,993	7,906

Source: Authors' calculations.

Note: * = significant at the 10 percent level; ** = significant at the 5 percent level; *** = significant at the 1 percent level. Robust standard errors are in brackets. The table reports the results of regressing the log of sales per worker on the investment climate attributes and firm controls in the first column. Column 1 uses 2SLS with region–industry–firm size sample averages as instruments; column 2 uses 2SLS with region–industry–firm size sample averages as instruments and replaces missing observations with the instrumental variable. 2SLS instruments are constructed using a minimum threshold of 10 observations. All regressions include country, industry, and region dummies.

Table 2A.4 Investment Climate Effect on Total Factor
Productivity

	Dependent variable: Log of value added per worker			Log sales per worker
	(1)	(2)	(3)	(4)
	OLS	2SLS	2SLS	2SLS
Substitution	No	No	Yes	Yes
Instruments		Sample averages	Sample averages	Sample averages
Investment climate attributes				
Bribes	0.001	−0.494**	−0.479***	−0.506***
	[0.047]	[0.216]	[0.138]	[0.135]
Security	−1.478***	−3.838**	−2.572*	−1.826
	[0.375]	[1.912]	[1.317]	[1.214]
Crime	−2.689***	−8.683***	−5.119**	−6.151***
	[0.770]	[3.283]	[2.216]	[2.261]
Regulatory compliance	0.318***	1.699***	1.518***	1.589***
	[0.064]	[0.302]	[0.209]	[0.205]
Audited	0.281***	0.353*	0.333**	0.379**
	[0.046]	[0.200]	[0.155]	[0.152]
Incorporated	0.262***	0.181	0.113	0.121
	[0.060]	[0.201]	[0.140]	[0.136]
Infrastructure	0.688*	2.65	1.306	1.421
	[0.377]	[1.667]	[1.084]	[1.061]
Access to finance	0.185***	−0.079	0.02	0.003
	[0.055]	[0.277]	[0.192]	[0.188]
Technology	0.131***	−0.019	−0.124	0.076
	[0.050]	[0.254]	[0.167]	[0.170]
Training	0.094**	0.195	0.213	−0.004
	[0.041]	[0.215]	[0.151]	[0.147]
Firm controls				
Unique establishment	−0.249***	−0.236***	−0.248***	−0.292***
	[0.054]	[0.062]	[0.048]	[0.047]
Log of firm's age	0.133***	0.124***	0.110***	0.078***
	[0.028]	[0.031]	[0.021]	[0.021]

(continued)

Table 2A.4 Investment Climate Effect on Total Factor
Productivity *(continued)*

	Dependent variable: Log of value added per worker			Log sales per worker
	(1)	*(2)*	*(3)*	*(4)*
	OLS	2SLS	2SLS	2SLS
Substitution	No	No	Yes	Yes
Instruments		Sample averages	Sample averages	Sample averages
Foreign owned	0.402***	0.325***	0.284***	0.330***
	[0.081]	[0.087]	[0.061]	[0.061]
Exporter	0.281***	0.269***	0.268***	0.262***
	[0.049]	[0.067]	[0.048]	[0.048]
20–99 employees	−0.024	−0.069	−0.011	0.038
	[0.048]	[0.093]	[0.068]	[0.068]
100+ employees	−0.122	−0.267*	−0.064	−0.02
	[0.074]	[0.157]	[0.109]	[0.111]
Log capital per worker	0.027***	0.024***	0.026***	
	[0.004]	[0.005]	[0.003]	
Observations	3,654	3,653	6,880	6,880

Source: Authors' calculations.

Note: * = significant at the 10 percent level; ** = significant at the 5 percent
level; *** = significant at the 1 percent level. Robust standard errors are in brackets.
Columns 1 to 3 report the results of regressing the log of value added per worker
on the investment climate attributes and firm controls in the first column. Column
1 uses OLS; column 2 uses 2SLS with region–industry–firm size sample averages as
instruments; column 3 uses 2SLS with region–industry–firm size sample averages as
instruments and replaces missing observations with the instrumental variable. 2SLS
instruments are constructed using a minimum threshold of 10 observations. Column
4 is as column 3 in table A.3 but restricts the sample to the one used in column 3. All
regressions include country, industry, and region dummies.

Table 2A.5 Investment Climate Effect on Wages

	Dependent variable: Log of wage		
	(1)	*(2)*	*(3)*
	2SLS-R	*2SLS*	*2SLS*
		Education not instrumented	*Education instrumented*
Substitution	Yes	Yes	Yes
Instruments	*Sample averages*	*Sample averages*	*Sample averages*
Investment climate attributes			
Bribes	−0.374***	−0.306***	−0.312***
	[0.070]	[0.098]	[0.099]
Security	0.278	−0.822	−0.838
	[0.563]	[0.810]	[0.813]
Crime	−1.812*	−1.938	−1.842
	[0.994]	[1.732]	[1.716]
Regulatory compliance	0.427***	0.570***	0.558***
	[0.101]	[0.133]	[0.135]
Audited	0.289***	0.449***	0.458***
	[0.059]	[0.115]	[0.114]
Incorporated	0.215***	0.220**	0.223**
	[0.060]	[0.086]	[0.087]
Infrastructure quality	−0.22	0.302	0.236
	[0.632]	[0.755]	[0.771]
Access to finance	0.211**	0.178	0.192
	[0.096]	[0.139]	[0.140]
Technology	0.039	0.287**	0.297***
	[0.061]	[0.113]	[0.114]
Training	−0.064	0.038	0.026
	[0.065]	[0.102]	[0.103]
Firm controls			
Unique establishment	−0.136***	−0.069**	−0.064*
	[0.020]	[0.033]	[0.034]
Log of firm's age	0.102***	0.089***	0.091***
	[0.009]	[0.014]	[0.014]

(continued)

Table 2A.5 Investment Climate Effect on Wages *(continued)*

	Dependent variable: Log of wage		
	(1)	*(2)*	*(3)*
	2SLS-R	*2SLS*	*2SLS*
		Education not instrumented	*Education instrumented*
Substitution	*Yes*	*Yes*	*Yes*
Instruments	*Sample averages*	*Sample averages*	*Sample averages*
Foreign owned	0.368***	0.216***	0.209***
	[0.025]	[0.044]	[0.045]
Exporter	0.173***	0.118***	0.115***
	[0.018]	[0.034]	[0.034]
20–99 employees	0.018	−0.128***	−0.124***
	[0.019]	[0.046]	[0.046]
100+ employees	0.048*	−0.268***	−0.268***
	[0.028]	[0.075]	[0.075]
Education of average worker 7–12 years	0.317***	0.081**	0.111
	[0.069]	[0.033]	[0.117]
Education of average worker 13+ years	0.579***	0.124**	0.420**
	[0.137]	[0.057]	[0.210]
Observations	10,205	10,205	10,205

Source: Authors' calculations.

Note: * = significant at the 10 percent level; ** = significant at the 5 percent level; *** = significant at the 1 percent level. Robust standard errors are in brackets. The table reports the results of regressing the log of wages per worker on the investment climate attributes and firm controls in the first column. Columns 1 to 3 use 2SLS with region–industry–firm size sample averages as instruments. Education is instrumented in column 3. All regressions include country, industry, and region dummies.

Table 2A.6 Investment Climate Effect on Labor Productivity, by Firm Size

	Dependent variable: Log of sales per worker	
	(1)	*(2)*
	2SLS	*2SLS*
Substitution	No	Yes
Instruments	Sample averages	Sample averages
Investment climate attributes		
Bribes	–0.265	–0.327**
	[0.222]	[0.129]
Security	–3.015*	–3.410***
	[1.746]	[1.164]
Crime	–13.404**	–8.599***
	[5.403]	[3.198]
Regulatory compliance	2.122***	1.143***
	[0.366]	[0.208]
Audited	0.531**	0.330**
	[0.219]	[0.140]
Incorporated	0.513**	0.528***
	[0.214]	[0.134]
Infrastructure quality	2.364	0.329
	[2.315]	[1.212]
Access to finance	0.112	0.255
	[0.378]	[0.237]
Technology	0.134	–0.009
	[0.254]	[0.147]
Training	0.036	0.386***
	[0.248]	[0.129]
Investment climate attributes interacted with small firm size (<20 employees)		
Bribes	–0.781***	–0.364**
	[0.270]	[0.142]
Security	–1.068	–3.875*
	[2.245]	[2.167]

(continued)

Table 2A.6 Investment Climate Effect on Labor Productivity, by Firm Size *(continued)*

	Dependent variable: Log of sales per worker	
	(1)	*(2)*
	2SLS	2SLS
Substitution	No	Yes
Instruments	*Sample averages*	*Sample averages*
Crime	7.388	1.675
	[6.567]	[3.818]
Regulatory compliance	−1.167**	−0.121
	[0.471]	[0.260]
Audited	−0.221	−0.024
	[0.238]	[0.131]
Incorporated	0.109	−0.065
	[0.192]	[0.123]
Infrastructure quality	1.826	3.438**
	[2.690]	[1.656]
Access to finance	−0.441	−0.065
	[0.431]	[0.282]
Technology	0.443	0.439***
	[0.278]	[0.152]
Training	−0.09	−0.19
	[0.332]	[0.195]

Source: Authors' calculations.

Note: * = significant at the 10 percent level; ** = significant at the 5 percent level; *** = significant at the 1 percent level. Robust standard errors are in brackets. The table reports the results of regressing the log of sales per worker on the investment climate attributes in the first column. All columns use 2SLS with region–industry–firm size sample averages as instruments. Column 2 replaces missing observations with the instrumental variable. Instruments are constructed using a minimum threshold of 10 observations. All regressions include country, industry, and region dummies and the set of controls used in table 2.3.

Notes

1. ICRG is updated monthly and is available on a subscription basis. For more information, visit http://www.adbi.org/3rdpartycdrom/2004/12/01/1359.international.country.risk/. Transparency International publishes the Corruption Perceptions Index. See http://www.transparency.org/news_room/in_focus/cpi_2006 for more information.

2. Enterprise Surveys are conducted by the Enterprise Analysis Unit of the World Bank. See http://www.enterprisesurveys.org/.

3. In turn, Investment Climate Surveys built on the World Business Environment Surveys launched in 1999. The latter relied on smaller samples and mainly on perception aspects.

4. Note that the questionnaire used for the current Enterprise Surveys is very similar to that used in the past in the Investment Climate Surveys. This report uses the denomination Enterprise Surveys to refer to both Enterprise Surveys and Investment Climate Surveys. Note also that although an Enterprise Survey has been collected for one additional Latin American country—Guyana—this report does not use it in estimations because of the relatively small sample of the survey. As explained later in this chapter, the small sample severely limits the potential for correcting for potential reverse causality using internal instruments (see later in this chapter for a discussion of how this report exploits the sample information to construct instruments that are valid under fairly general conditions).

5. For more information about the Doing Business project, see http://www.doingbusiness.org/.

6. For example, the Doing Business project collects the procedures, time, and cost involved in launching a commercial or industrial firm with up to 50 employees and start-up capital of 10 times the economy's per capita gross national income. Similarly, it reports the administrative burden of paying taxes according to a case study that assumes a firm that has 60 employees—4 managers, 8 assistants, and 48 workers—and a start-up capital of 102 times income per capita at the end of 2004.

7. Worth noting, however, is that for those investment climate attributes that do vary at the subnational level, the use of individual country samples has the advantage of uncovering possible cross-country heterogeneities in the effect of the investment climate on firm performance—as opposed to analyses based on pooled samples, which only allow estimation of average effects across countries.

8. Although in many cases an indicator is unambiguously objective, in other cases indicators are in a gray area. In those middle-ground situations, this study has conservatively avoided the indicator.

9. See Perry and others (2007) for a review of the links between regulatory noncompliance and the quality of governance and institutions.

10. For instance, Demirgüç-Kunt, Love, and Maksimovic (2006) argue that firms are more likely to be incorporated in countries with a well-functioning legal system.

11. In principle, one could argue that dropping variables, even if they are not significant, can affect the results because of the existing covariance structure. The fact that preliminary analysis trying to reduce the number of variables through principal components suggested only modest correlation among the different variables provides some comfort.

12. Although some of these specific analyses could be performed using Enterprise Survey data, one would have to focus on different specific subsamples of firms.

13. As mentioned previously, principal component analysis was used in an effort to reduce the dimension of the different areas, but the analysis indicated that the number of principal components needed to explain a significant share of the variance would be quite close to the number of original variables in the exercise.

14. The number of "cells" thus constructed for each variable varies from 560 (for bribes) to 754 (for the dummy variable for incorporated firms). The median number of firms per cell is between 19 and 22, and the mean is between 32 and 40.

15. The new wave of surveys uses stratified sampling, whereas previous waves have used random sampling.

16. The authors thank Luis Servén for pointing this out. For example, assume for simplicity that there are N groups, each of which has K observations. Equation 2.7 could then be expressed in vector form as

$$IC_j = P * IC_{.j} + w_j,$$

where IC_j is a $NKx1$ vector, $IC_{.j}$ is $Kx1$, and P is a matrix $NKxK$ that is given by $P = (I_N \otimes 1_K)$, where I_N is an identity matrix of size N, and 1_K is a vector of ones of size $Kx1$, and $\otimes$ indicates a Kronecker product. Thus, the instrumental variable for the first-stage regression would be

$$\hat{IC}_j = P'(P'P)^{-1}P * IC_j = T^{-1}PP'IC_j,$$

which in turn is just an $NKx1$ vector equal to the sample mean of each group (that is, each K-th group sample mean is repeated N times).

17. Debate is still ongoing about whether one should use survey weights in regression. As argued by Deaton (1997), if, on the one hand, regressions are being used for primarily descriptive purposes—for example, to explore association by looking at the mean of one variable conditional on others—it is better to use weights in the regressions. On the other hand, if one is interested in estimating behavioral models, then both weighted and unweighted regression estimates are inconsistent when behavior is heterogeneous across strata, but unweighted estimates are more efficient if behavior is homogeneous across strata.

18. In such a case, the resulting 2SLS estimator would not be identical to the OLS estimator obtained by replacing the explanatory variables with the group means:

$$\tilde{IC}_j = K^{-1}PW'IC_j,$$

where now $W = (I_N \otimes w_K)$, with w_K being a vector of weights of size $Kx1$, so that plim $(\tilde{IC}_{ij}) \neq IC_{sj}$.

19. A minimum size of 10 observations is imposed to compute the region–industry–firm size average. If every group had at least 10 observations, the estimates corresponding to the group sample average and weighted average should be the same because the weights are identical for firms within a region–industry–firm size group. However, in some cases, a minimum of 10 observations is not available to compute IC_i. In those circumstances, the same procedure is followed as for calculating group means for the purpose of constructing instrumental variables (that is, using the average of the corresponding region-industry regardless of firm size and, if still short of 10 observations, using industry or region averages, or in the worst-case scenario treating the observation as missing). In the cases where weighted averages have to be computed at higher levels of aggregation than region–industry–firm size, the weights are redefined to take into account the different probability of selection associated with the different groups. Finally, for the estimates based on instruments constructed as sample averages (reported in annex 2A), sample averages are also used for substitution purposes.

20. See the previous section for a methodological discussion on the advantages and disadvantages of using simple compared with weighted averages as instruments.

21. Annex 2A reports the models of columns 2 and 3 of table 2.3 using sample averages instead of weighted means. The comparison of tables 2.3 and 2A.2 (in the annex) indicates that using instruments based on sample or on weighted averages affects only modestly the magnitude of the estimated coefficients, although it may affect their statistical significance. The one exception is the indicator of access to external finance, whose coefficient increases considerably when moving from using sample to using weighted averages as instrumental variables.

22. See chapter 3 for a discussion of the magnitudes of the estimated coefficients in terms of policy priorities.

23. The possibility was also considered of a nonlinear relationship between firm's age and productivity by including a quadratic term. The coefficient for age squared, however, was never significantly different from zero.

24. In fact, these results are now even more robust to changes in the calculation of group means—that is, sample as opposed to weighted averages—for the purpose of constructing instrumental variables, which is illustrated by the fact that the variables proxying access to finance and technology adoption are now significant in both column 2 of table 2.6 and column 2 of table 2A.3 in the annex. Apart from the *audit* variable, which now is not significantly different from zero when sample means are used rather than weighted averages as instrumental variables, the differences in parameter estimates across different estimation methods are quite modest.

25. The results on the effect of the investment climate on TFP reported in table 2.7 are based on the estimation of equation 2.5. As an alternative, an estimation of equation 2.4 was also attempted by calculating TFP as a "Solow residual," assuming that factor shares (Sl, Sk, Sm) are equal across industries and countries. This nonparametric approach requires the computation of input cost shares and is based on the assumption of constant returns to scale. The results are qualitatively similar to those in table 2.7, with only *corruption*, *crime*, and *regulatory compliance* having a significant effect on TFP.

26. This issue is addressed in more depth in chapter 7 of this report.

27. Table 2A.6 reports the results using sample averages.

28. Admittedly, if one takes into account the decline in the sample size and, as already discussed, the effects of this decrease on the results of the estimation, it is difficult to say whether the observed changes are caused by parameter heterogeneity or by working with sample sizes that are one-third the size of the full samples.

29. They construct their governance variable as the first principal components of four indicators produced by the ICRG—namely, the prevalence of law and order, the prevalence of corruption, the quality of bureaucracy, and the accountability of public officials.

30. Dollar and Kraay (2003) obtain a similar result. When they control for trade openness, various measures of governance turn out to have a relatively weak effect on growth, particularly over medium-term horizons (that is, decadal growth).

31. It is worth noting, however, that high regulatory noncompliance can also have negative direct effects on firm productivity if it is associated with lower firm size—either to avoid detection or as a result of lower access to markets and services—or if it reduces the market share and investments of formal competitors. These effects, however, can potentially be compensated for by the higher flexibility enjoyed by firms operating in areas where noncompliance is lower because of reduced enforcement (see Perry and others 2007).

References

Barro, R. 1991. "Economic Growth in a Cross Section of Countries." *Quarterly Journal of Economics* 106 (2): 407–43.

Beck, T., R. Levine, and N. Loayza. 2000. "Finance and the Sources of Growth." *Journal of Financial Economics* 58 (1–2): 261–300.

Canning, D., M. Fay, and R. Perotti. 1994. "Infrastructure and Growth." In *International Differences in Growth Rates: Market Globalization and Economic Areas*, ed. M. Baldassarri, L. Paganetto, and E. S. Phelps, 113–47. New York: St. Martin's Press.

Deaton, A. 1997. *The Analysis of Household Surveys: A Microeconometric Approach to Development Policy.* Baltimore, MD: Johns Hopkins University Press and World Bank.

Demirgüç-Kunt, A., I. Love, and V. Maksimovic. 2006. "Business Environment and the Incorporation Decision." *Journal of Banking and Finance* 30 (11): 2967–93.

Dollar, D. 1992. "Outward-Oriented Developing Economies Really Do Grow More Rapidly: Evidence from 95 LDCs, 1976–1985." *Economic Development and Cultural Change* 40 (3): 523–44.

Dollar, D., M. Hallward-Driemeier, and T. Mengistae. 2005. "Investment Climate and Firm Performance in Developing Economies." *Economic Development and Cultural Change* 54 (1): 1–31.

Dollar, D., and A. Kraay. 2003. "Institutions, Trade, and Growth: Revisiting the Evidence." Policy Research Working Paper 3004, World Bank, Washington, DC.

Easterly, W., and R. Levine. 2001. "It's Not Factor Accumulation: Stylized Facts and Growth Models." *World Bank Economic Review* 15 (2): 177–219.

Escribano, A., and J. L. Guasch. 2005. "Assessing the Impact of the Investment Climate on Productivity Using Firm-Level Data." Policy Research Working Paper 3621, World Bank, Washington, DC.

Escribano, A., J. L. Guasch, and M. de Orte. 2006. "Investment Climate Assessment (ICA) on Productivity and on Allocative Efficiency: Effects on Exports, Foreign Direct Investment, Wages, and Employment Analysis Based on Firm Level Data from 2001–2003." World Bank, Washington, DC.

Hallward-Driemeier, M., and D. Stewart. 2004. "How Do Investment Climate Conditions Vary across Countries and Types of Firms?" World Bank, Washington DC.

Loayza, N., P. Fajnzylber, and C. Calderón. 2005. *Economic Growth in Latin America and the Caribbean: Stylized Facts, Explanations, and Forecasts.* Washington, DC: World Bank.

Loayza, N., and N. Sugawara. 2007. "Fundamental and Proximate Sources of Economic Growth." World Bank, Washington, DC.

Perry, G., W. Maloney, O. Arias, P. Fajnzylber, A. Mason, and J. Saavedra. 2007. *Informality: Exit and Exclusion.* Washington DC: World Bank.

World Bank. 2005. *World Development Report: A Better Investment Climate for Everyone.* Washington, DC: World Bank.

3

What Would Be the Effect of a Better Investment Climate for All?

Verónica Alaimo, Pablo Fajnzylber,
J. Luis Guasch, J. Humberto López, and
Ana María Oviedo

A better investment climate will contribute to improvements in the performance of firms and more importantly to higher growth rates. In principle, this effort will require concerted action along several fronts. Yet from an operational perspective, a number of questions need to be addressed: Should all countries focus on the same areas, or should each country follow a different path? What are the potential gains of making progress in a particular area? What are the main priority areas of the different countries?

So far, this study has analyzed the effect of the investment climate on firms' productivity in Latin America and has found several areas where progress will likely lead to better firm performance and hence faster growth. However, should all countries focus on the same areas, or should each country follow a different path? After all, there are important differences across countries that must be kept in mind when formulating policy recommendations. For example, reducing corruption can be extremely useful in all countries, but the sense of urgency and the returns to any potential intervention will likely be different in, say, Chile, where only 6 percent of firms report paying bribes, than in, say, Ecuador, where as much as 68 percent of firms pay bribes (see chapter 4). Similarly, making progress on the regulatory framework may lead to higher firm productivity and growth, but it would not be very reasonable to stress this area the same way in Panama, where 92 percent of firms are incorporated and 85 percent have external audits, as in Nicaragua, where the same shares are 2 and 27 percent, respectively. Or consider the variable that captures the use of technology. In Argentina, 73 percent of firms use the Internet, whereas in Honduras, only 22 percent do. Once again, it does not seem reasonable to emphasize the need to make equal progress in this area in those two countries.

In other words, beyond the effect that a marginal change in one of the variables under analysis has on firm productivity (estimated in chapter 2), policy makers will likely also want to consider the potential for improvement in the different areas. Following this line of argument, one could obtain a simulation of potential gains of progress in a particular area by merging two pieces of information. The first is the magnitude of a marginal improvement in a specific area or investment climate attribute. The second is the potential for improvements in the attribute as measured by the distance between the country's current situation and a prespecified target. Thus, this exercise is very similar to the one reported by Loayza, Fajnzylber, and Calderón (2005) in their analysis of economic growth in Latin America, using macrodata in this case.

This type of exercise has a number of limitations. First, because it relies on the results of chapter 2, it is subject to the same caveats mentioned there. That is, although an attempt was made to control for the endogeneity of investment climate variables through the use of instrumental variables, data limitations suggest that the estimated coefficients should not be given a strict causal interpretation. The reader is therefore advised to emphasize the qualitative rather than the quantitative aspects of the results presented in this chapter. Second, although the exercise introduces some country specificity by simulating on a country-by-country basis the distance between an indicator and the prespecified target, the elasticities used are based on a pooled regression and hence would correspond to the average Latin American firm rather than to the average firm of a specific country. Similarly, the simulations look at progress in one area or attribute in isolation, neglecting cross-correlations. For example, as discussed in chapter 4, progress on the regulatory compliance front will also lead to progress on the corruption front. That is, there will be a double payoff associated with improvements in some indicators.

One should note, however, that in principle, there will likely be significant trade-offs between breadth and depth. For example, chapter 2 attempted to estimate the determinants of firm productivity for subgroups of countries rather than for the pooled sample (that is, it attempted to make the estimates more country specific). On the one hand, as discussed there, the results were somewhat disappointing, in part because country variability is not exploited as in the pooled sample. On the other hand, having a complex model that takes into account potential interrelations among a large set of variables can be quite intractable. Thus, in practice, there are no straightforward solutions to these problems other than being extremely careful with the results of the exercise and taking those results as just an additional piece of information.

To anticipate some of the results below, when one looks at the areas that appear to have more potential to unleash growth in the region, one finds that the regulatory framework (regulatory compliance and audited and incorporated) and the rule of law (corruption and crime and security expenses) are the areas that generate the largest gains in labor productivity for all the Latin American countries in the sample. The importance of the regulatory framework is driven by improvements in regulatory compliance. The gains from a more efficient legal system and strong shareholders' and creditors' rights (captured here in audited and incorporated) could generate important productivity gains. Within the rule of law, reductions in losses caused by crime and in security expenses are the biggest source of potential productivity gains for the region. Gains from improvements in other areas are relatively small for almost every country.

At the country level, the countries with the most potential to gain from improvements in the investment climate are Ecuador, El Salvador, Honduras, and Nicaragua. At the other extreme is, not surprisingly, Chile, the country with the best investment climate in the region. This ordering is robust to the use of different prespecified targets. For example, if all the firms improve their attributes to the level of the Chilean firms (within the same industry and size), Ecuador, El Salvador, Honduras, and Nicaragua could almost double their labor productivity.

The chapter also notes differences in productivity gains by firm size. Its findings indicate that small firms with fewer than 20 workers stand to gain the most from improvements in the investment climate. Small firms gain more than medium and large firms from improvements in regulatory compliance, audited and incorporated, infrastructure quality, technology, and access to finance. Although small firms could benefit from lower corruption and crime, their potential gains are smaller than those that medium and large firms could obtain.

Finally, as noted in chapter 2, improvements in the investment climate may have a positive effect on poverty reduction, because the main source of income for the poor is wage labor. Using the same methodology described above, the study simulates the gains in wages under different scenarios of investment climate improvements. It finds that there are potential wage gains from a better investment climate in all the countries of the region. The potential gains are slightly smaller than those of labor productivity, but they reinforce the importance that a better investment climate could have not only for producers, but also for consumers in Latin America.

Potential Productivity Gains under Alternative Scenarios

As noted above, the mechanics of the exercise are quite simple. Starting from the general equation that relates firm productivity to the investment climate and firm attributes,

$$\log(Y_i / L_i) = \sum_j \beta_{1j} IC_{ij} + \sum_j \delta_{1j} C_{ij} + v_{1i}, \tag{3.1}$$

the gain associated with making progress in a particular attribute from IC_{ij} to IC_{ij}^b, everything else constant, would be given by

$$Gain_{ij} = \beta_{1i}^* (IC_{ij}^b - IC_{ij}). \tag{3.2}$$

Clearly in practice, a value is needed for β_{1j}, which, as noted above, should be country specific and perhaps even firm specific. In absence of reliable parameters at that low level of aggregation, one possibility is the estimated parameters obtained in chapter 2.

The other ingredient needed in this context is the value of IC_{ij}^b. Here the results are presented for five alternative benchmarks. Two scenarios take a country as a reference. The first considers the potential gains of moving to Ireland's investment climate. Ireland was chosen because it is the best performer in the global sample estimates (see table 2.11 in chapter 2). The second considers the potential gains of moving to Chile's investment climate.[1] Chile was chosen because it is the Latin American country that grew the most in the 1990s, and it has often been cited in policy circles as a successful case of policy reforms. Moreover, Chilean firms exhibit the best indicators of investment climate conditions of all 16 Latin American countries in the sample.[2]

The other three scenarios take as a benchmark a hypothetical firm at the 75th percentile of the Latin American firms. More specifically, the most optimistic scenario takes as potential gains the difference between the value of an attribute for a particular firm and the value corresponding to a firm at the 75th percentile of the entire sample of Latin American firms. To do so, the study sorts the entire sample according to investment climate variables and takes the values of the firm at the 75th percentile as the benchmark. So every firm is compared with this benchmark firm regardless of the country of origin, industry, or firm size. The other two scenarios take some characteristics of firms into account. For example, the fourth scenario simulates the potential gains for a firm as the difference between the value of the attribute in question and the value corresponding to a firm at the 75th percentile within the same industry and firm size. Finally, a fifth scenario takes as potential gains the difference between the value of the attribute and that corresponding to a firm in the top 75th percentile, not only within industry and firm size, but also within the country.

One clarification is necessary; in many cases, the simulated gains are far from realistic over the short run. In other words, although this study refers to the potential gains associated with progress in each area, the progress is likely to be beyond what is reasonable, and therefore the gains will also be unreasonable. This problem, however, does not rest interest in the simulations, because they can be viewed as a priority-setting exercise.

Results

Figure 3.1 shows the average productivity gains of moving to those five different benchmarks. This figure indicates that the most modest gains are generally associated with the fifth scenario. Moreover, although there are important quantitative differences among the five scenarios, the qualitative results are very similar (with the exception of the estimated gains of audited and incorporated in the first and last scenarios). For simplification, the contributions of crime and security, as well as the contributions of audited and incorporated firms, are merged. Overall, the investment

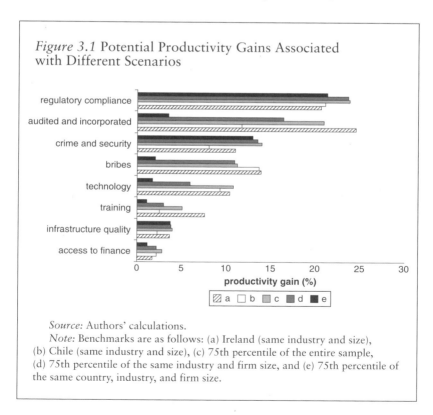

Figure 3.1 Potential Productivity Gains Associated with Different Scenarios

Source: Authors' calculations.
Note: Benchmarks are as follows: (a) Ireland (same industry and size), (b) Chile (same industry and size), (c) 75th percentile of the entire sample, (d) 75th percentile of the same industry and firm size, and (e) 75th percentile of the same country, industry, and firm size.

climate areas that yield the largest gains are related to the regulatory framework (regulatory compliance and audited and incorporated) and to the rule of law (crime and security expenses and corruption). They are followed by improvements in technology and corruption. Somewhat surprisingly, at the end of this classification is access to finance, which, as noted in chapter 2, was identified by firms as one of the top five obstacles to growth in half of the countries. The maximum productivity gains (regulatory compliance) imply productivity improvements of 20 percent or more. The minimum productivity gains (access to finance) would be 10 times lower, around 2 percent.

Under the Irish benchmark (benchmark a in figure 3.1), improvements in audited and incorporated would generate a larger gain than improvements in regulatory compliance, whereas the former would generate the fourth-largest gain under the most realistic scenario (benchmark e) and the third-largest gain under the Chilean benchmark (benchmark b). In the other two scenarios (benchmarks c and d), improvements in audited and incorporated would generate the second-largest gain for the region. Reducing government corruption would generate the second-largest gain under the Chilean benchmark (benchmark b), whereas reductions in crime and security expenses appear as the second priority if firms moved to the practice of the 75th percentile of the same country, industry, and firm size (benchmark e). In this scenario, technology, training, and infrastructure quality also appear among the top four constraints for the region. Increased Internet use for communicating with clients and suppliers could generate productivity gains, especially if firms were to move to the top 75th percentile of the entire sample (11 percent), or to their Irish or Chilean counterparts (10 and 9 percent, respectively). Losses from power outages cause considerable competitive disadvantages for Latin American firms, as the average productivity gain from moving to the 75th percentile of the same industry and firm size (benchmark d) would be 4 percent. In the same scenario, firms could increase their labor productivity by 3 percent through training their workers.

However, are these areas the top priorities for each country in the sample? Before answering that question, one must look at the aggregate potential gains for each country if the country were to improve all areas of investment climate at once. Figure 3.2 shows the aggregate gains of moving to the five different benchmarks for each country. To ease the presentation of the results, focus on benchmarks a, b, and d and consider the potential gains of moving to the investment climate of Ireland, to that of Chile, and to the 75th percentile of the same industry and firm size. These results are shown in panels a, b, and d of figure 3.2.

The largest gains for the Latin American countries could be achieved by moving to Ireland's investment climate. As panel a of figure 3.2 shows, Chile could increase its labor productivity by more than 30 percent, and all other countries would gain more than 50 percent in this scenario. In

Figure 3.2 Aggregate Labor Productivity Gains, by Country

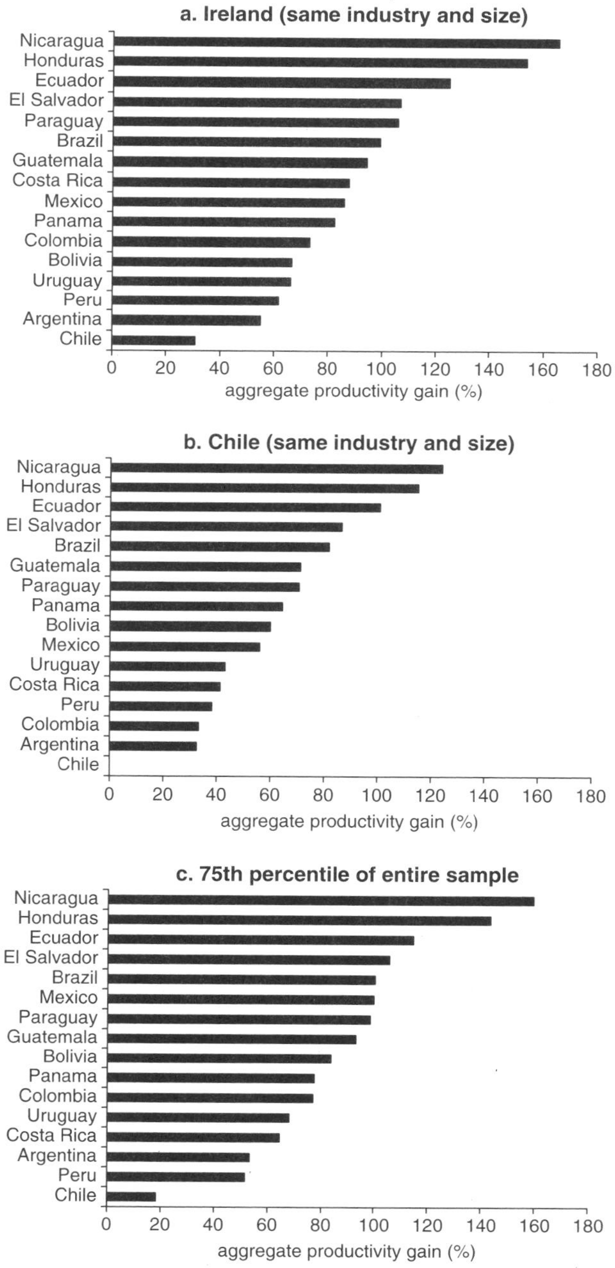

a. Ireland (same industry and size)
Nicaragua
Honduras
Ecuador
El Salvador
Paraguay
Brazil
Guatemala
Costa Rica
Mexico
Panama
Colombia
Bolivia
Uruguay
Peru
Argentina
Chile
0 20 40 60 80 100 120 140 160 180
aggregate productivity gain (%)
b. Chile (same industry and size)
Nicaragua
Honduras
Ecuador
El Salvador
Brazil
Guatemala
Paraguay
Panama
Bolivia
Mexico
Uruguay
Costa Rica
Peru
Colombia
Argentina
Chile
0 20 40 60 80 100 120 140 160 180
aggregate productivity gain (%)
c. 75th percentile of entire sample
Nicaragua
Honduras
Ecuador
El Salvador
Brazil
Mexico
Paraguay
Guatemala
Bolivia
Panama
Colombia
Uruguay
Costa Rica
Argentina
Peru
Chile
0 20 40 60 80 100 120 140 160 180
aggregate productivity gain (%)

(continued)

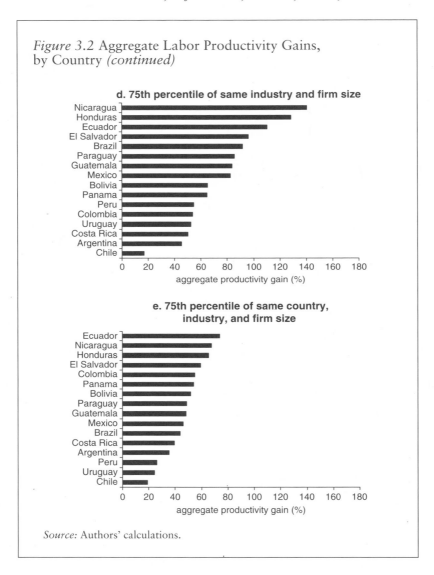

Figure 3.2 Aggregate Labor Productivity Gains, by Country *(continued)*

d. 75th percentile of same industry and firm size

e. 75th percentile of same country, industry, and firm size

Source: Authors' calculations.

particular, Ecuador, El Salvador, Honduras, Nicaragua, and Paraguay could more than double their labor productivity, with an average gain for those countries of 131 percent.

Panel b indicates that if firms in each country were to move to the Chilean average (by industry and firm size), Ecuador, Honduras, and Nicaragua could more than double their labor productivity. Brazil, El Salvador, Guatemala, Panama, and Paraguay could also obtain gains above the regional average (64 percent). On the other side of the distribution, Argentina, Colombia, and Peru could gain between 33 and 38 percent of labor productivity, whereas Bolivia, Costa Rica, Mexico, and Uruguay could obtain gains between 60 and 40 percent. Chile, obviously, would get no gains.

Panel d of figure 3.2 shows that Ecuador, Honduras, and Nicaragua could still obtain labor productivity gains above 100 percent if they were to move to the 75 percentile of the same industry and firm size. Chile appears as the country with the smallest gain (17 percent) followed by Argentina, Colombia, Costa Rica, Peru, and Uruguay with gains between 45 and 55 percent. Note that to a large extent, the results of panels a, b, and d are similar, at least with respect to the ordering.

Country Detail

So far, the discussion has considered the potential productivity gains by country (figure 3.2) and the gains associated with the different investment climate areas (figure 3.1). Tables 3.1 and 3.2 cross the information of the two previous exercises and present the potential labor productivity gains by country and by investment climate attribute of moving to Irish and Chilean levels, respectively. Table 3.3 presents the results of using the 75th percentile of the same industry and firm size as the benchmark. The last column provides the total percentage gain in labor productivity, and under each of the remaining columns is the contribution of each attribute to this gain.

The results of these tables, while consistent, present some subtle differences. For example, table 3.1 shows that improvements in audited and incorporated would be the priority for the region, followed by improvements in regulatory compliance, reductions in corruption, increased Internet use, and reductions in crime and security expenses. According to table 3.2, the priority for the region (represented by the average country) would be improvements in regulatory compliance, followed by reductions in corruption and improvements in audited and incorporated. Improvements in technology and reductions in crime and security expenses would follow in the list. These priorities are confirmed in table 3.3, although the ordering is somewhat different. Improvements in regulatory compliance continue to score high, but now that priority is followed by audited and incorporated, crime and security, corruption, and technology.

The information in tables 3.2 and 3.3 is summarized in tables 3.4 and 3.5, which list the top three priorities for each country under both benchmarks. Improvements in regulatory compliance appear as the top priority for the region under both scenarios. If firms move to the benchmark of a firm in the 75th percentile (same industry and firm size), regulatory compliance is the top priority in 10 of the 16 countries in the sample, and it

Table 3.1 Investment Climate Contributions to Labor Productivity Gains from Moving to the Irish Benchmark: Same Industry and Firm Size

| Country | Contribution of each variable to the total gain (%) | | | | | | | | | Labor productivity gain |
	Bribes	Crime and security	Regulatory compliance	Audited and incorporated	Infrastructure quality	Access to finance	Technology	Training	Total	
Argentina	24.9	12.9	22.5	20.0	1.5	1.1	2.5	14.7	100	55.1
Bolivia	25.7	9.4	24.0	18.0	2.5	3.3	11.8	5.2	100	66.8
Brazil	32.8	7.2	26.3	25.3	2.0	0.9	1.4	4.1	100	99.4
Chile	10.3	15.5	3.5	45.8	7.4	0.0	0.0	17.4	100	31.0
Colombia	8.3	11.2	23.5	23.4	3.1	0.7	16.1	13.5	100	73.1
Costa Rica	12.8	8.7	36.6	24.5	5.7	0.0	2.5	9.2	100	87.7
Ecuador	24.3	26.3	16.7	13.7	6.5	2.9	5.0	4.7	100	124.7
El Salvador	12.7	20.9	16.0	26.6	3.7	0.0	11.5	8.5	100	106.7
Guatemala	9.4	18.9	24.8	26.3	2.2	1.3	10.2	6.9	100	94.3
Honduras	12.3	10.8	20.0	34.9	4.4	1.6	12.0	3.9	100	153.7
Mexico	2.0	7.4	23.4	31.3	2.4	2.3	15.9	15.2	100	86.2

(continued)

Table 3.1 Investment Climate Contributions to Labor Productivity Gains from Moving to the Irish Benchmark: Same Industry and Firm Size (continued)

Country	Bribes	Crime and security	Regulatory compliance	Audited and incorporated	Infrastructure quality	Access to finance	Technology	Training	Total	Labor productivity gain
					Contribution of each variable to the total gain (%)					
Nicaragua	11.2	6.9	20.5	36.5	5.0	1.4	13.0	5.4	100	165.6
Panama	2.9	11.6	46.9	5.8	6.1	0.0	16.6	10.2	100	82.6
Uruguay	0.0	6.8	20.2	37.9	0.0	3.9	17.4	13.8	100	66.0
Paraguay	19.4	9.8	15.6	26.8	4.1	1.1	14.3	8.9	100	105.8
Peru	15.4	4.9	17.6	35.9	0.3	1.6	13.9	10.4	100	61.8
Mean	14.9	11.8	22.1	26.3	3.9	1.8	11.1	8.1	100	91.3
Median	15.5	9.1	21.5	27.0	2.6	1.8	13.2	9.3	100	87.0

Source: Authors' calculations.
Note: The table reports only potential gains. When a country is already above the Irish average in one area, the gains would be negative; those cases are excluded from the analysis and the contribution to the total gain is shown as 0.0.

Table 3.2 Investment Climate Contributions to Labor Productivity Gains from Moving to the Chilean Benchmark: Same Industry and Firm Size

Country	Bribes	Crime and security	Regulatory compliance	Audited and incorporated	Infrastructure quality	Access to finance	Technology	Training	Total	Labor productivity gain
				Contribution of each variable to the total gain (%)						
Argentina	41.7	6.4	38.7	0.0	0.0	6.7	0.0	6.4	100	32.6
Bolivia	29.5	7.8	30.8	14.6	0.0	4.5	12.8	0.0	100	60.1
Brazil	38.5	4.9	36.2	17.0	0.5	2.9	0.0	0.0	100	81.8
Chile										
Colombia	13.8	9.9	43.8	6.0	0.0	1.8	22.5	2.1	100	33.3
Costa Rica	17.2	1.5	70.6	1.9	1.2	4.9	0.0	2.7	100	41.2
Ecuador	28.5	35.9	18.9	4.0	3.5	4.5	4.7	0.0	100	101.1
El Salvador	13.0	19.5	21.6	27.7	0.2	1.2	13.6	3.2	100	86.7
Guatemala	21.4	16.5	27.0	19.4	0.0	0.4	10.4	4.8	100	71.0
Honduras	13.6	10.7	24.3	32.6	2.7	3.0	12.2	0.9	100	115.0
Mexico	3.0	4.3	37.0	21.7	0.0	5.5	17.4	11.0	100	56.2
Nicaragua	12.4	7.5	24.9	32.1	5.3	4.8	11.4	1.7	100	123.8
Panama	5.1	9.0	63.3	0.0	2.5	0.3	15.7	4.0	100	64.3

(continued)

Table 3.2 Investment Climate Contributions to Labor Productivity Gains from Moving to the Chilean Benchmark: Same Industry and Firm Size (continued)

				Contribution of each variable to the total gain (%)						
Country	Bribes	Crime and security	Regulatory compliance	Audited and incorporated	Infrastructure quality	Access to finance	Technology	Training	Total	Labor productivity gain
Paraguay	26.7	13.1	23.0	18.5	0.0	2.4	12.4	3.8	100	70.8
Peru	43.7	3.7	11.3	20.8	0.0	1.1	19.5	0.0	100	38.0
Uruguay	10.2	0.9	32.6	22.4	0.0	3.7	18.0	12.2	100	43.3
Mean	21.2	10.1	33.6	15.9	1.1	3.2	11.4	3.5	100	67.9
Median	17.2	7.8	30.8	18.5	0.0	3.0	12.4	2.7	100	64.3

Source: Authors' calculations.

Note: The table reports only potential gains. When a country is already above the top 75th percentile in one area, the gains would be negative; those cases are excluded from the analysis and the contribution to the total gain is shown as 0.0. The survey for Chile includes firms from the food, metals and machinery, chemicals, other manufacturing, and information technology services. The simulation of the gains of moving to the Chilean benchmark controls for industry; the results reported correspond to the gains for firms in those industries in the other 15 Latin American countries.

Table 3.3 Investment Climate Contributions to Labor Productivity Gains from Moving to the Top 75th Percentile of the Same Industry and Firm Size

	Contribution of each variable to the total gain (%)									*Labor productivity gain*
Country	*Bribes*	*Crime and security*	*Regulatory compliance*	*Audited and incorporated*	*Infrastructure quality*	*Access to finance*	*Technology*	*Training*	*Total*	
Argentina	23.0	20.1	38.1	5.5	1.8	5.1	0.0	6.4	100	45.2
Bolivia	19.5	14.3	32.9	18.0	4.5	4.2	5.5	1.1	100	65.0
Brazil	28.7	10.4	37.3	16.8	3.6	2.4	0.4	0.3	100	91.6
Chile	0.0	32.9	18.8	30.0	14.7	1.2	1.2	1.2	100	17.0
Colombia	1.3	16.6	35.6	21.4	6.1	0.7	11.4	6.9	100	53.7
Costa Rica	3.0	16.6	59.3	4.2	10.2	2.6	0.0	4.2	100	50.1
Ecuador	22.8	37.3	19.5	6.2	6.8	4.4	3.1	0.0	100	110.3
El Salvador	10.7	21.9	25.2	24.9	3.5	1.5	9.7	2.6	100	96.2
Guatemala	7.8	23.7	28.1	21.4	4.2	1.1	8.1	5.6	100	83.6
Honduras	7.2	14.4	25.8	34.3	6.3	2.0	9.1	0.9	100	128.4
Mexico	0.0	11.3	34.3	29.9	1.7	4.7	9.0	9.1	100	82.4
Nicaragua	6.9	12.0	25.1	34.0	7.5	3.5	9.1	2.1	100	140.5
Panama	1.7	15.4	61.9	1.5	6.5	0.0	6.5	6.5	100	64.8

(continued)

Table 3.3 Investment Climate Contributions to Labor Productivity Gains from Moving to the Top 75th Percentile of the Same Industry and Firm Size *(continued)*

Country	Bribes	Crime and security	Regulatory compliance	Audited and incorporated	Infrastructure quality	Access to finance	Technology	Training	Total	Labor productivity gain
				Contribution of each variable to the total gain (%)						
Paraguay	19.7	16.6	23.8	21.5	5.0	1.4	7.5	4.6	100	85.7
Peru	21.1	13.0	24.0	27.5	1.5	1.6	9.2	2.2	100	54.6
Uruguay	0.0	14.8	27.3	29.4	0.2	5.2	11.1	12.1	100	52.1
Mean	10.8	18.2	32.3	20.4	5.3	2.6	6.3	4.1	100	76.3
Median	7.5	16.0	27.7	21.4	4.7	2.2	7.8	3.4	100	73.7

Source: Authors' calculations.

Note: The table reports only potential gains. When a country is already above the top 75th percentile in one area, the gains would be negative; those cases are excluded from the analysis and the contribution to the total gain is shown as 0.0.

Table 3.4 Top Three Priorities for Firms Moving to the 75th Percentile of the Same Industry and Firm Size

| Country | *Order of priorities* | | |
	First	*Second*	*Third*
Argentina	Regulatory compliance	Bribes	Crime and security expenses
Bolivia	Regulatory compliance	Bribes	Audited and incorporated
Brazil	Regulatory compliance	Bribes	Audited and incorporated
Chile	Crime and security expenses	Audited and incorporated	Regulatory compliance
Colombia	Regulatory compliance	Audited and incorporated	Crime and security expenses
Costa Rica	Regulatory compliance	Crime and security expenses	Infrastructure quality
Ecuador	Crime and security expenses	Bribes	Regulatory compliance
El Salvador	Regulatory compliance	Audited and incorporated	Crime and security expenses
Guatemala	Regulatory compliance	Crime and security expenses	Audited and incorporated
Honduras	Audited and incorporated	Regulatory compliance	Crime and security expenses
Mexico	Regulatory compliance	Audited and incorporated	Crime and security expenses
Nicaragua	Audited and incorporated	Regulatory compliance	Crime and security expenses
Panama	Regulatory compliance	Crime and security expenses	Technology, infrastructure quality, and training
Paraguay	Regulatory compliance	Audited and incorporated	Bribes
Peru	Audited and incorporated	Regulatory compliance	Bribes

(continued)

Table 3.4 Top Three Priorities for Firms Moving to the 75th Percentile of the Same Industry and Firm Size *(continued)*

Country	Order of priorities		
	First	*Second*	*Third*
Mean	Regulatory compliance	Audited and incorporated	Crime and security expenses
Median	Regulatory compliance	Audited and incorporated	Crime and security expenses

Source: Authors' calculations.

Table 3.5 Top Three Priorities for Firms Moving to the Chilean Benchmark: Same Industry and Firm Size

Country	Order of priorities		
	First	*Second*	*Third*
Argentina	Bribes	Regulatory compliance	Access to finance
Bolivia	Regulatory compliance	Bribes	Audited and incorporated
Brazil	Bribes	Regulatory compliance	Audited and incorporated
Colombia	Regulatory compliance	Technology	Bribes
Costa Rica	Regulatory compliance	Bribes	Access to finance
Ecuador	Crime and security expenses	Bribes	Regulatory compliance
El Salvador	Audited and incorporated	Regulatory compliance	Crime and security expenses
Guatemala	Regulatory compliance	Bribes	Audited and incorporated
Honduras	Audited and incorporated	Regulatory compliance	Bribes
Mexico	Regulatory compliance	Audited and incorporated	Technology
Nicaragua	Audited and incorporated	Regulatory compliance	Bribes
Panama	Regulatory compliance	Technology	Crime and security expenses

(continued)

Table 3.5 Top Three Priorities for Firms Moving to the Chilean Benchmark: Same Industry and Firm Size *(continued)*

Country	First	Second	Third
		Order of priorities	
Paraguay	Bribes	Regulatory compliance	Audited and incorporated
Peru	Bribes	Audited and Incorporated	Technology
Mean	Regulatory compliance	Bribes	Audited and incorporated
Median	Regulatory compliance	Audited and incorporated	Bribes

Source: Authors' calculations.

is a second or third priority for the other 6 countries. Under the Chilean benchmark, it is a top priority for seven countries and is among the top three priorities for all countries except Peru. However, the other priority areas change with the benchmark under consideration. In table 3.4, audited and incorporated and crime and security expenses appear within the top three priorities in 12 countries of the sample. In particular, improving the legal system's efficiency, enhancing shareholder and creditor rights, and reducing regulatory burdens, as measured by the audited and incorporated variable, are the top priority in Honduras, Nicaragua, Peru, and Uruguay. Reductions in crime and in security expenses could yield the highest gains in Chile and Ecuador. For example, progress in the crime and security expenses area as the top priority in Chile and Ecuador does not tell the whole story. As table 3.3 shows, on the one hand, Chilean firms could obtain productivity gains of 5.6 percent, which represents 33 percent of the total potential gains for the country. On the other hand, firms in Ecuador could gain as much as 41 percent from improvements in this area, which represents 37 percent of the total potential gain for Ecuador under this scenario.

Corruption appears as the second priority for Argentina, Bolivia, Brazil, and Ecuador and as the third priority for Paraguay and Peru. Improvements in infrastructure quality (measured by losses caused by power outages), in technology (measured by Internet use), and in training appear as a top three priority in a few cases. Infrastructure quality is a top three priority in Costa Rica and Panama. The latter could make the same gains from improvements in technology and training.

Reducing corruption appears as the second priority for the region under the Chilean benchmark (table 3.5). This result means that Chile is well above the 75th percentile of the Latin American distribution. Therefore, moving to the Chilean average would yield a larger gain from fighting corruption than moving to the performance of a firm at the 75th percentile of the same industry and firm size. Improvements in audited and incorporated appear as the third priority in this scenario (it is a top priority for El Salvador, Honduras, and Nicaragua). Interestingly, improvement in technology is among the top three priorities for Colombia, Mexico, Panama, Peru, and Uruguay. Reductions in crime and security expenses do not yield gains as large as in the previous scenario; this variable is a top priority only for Ecuador and a third priority for El Salvador and Panama. This result is consistent with the relatively low performance of Chile in this front, as crime and security expenses appear in table 3.4 as a top three priority for Chilean firms. Finally, the enhancement of access to finance is a priority for Argentina and Costa Rica.

Are There Any Differences by Firm Size?

As discussed in chapter 2, some empirical evidence indicates that smaller firms would benefit more than proportionally from improvements in the investment climate. However, this judgment was based on the elasticities of the estimated equations rather than on the potential gains. This issue can be explored in the context of the simulation exercises. Figure 3.3 reports the results of two of the simulations by firm size.

Overall, small firms with fewer than 20 workers stand to gain the most from improvements in the investment climate: on average, 76 percent in a scenario of moving to the region's 75th percentile of the same industry and firm size, compared with 69 percent and 49 percent for medium (20–99 workers) and large firms (more than 100 workers), respectively. In terms of the areas that yield the largest benefits, figure 3.3 shows that firms would benefit the most from improvements in regulatory compliance. The estimated gain would be bigger for small firms (26 percent, against 23 and 17 percent for medium and large firms, respectively). The sum of audited and incorporated appears as the second priority for small firms, with potential productivity gains of 16 percent. Medium and large size firms would obtain productivity gains of 13 and 9 percent from reductions in crime and security expenses, respectively.

The importance of the other areas of investment climate is very similar for all firm sizes; the order is corruption, technology, infrastructure quality, training, and access to finance. In the case of corruption, medium firms would benefit the most, with average gains of 10 percent. In the remaining areas, small firms could obtain the largest gains in labor productivity, ranging from about 5 percent in technology to 3 percent in access to finance.

The difference between small and medium firms and larger firms is more extreme when the gains of moving to the Chilean standards are considered. The overall potential gain is almost 60 percent for small firms and

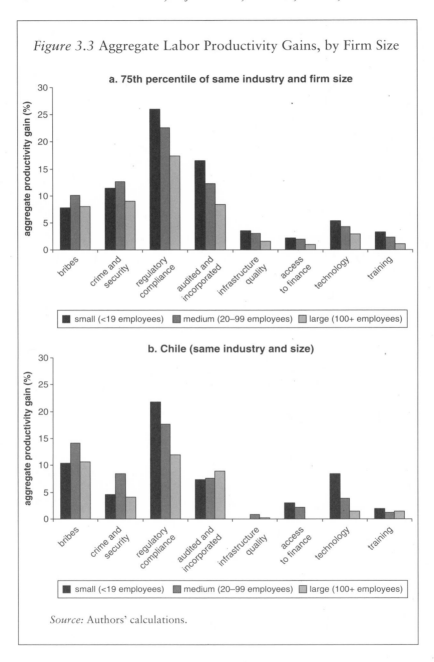

Figure 3.3 Aggregate Labor Productivity Gains, by Firm Size

Source: Authors' calculations.

56 percent for medium firms versus 39 percent for large firms. The same is observed in terms of gains from regulatory compliance improvements (22 and 18 percent versus 12 percent). In this scenario, the second priority for all firms is reduction in corruption, especially important for medium firms, which could increase their labor productivity by 14 percent. In this case, an interesting difference comes from improvements in technology. If firms move to the Chilean standard, using the Internet to communicate with clients and suppliers could generate a gain of 8 percent for small firms, 4 percent for medium firms, and 2 percent for large firms.[3]

Are There Potential Gains for Wages?

As noted in chapter 2, improvements of the investment climate may have a positive influence on poverty reduction, because the main source of income for the poor is wage labor. However, what gains could be expected from improvements in the investment climate? The same methodology described in "Potential Productivity Gains under Alternative Scenarios" is used to simulate the gains in wages under the different scenarios of investment climate improvements. Figure 3.4 reports the results of the different simulations.

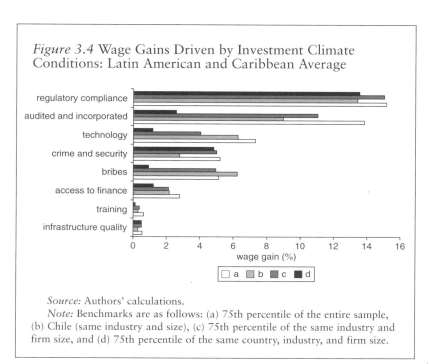

Figure 3.4 Wage Gains Driven by Investment Climate Conditions: Latin American and Caribbean Average

Source: Authors' calculations.
Note: Benchmarks are as follows: (a) 75th percentile of the entire sample, (b) Chile (same industry and size), (c) 75th percentile of the same industry and firm size, and (d) 75th percentile of the same country, industry, and firm size.

Consistent with the regression analysis of chapter 2, the simulation shows that there are wage gains from a better investment climate, ranging from 48 percent when firms move to the 75th percentile of the entire sample (benchmark a) to nearly 25 percent when firms move to the top 75th percentile of the same country, industry, and firm size (benchmark d). If firms were to move to the Chilean benchmark (benchmark b), wages could rise by 37.8 percent. These gains are smaller than the productivity gains described previously, but they show that a better investment climate would benefit not only firms, but also their workers in terms of their standard of living.

Regulatory compliance is again the area that could generate the biggest gain for workers in Latin American firms. Under benchmarks a, b, and c, the second priority would be audited and incorporated, and crime and security expenses would be the second under benchmark d (75th percentile of the same country, industry, and firm size). If Chile is the benchmark, the third priority is improvements in corruption.

Are there any differences across countries? Indeed there are. Overall, the average wage gain for the region ranges from 75 percent for Nicaragua to 9 percent for Chile, if all areas of investment climate were to move to the top 75th percentile of the same industry and firm size (see figure 3.5, panel a). Brazil, Ecuador, El Salvador, Honduras, Mexico, and Paraguay could also increase worker wages by more than 45 percent (their average is 53 percent). Bolivia, Guatemala, Panama, Peru, and Uruguay could obtain wage gains of 36 percent on average, and Argentina, Colombia, and Costa Rica could gain 27 percent on average.

Table 3.6 reports the contribution of each investment climate to the total wage gain (reported in the last column) if the countries move to the 75th percentile of the same industry and firm size. As with labor productivity, most of the wage gains in this simulation come from improvements in the rule of law and the regulatory framework. More than 60 percent of the potential wage gain of moving to the 75th percentile of the same industry and firm size comes from the enhancement of the regulatory framework, approximated by the level of regulatory compliance and the proportion of firms that are audited and incorporated. Another 20 percent of the total potential gain comes from reductions in corruption and crime and security expenses. Another 8 percent of the wage gains would come from better use of the Internet, with values ranging from 14 percent for Colombia to no gain for Argentina and Costa Rica, which are already at or above the 75th percentile. Surprisingly, the wage gain related to training is very small. Uruguay would get the greatest benefit from this source, with a potential gain of only 2.3 percent, followed by Mexico with a potential 2.0 percent gain.

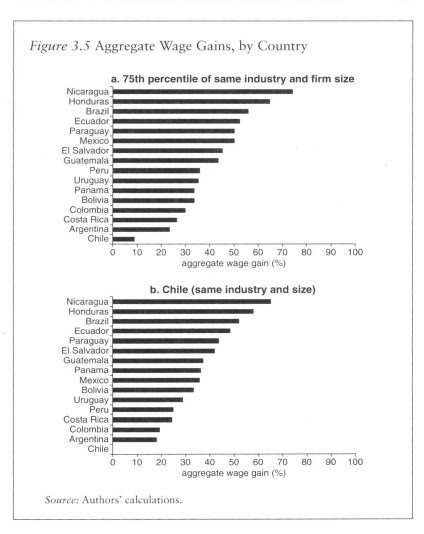

Figure 3.5 Aggregate Wage Gains, by Country

a. 75th percentile of same industry and firm size

aggregate wage gain (%)

b. Chile (same industry and size)

aggregate wage gain (%)

Source: Authors' calculations.

Conclusions

The simulations indicate that significant gains exist in terms of labor productivity and wages for all the Latin American countries in the sample. Progress in the regulatory framework and the rule of law would generate the two most significant gains for producers and consumers in the region. These results are driven by regulatory compliance in the first area and crime and security expenses in the second area. Corruption also appears as a constraint for labor productivity and wage gains for the region. The

Table 3.6 Investment Climate Contributions to Wage Gains from Moving to the Top 75th Percentile of the Same Industry and Firm Size

Country						Contribution of each variable to the total gain (%)					
	Bribes	Crime and security	Regulatory compliance	Audited and incorporated	Infrastructure quality	Access to finance	Technology	Training	Total	Wage gain
Argentina	20.0	17.4	46.4	4.3	0.4	9.8	0.0	1.7	100	23.5
Bolivia	17.0	11.3	40.6	14.0	1.2	8.1	7.5	0.3	100	33.5
Brazil	21.3	6.3	39.1	28.1	0.7	3.9	0.5	0.0	100	55.8
Chile	0.0	25.8	22.5	44.9	3.4	2.2	1.1	0.0	100	8.9
Colombia	1.0	11.7	40.5	28.4	1.3	1.3	14.0	1.7	100	29.9
Costa Rica	2.7	13.3	71.9	3.4	2.7	4.9	0.0	1.1	100	26.3
Ecuador	21.8	23.1	26.2	13.6	1.9	9.0	4.4	0.0	100	52.3
El Salvador	10.2	15.7	34.1	21.5	0.9	3.1	13.9	0.7	100	45.2
Guatemala	6.7	20.5	34.3	23.4	1.1	2.1	10.6	1.4	100	43.5
Honduras	6.5	9.4	32.6	33.5	1.7	3.9	12.2	0.3	100	64.8
Mexico	0.0	8.4	35.9	35.9	0.4	7.6	10.0	2.0	100	50.2
Nicaragua	5.9	7.8	30.2	35.4	1.9	6.5	11.7	0.5	100	74.1

(continued)

Table 3.6 Investment Climate Contributions to Wage Gains from Moving to the Top 75th Percentile of the Same Industry and Firm Size (continued)

				Contribution of each variable to the total gain (%)						
Country	Bribes	Crime and security	Regulatory compliance	Audited and incorporated	Infrastructure quality	Access to finance	Technology	Training	Total	Wage gain
Panama	1.5	10.1	75.7	1.2	1.8	0.0	8.3	1.5	100	33.7
Paraguay	15.1	10.4	25.7	35.7	1.2	2.4	8.6	1.0	100	50.2
Peru	14.5	8.1	23.1	41.5	0.3	2.5	9.5	0.6	100	35.9
Uruguay	0.0	9.0	25.4	44.6	0.0	7.6	11.0	2.3	100	35.4
Mean	9.0	13.0	37.7	25.6	1.3	4.7	7.7	0.9	100	41.5
Median	6.6	10.9	34.2	28.3	1.2	3.9	9.0	0.8	100	39.7

Source: Authors' calculations.

Note: The table reports only potential gains. When a country is already above the top 75th percentile in one area, the gains would be negative; those cases are excluded from the analysis and the contribution to the total gain is shown as 0.0.

gains from improvements in other areas, such as technology, infrastructure quality, access to finance, and training, are smaller and more heterogeneous across countries. However, studies that look at the effect of investment climate on aggregate growth find that the quality of the banking system, of public infrastructure, and of education are important sources of growth.

Firm size matters for the magnitude of potential gains. In particular, small firms would benefit relatively more than medium and large firms, especially from improvements to the regulatory framework. The benefits from Internet use to communicate with suppliers and clients are also bigger for smaller firms than for larger firms, whereas the opposite is observed for reductions in corruption.

Notes

1. It is important to note that the Enterprise Survey for Chile is not representative of all the industries covered in other countries. In particular, the Chilean survey collects information of firms in the food, metals and machinery, chemicals, other manufacturing, and information technology services industries. Hence, when Chile is the benchmark, only firms in those industries are considered.

2. Clearly, if one operates mechanically with these simple rules, it would imply that if a country is already in a better situation than the reference group, the gains would be negative. Given that this does not seem a very realistic policy recommendation, those cases are excluded in the computation of aggregate gains.

3. These results could be altered by the fact that not all industries are included in the comparison. Recall that the survey for Chile only includes firms from the food, metals and machinery, chemicals, other manufacturing, and information technology services industries. In the simulation, the results reported correspond to the gains for firms in those industries in the other 15 Latin American countries.

Reference

Loayza, N., P. Fajnzylber, and C. Calderón. 2005. *Economic Growth in Latin America and the Caribbean: Stylized Facts, Explanations, and Forecasts.* Washington, DC: World Bank.

4

Behind the Investment Climate: Back to Basics—Determinants of Corruption

*Verónica Alaimo, Pablo Fajnzylber,
J. Luis Guasch, J. Humberto López, and
Ana María Oviedo*

Previous chapters discussed the role of the investment climate as a determinant of growth in Latin America and suggested priority areas of reform for each country. Yet to effectively tackle reform, one needs to understand in more depth the mechanisms behind the investment climate determinants. For example, what are the mechanisms behind corruption activities? What incentives sustain corruption activities, which firms are more likely to pay bribes, and why? What is the role played by regulation, oversight, and the courts? What are the policy implications of these aspects and instruments for reform?

One of the main messages emerging from chapter 2 is that bribe payments—and more generally corruption—have a strong negative impact on firm labor productivity. Moreover, in chapter 3, the assessment of the relative importance of the different investment climate attributes revealed that in 7 of the 16 Latin American countries under analysis, corruption appears among the top three areas where progress can be expected to contribute the most to firm performance improvements. The finding that corruption is a barrier to firm performance is consistent with a large number of cross-country econometric studies that have found that poor governance—fueled, among other factors, by rampant corruption—negatively affects economic outcomes such as per capita income, growth, infant mortality, literacy, macroeconomic stability, and so forth (see, for instance, Kaufmann, Kraay, and Zoido-Lobatón 1999; Loayza, Oviedo, and Servén 2004, 2005; Mauro 1995).

This evidence suggests that reducing corruption is a significant priority and should be placed at the top of the reform agenda. From a policy perspective, however, the critical issue is identifying and deciding which actions need to be implemented to attack the problem. After all, the existence (or absence) of bribe payments is just the outcome of a wide range of factors and country circumstances that breed corruption, rather than a policy variable that can be changed at the will of policy makers. In fact, from a policy perspective, if the objective is attacking corruption, it is extremely important to identify those factors and country circumstances that are behind corruption practices so that appropriate and effective interventions can be designed.

Against this background, what does the existing literature tell us?[1] The past few years have witnessed the emergence of a booming literature (mainly based on cross-country aggregate regressions) on the causes of corruption. The literature tries to explain why the incidence of corruption is higher in some countries than in others.[2] For example, Montinola and Jackman (2002) find that political competition affects the level of corruption in a nonlinear way. At low levels of democracy, corruption is lower in dictatorships than in partially democratic countries. But at higher levels of democracy, democratic practices tend to lower corruption. Treisman (1999), however, argues that the current degree of democracy may not be that relevant—the effect of democracy on corruption breaks down once the regression controls for per capita income—and what matters is a long period of exposure to democracy. In his regressions, Treisman finds a significant effect when testing for countries that have been democracies since 1950. In a somewhat related study, using data for 125 countries compiled by Freedom House, Brunetti and Weder (2003) find that a free press appears to deter corruption. They argue that a free press can play a strong oversight role and that any independent journalist has a strong incentive to investigate and uncover stories on wrongdoing, given the prominence and attention that those issues draw from most of the relevant stakeholders, mostly members of civil society.

Corruption is also more present in low-income countries (see also Lambsdorff 1999; Mauro 1995; and Paldam 1999), something that Montinola and Jackman (2002) relate to the tendency of poorer countries to underpay public sector employees and to have weaker oversight institutions. In this vein, Rauch and Evans (2000) analyze the effect of merit-based recruitment on corruption in 35 developing countries. Using a merit-based recruitment index, they find that higher values of this index are associated with a larger share of high-level officials either having a college degree or entering the civil service through a formal examination system. Moreover, when they control for income, Rauch and Evans find that the merit-based recruitment index is negatively associated with corruption.

Other authors have emphasized low institutional capacity and quality and policy distortions as cause for corruption. On the judiciary front, the *World Development Report 1997* (World Bank 1997) focuses on the quality of the judiciary and finds that if one controls for other factors, the predictability of the judiciary appears to lower the level of corruption. A similar correlation between corruption and the independence of the judicial system is presented by Ades and Di Tella (1996). Similarly, Ades and Di Tella (1997: 1040) rely on two indexes that measure "the extent to which public procurement is open to foreign bidders" and "the extent to which there is equal fiscal treatment to all enterprises," respectively, and find that both variables appear to contribute to higher levels of corruption even when the authors control for other explanatory variables.

The degree of government involvement in the economy—as measured by the size of the budget to gross domestic product (GDP)—has also been found to affect the level of corruption. The idea here is that state intervention and public spending give rise to rent-seeking activities and hence to corruption. For example, Goel and Nelson (1998) relate the number of public officials convicted for abuse of public office in various states of the United States to the real per capita total expenditures of the local government and find a positive and significant association. LaPalombara (1994) relies on a sample of countries finding that the overall share of the government budget relative to GDP is positively correlated with levels of corruption (he excludes Scandinavian countries from the analysis).

Competition and openness to trade have also deserved some attention in the literature. To the extent that competition lowers the rents of economic activities, one could expect that it also reduces the motive of public officials to capture a share of these rents through extortion and corruption. In this regard, Ades and Di Tella (1995, 1997) use openness to trade (as measured by imports to GDP) as an indicator of competition, finding that it is negatively related to corruption in a cross-section of 55 countries. Similar results are found by Brunetti and Weder (2003) in a cross-section of 122 countries. Leite and Weidmann (1999) and Treisman (1999) use the Sachs and Warner index to measure the number of years that a country has been open to trade and find that this variable is also negatively correlated with the level of corruption.

On the whole, previous studies suggest that a number of policy interventions may lead to lower levels of corruption. For example, transparency in the form of laws protecting free speech and independent media outlets would likely result in a freer press. Having well-paid, professional civil servants would reduce their incentives to undertake extortion, while limiting their discretionary powers would reduce their leverage to extract bribes. Extensively using e-government, providing online access for fulfilling procedures, and implementing "administrative silence" procedures also limit corruption practices. On the macrofront, keeping public spending at reasonable levels and opening the economy to trade and foreign competition would also be steps in the right direction.

Yet, as argued by Svensson (2003), one must also acknowledge a number of limitations to the use of cross-country data in this context. First, in most of the studies mentioned, corruption is measured using a perceptions-based index, like those collected by Transparency International or similar organizations. Such indexes could raise a number of questions regarding perception biases. Second, many of the aggregate indicators are unique by country, which makes it difficult to explain why some firms pay bribes and others do not. That is, they reveal little about the mechanics of corruption.

As a response to those concerns, a (much more limited) number of studies have looked at the issue from a microeconomic perspective. For example, Kaufmann and Wei (1999) use data from three worldwide, firm-level surveys to examine the relationship between bribe payment, management time wasted with bureaucrats, and cost of capital, finding that firms that pay more bribes are also likely to face higher costs of capital and to spend more time with bureaucrats negotiating regulations. Likewise, corruption is also found to be positively associated with two subjective indicators: the degree to which "government regulations impose a heavy burden on business competitiveness" and the degree to which the "government regulations are vague and lax" (Kaufmann and Wei 1999: 7).

Similarly, Hellman, Jones, and Kaufmann (2000) rely on the Business Environment and Enterprise Performance Survey data for a number of transition economies. They find that new firms trying to compete in a market dominated by established incumbents in states that lack contract and property rights enforcement resort more easily to corrupt practices to compensate for existing weaknesses in the overall legal framework.

Svensson (2003) uses a survey of Ugandan firms to study "who must pay bribes and how much." Svensson proposes an explanation for the pattern of corruption in Uganda and finds that firms that have more frequent contact with the government, firms that are more profitable, and firms that have lower bargaining power (that is, firms with no outside option) are more likely to pay bribes.

Looking at the effect of corruption on the society at large, Seligson (2006) examines corruption-victimization measures from public opinion surveys in Latin America and concludes that corruption weakens democracy and people's trust in their fellow citizens, something that, in turn, negatively affects the efficiency of the state.

This chapter enters the debate and explores the determinants of corruption in Latin America from a microperspective—and, more specifically, from an investment climate perspective. It implicitly assumes that there may be a double payoff to improvements in some of the investment climate determinants. On the one hand, one has to consider the direct effect already discussed in chapter 2. On the other hand, there is also a possible indirect effect that works through a potential relationship between the different investment climate attributes. Improved governance is likely to make investment across sectors in education, technology, infrastructure, and so on more effective and cost-efficient.

The analysis in this chapter relies to a large extent on the conceptual framework put forward by Svensson (2003), which explains the incidence of corruption by the amount of regulation across industries (that is, the "control rights" hypothesis) and by the bargaining position of the firm, where the firm's ability to pay plays a crucial role (for example, more solvent firms may be in a weaker bargaining position). In other words, public officials demand bribes, and firms decide to obey to varying extents, depending on their leverage and on the cost of not paying.

In the econometric specifications, however, this chapter also considers the hypothesis that firms not only endure extortion from corrupted officials, but also play an active role in benefiting from corrupt practices. In this view, firms may have an incentive to bribe, provided that the gain for the firm is larger than the bribe plus the expected cost of being caught and fined (or any other punishment that might apply, such as jail time or public exposure). After all, it takes two to tango. Moreover, the analysis allows for the possibility that countries' attitudes toward corruption vary as well. As long as such behavior by public servants is implicitly condoned and generally accepted as part of business as usual—at least sotto voce—and not sanctioned, public servants may have incentives to engage in that type of activity, extracting rents under the belief that the chance of being caught and punished is quite small.

What are the main findings of this empirical analysis? First, the quantity and quality of regulations, proxied by the degree of regulatory compliance, affect the probability of paying bribes. These findings complement those of Recanatini, Prati, and Tabellini (2005), who study corruption in public agencies in eight countries using microdata, and find that agencies that provide services to firms (rather than to individuals) tend to be more corrupt, as are agencies that are the sole providers of basic services (electricity and water).[3] Both the findings of this analysis and the large variation in corruption behavior across agencies found by Recanatini, Prati, and Tabellini (2005) support the control rights hypothesis, as they show that public officials' demand for bribes will vary depending on their power to extract rents (which is itself directly related to the amount and the quality of regulation) and on the management of their agency.

Second, there is not enough evidence to support the "bargaining position" hypothesis. Indeed, the analysis finds that more solvent firms (as measured by having access to finance) tend to pay fewer bribes.[4] Third, domestically owned firms are more likely to pay bribes. This result is could be interpreted two ways: First, there could be an intrinsic difference between the degree to which local and foreign firms perceive corruption as improper conduct. In that case, local firms could consider bribe payments to be a normal part of doing business, whereas foreign firms are held to higher standards. Second, because local firms function in a particular "bad equilibrium" situation, they are more likely to resort to bribe payments in order to expedite procedures; that is, they use corruption as a way to "grease the wheels." The analysis also finds that the overall country attitude toward corruption, as measured by the Index of Economic Freedom or by the World Economic Forum's Business Costs of Corruption, is strongly related to the incidence of bribes. The better the index is or the lower the costs are, the lower the incidence of bribes is. This finding is consistent with the interpretation of the higher likelihood of bribe payments for domestically owned firms.

Fourth, a more credible judicial system is associated with lower levels of graft. This finding has important consequences, because a credible judicial system, in addition to reducing corruption, increases the likelihood of regulatory compliance (that is, improving the judicial system would have a double payoff in terms of the incidence of corruption).

These results have clear policy implications. Even though the appropriate policy mix will clearly depend on country circumstances, reducing corruption will require a combination of carrots and sticks. On the one hand, countries should assess their regulatory frameworks to distinguish between regulations that are justified by public interest and those that are outdated or plainly benefit certain interest groups. On the other hand, countries should consider the regulatory framework from an administrative perspective. A good regulatory framework could still suffer from bad enforcement (because of cumbersome procedures or lack of qualified personnel) or untimely implementation, which leads to increased costs for the private sector. Thus, administrative simplification, together with a more professional civil service, can be an effective tool for lowering the cost and improving the efficiency of regulations, thereby increasing compliance and reducing the power of public officials to demand bribes.

But countries should also look for solutions on the stick side, such as increasing efforts to monitor regulatory compliance and raising the costs of regulation infringement by increasing fines and sanctions for those being caught in an irregular situation. Similarly, improvements to the judicial system that increase the likelihood of punishment for both parties in a corrupting agreement (and hence increase the expected cost of entering in such agreements) are likely to lead to lower corruption levels.

The rest of the chapter is structured as follows. The chapter first reviews the conceptual framework and the econometric details. Next, it presents the main results and discusses the robustness of those results. Finally, it closes with some reflections.

A Conceptual Framework

What is the incidence of bribes in the different Latin American countries? Figure 4.1 presents the frequency of bribe payment across the different

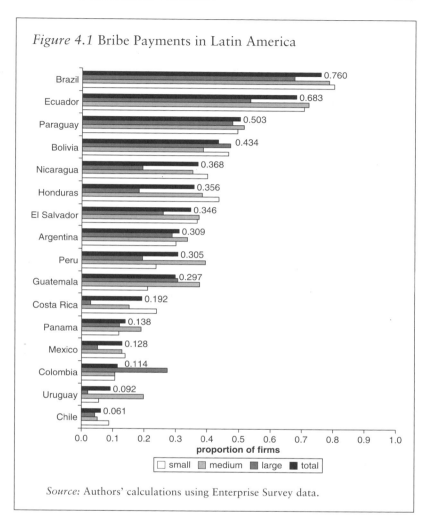

Figure 4.1 Bribe Payments in Latin America

Source: Authors' calculations using Enterprise Survey data.

countries in the region, breaking the sample down by firm size. *Bribe payments* are measured as a variable that equals one in these instances:

- If, when the interviewer asks, "When establishments like this one do business with the government, what percentage of the contract value would typically be paid in additional or informal payments or gifts to secure the contract?" the firm's manager answers with a percentage greater than zero.
- If the firm answers affirmatively to this question in reference to a telephone, water, or electricity connection; an import, or operating

license; or a construction permit: "Was an informal gift or payment expected or requested to obtain the [service]?"

Bribe payments equals zero if the manager answers "zero" to the first question (procurement) and "no" to the second question (public services). As in previous chapters, all the data used in the empirical analysis come from the Enterprise Surveys.

Inspection of figure 4.1 indicates significant variation in reported bribe payments across countries. Firms report the lowest frequency of bribes in Chile, Colombia, and Uruguay. At the other extreme, in Brazil, Ecuador, and Paraguay, firms report large levels of graft with frequencies in the 50 to 75 percent range. In between, almost one-third of the firms of the median Latin American country pay bribes. Figure 4.1 also indicates that there is significant country heterogeneity in the way firm size affects the frequency of bribes. Yet small and mainly medium firms appear to pay more bribes than larger firms: in the median Latin American country, the frequency of bribe payments among small, medium, and large firms is 27, 36, and 22 percent, respectively.

What are the reasons behind (a) the significant differences in graft levels across countries and (b) why within a given country some firms pay bribes and others do not?

To study these issues, the analysis follows Svensson (2003), who proposes an explanation based on the control rights hypothesis, defined as the implicit control that public officials exert on firms, which stems from inherent features of regulations and from the discretionary power that officials have in enforcing regulations. In this regard, one would expect that too much regulation or too low a quality of regulation (either de jure or de facto) would increase the control that public officials exert over firms and, hence, their power to obtain bribes. Differences in control rights across countries would be easy to understand because of differences in the regulatory framework across borders. But even within a country, public officials can affect firms' decisions differently across sectors, sizes, and locations, partly because of the natural variation of regulations across these dimensions, but also because of differences in enforcement and in the management of regulatory agencies.

If, however, all firms face the same regulations but only some of them pay bribes, one should be able to identify the characteristics that make firms more or less likely to pay. This is the idea behind the bargaining hypothesis. Specifically, the bargaining power of the firm facing a rent-maximizing public official trying to extract a bribe will depend on combination of current and expected profit (that is, on the current solvency and prospects for the firm) and on the opportunity cost of not paying. In principle, higher current and future expected profits should mean that the firm has more potential to pay and hence is in a weaker position to bargain. At the same time, higher future profits would also imply that the exit price[5] for the company is larger in term of forgone profits. Svensson (2003) further assumes that the combination of current and expected profits can be expressed as an increasing function of the observed capital stock, so that firms with a higher capital stock should pay more (and larger) bribes.

Most often, the problem of corruption is attacked from the perspective of a public official who extorts a firm, rather than from the perspective of a firm that decides to bribe a public official. However, there is an alternative (and admittedly less romantic) view of corruption, in which firms are not just "victims" but actually adopt corrupt practices themselves to speed up procedures; avoid red tape; and, in general, to grease the wheels of the administrative system. If being caught in corrupt behavior had no cost (moral considerations apart), profit-maximizing firms would be willing to pay bribes when the gains in time or contracts exceeded the bribe amounts. To the extent that firms caught being corrupt are punished, then one also needs to factor the chances and the costs of being caught.

In short, the incidence of bribes is the result of firms' as well as public servants' cost-benefit analysis. That is, in an environment where corruption does little or no damage to reputation and where corrupt behavior is not systemically monitored and punished, firms as well as public servants will have incentives to engage in that behavior. For illustrative purposes, this situation can be stated as follows:

$$E(\Pi) = Z - b - E(f) \quad \text{firm's behavior} \tag{4.1a}$$

$$E(G) = b - E(L) \quad \text{public servant's behavior} \tag{4.1b}$$

where Π is the net profit for the firm of bribing a pubic official; Z is the gross profit (time saved, contract awarded, and so forth); b is the bribe; f is the fine to pay if the firm gets caught; and $E(.)$ is the expectation operator.[6] Thus, a firm will have incentives to bribe provided that $E(\Pi) > 0$.[7] Likewise, G is the expected gains of a public servant asking for or accepting bribes, and L is the fine or sanction (such as loss of employment) if the public servant is caught. Thus, a public servant will have incentives to accept or request bribes if $E(G) > 0$.

From equations 4.1a and 4.1b, it follows that in countries where the rule of law is maintained and in cases where $E(f)$ and $E(L)$ are large, either because there is a high probability of getting caught or because there is a large fine associated with it, then firms and public servants have a lower incentive to offer or demand bribes. Within countries, firms that, for example, have more information on which officials are more prone to corrupt behavior also face a lower value of $E(f)$ and hence will have more incentives to pay bribes. Thus, differences in firms' attitudes toward greasing the wheels can explain why some firms engage in that type of behavior while others do not.

In practice, the study did not explicitly observe the information that individual firms have and hence did not observe $E(f)$ at the firm level, so it cannot directly test this hypothesis. However, one variable can be used to discriminate between at least two broad segments of firms—namely, domestic and foreign firms. If domestic firms have more information, or if attitudes toward corruption differ between domestic and foreign firms, then one can expect to observe differences in how often they pay bribes.

From an empirical point of view, this strategy relies on the following econometric model:

$$\Pr(bribe)_{j,c,i,r,s} = \beta_c + \beta_i + \beta_r + \varphi X_{j,c,i,s} + \upsilon_{j,c,i,s}, \tag{4.2}$$

where j = firm; c = country; i = industry; r = region; and s = size. $\Pr(bribe)$ is the probability that the firm in question pays bribes, and X is a set of controls aimed at testing the three hypotheses discussed above: "control rights," "bargaining," and "grease the wheels." More specifically, among the control set, the following variables are included. First is the degree of *regulatory compliance*, used in previous chapters, which should proxy for the quantity and quality of regulations and would thus capture the forces underlying the control rights hypothesis. Evidence in the empirical literature supports the view that regulatory compliance is directly related to the quantity, quality, and enforcement of regulations (see, for instance, Olson 1999); hence, this proxy should correctly reflect regulatory differences within a country. Regulatory differences, in turn, would explain why public officials in certain sectors or agencies can extract rents more easily than in others. The hypothesis is then that higher compliance will be associated with less frequent bribe payments.

Second, two variables are included to measure the bargaining power of the firm. One is in line with Svensson (2003)—namely, the capital stock per worker of the firm. The other is whether the firm has access to credit in the financial sector, which would give an idea of the solvency of the firm and hence of its future profitability. It is measured as a dummy variable that equals one if the firm has a loan, credit line, or overdraft facility or if the firm does not need any credit. If the bargaining hypothesis holds, both variables would be expected to carry negative parameters. (That is, more solvent firms have higher current and expected profits, so they can afford to pay more bribes and, hence, are in a disadvantageous bargaining position.)

Third, two additional variables are included to account for the grease the wheels hypothesis:

- A dummy variable for foreign-owned firms, in line with the idea that domestic firms have better information about the integrity of public officials and may have lower ethical standards about corruption
- The level of trust in the courts' enforcement power

Thus X contains a variable that equals one if the manager agrees (at least partially) with this statement: "I am confident that the judicial system will enforce my contractual and property rights in business disputes."[8] Here these variables are expected to carry negative coefficients.

The study also experiments with other variables that can be seen as reinforcing those used in the tests of the different hypothesis behind corruption. For example, in one of the specifications, a variable is included that equals one if in the past three years the firm requested any public service (a telephone, water, or electricity connection; an import or operating license; or a construction permit) and zero if it requested no service at all. This variable is intended to measure the extent to which the firm has contact with the government. Under the control rights hypothesis, it should carry a positive coefficient. Also, a dummy variable is introduced that equals one if the government (or a government-owned enterprise) is the firm's main client. Again, one would expect it to carry a positive sign. Finally, a variable is introduced for the number of times the firm was visited by tax inspectors in the previous fiscal year. This variable measures the degree of regulatory enforcement.

Country-level measures are needed to account for the effect of the overall country's attitude towards corruption, which affects the cost of the firm being caught in corrupt behavior $E(L)$. The analysis uses measures such as the Index of Economic Freedom or the World Economic Forum's Business Costs of Corruption to test whether bribe payments are more frequent in countries with a wider tolerance of corrupt practices.

Finally, in all the specifications, a set of controls is included that is aimed at capturing other unobserved firm characteristics. In addition to country, industry, and region dummies, the study includes the (log) age of the firm and dummy variables for exporters, medium firms (20 to 100 employees), and large firms (more than 100 employees).[9]

Results

Table 4.1 reports the results from the pooled probit estimations.[10] Column 1 corresponds to a baseline regression that, in addition to the firm controls used in all the specifications, includes regulatory compliance, the capital stock per worker, and a dummy for foreign-owned firms. This basic regression includes a single variable to capture each of the hypotheses behind corruption discussed previously. Inspection of table 4.1 indicates that, as predicted by the control rights hypothesis, the amount and variation of regulation, as captured by the degree of regulatory compliance, is negatively associated with the probability of paying bribes. Similarly, as predicted by the grease the wheels hypothesis, foreign-owned firms have a lower probability of paying bribes. In contrast, there is no evidence that the stock of capital has an effect on the probability of paying bribes (that is, there is no support for the bargaining hypothesis).

As for the coefficients of the control variables, the only one that appears to be significantly different from zero is the one corresponding to the

Table 4.1 Determinants of Bribe Payments in Latin America

	(1)	(2)	(3)	(4)	(5)	(6)
Regulatory compliance	-0.002*** [6.99]	-0.002*** [6.95]	-0.002*** [6.80]	-0.002*** [6.71]	-0.002*** [6.79]	-0.002*** [6.79]
Log of capital per worker	0.001 [0.50]	0.001 [0.55]	0.001 [0.62]	0.000 [0.41]	0.001 [0.62]	0.001 [0.62]
Foreign owned	-0.086*** [3.11]	-0.086*** [3.13]	-0.084*** [3.05]	-0.088*** [3.19]	-0.084*** [3.05]	-0.084*** [3.02]
Access to finance		-0.058*** [2.77]	-0.058*** [2.77]	-0.063*** [3.02]	-0.058*** [2.77]	-0.058*** [2.78]
Trust in courts' enforcement power			-0.050*** [3.15]	-0.049*** [3.07]	-0.050*** [3.15]	-0.050*** [3.16]
Requested public services				0.071*** [4.56]		
Government as main client					-0.014 [0.33]	
Number of tax inspections						0.000 [0.46]
Log of firm's age	-0.018* [1.76]	-0.017* [1.68]	-0.017 [1.63]	-0.011 [1.05]	-0.017 [1.62]	-0.017 [1.63]

(continued)

Table 4.1 Determinants of Bribe Payments in Latin America *(continued)*

	(1)	(2)	(3)	(4)	(5)	(6)
Exporter	-0.015	-0.013	-0.013	-0.019	-0.013	-0.012
	[0.81]	[0.70]	[0.69]	[1.04]	[0.70]	[0.68]
20–99 employees	0.014	0.019	0.017	0.008	0.017	0.018
	[0.80]	[1.05]	[0.97]	[0.46]	[0.98]	[0.99]
100+ employees	-0.03	-0.024	-0.022	-0.036	-0.023	-0.022
	[1.24]	[0.99]	[0.91]	[1.47]	[0.91]	[0.87]
Observations	4,870	4,870	4,870	4,870	4,870	4,870

Source: Authors' calculations.

Note: * = significant at the 10 percent level; ** = significant at the 5 percent level; *** = significant at the 1 percent level. Robust z statistics are in brackets. The table reports the results of a probit regression of the frequency of bribe payments on the variables in the first column. The coefficients reported correspond to marginal effects; that is, they reflect the (percentage) change in the probability of paying bribes if there is a one (percentage) point increase in the explanatory variable. All regressions include country, industry, and region effects.

variable measuring the age of the firm, which is negative. That is, established firms have a lower probability of paying bribes. Although (as will be seen) this finding is not very robust to departures from this basic specification, it would, in principle, lend some support to a view consistent with the grease the wheels hypothesis, which holds that new firms entering a market with weak contract and property rights try to counterbalance the power of firms already established and that older firms have found ways to circumvent bribe payments.

Column 2 expands the previous results and adds an additional variable that measures the solvency and potential profitability of the firm—namely, whether the firm has access to finance. Recall that, according to the bargaining hypothesis, this variable should carry a positive coefficient. In fact, it carries a negative coefficient (that is, firms with higher expected profitability pay fewer bribes). The other coefficients remain basically unchanged with respect to the findings in column 1. In other words, the evidence that emerges from this specification does not lend support to the bargaining hypothesis.

Column 3 explores whether trust in the judicial system plays a role in explaining the incidence of corruption. This specification suggests that when courts are trusted firms pay fewer bribes. The only noticeable change with respect to the previous specifications is that the coefficient of the variable measuring the age of the firm is not significant any longer at standard significance levels (although it continues to be significant at 15 percent). Access to finance continues to carry a negative and significant coefficient.

Additional support for the control rights hypothesis is also found in column 4, which explores whether firms that deal more often with government officials are more likely to pay bribes. However, somewhat surprisingly, firms that have the government as their main client do not seem to have higher probability of paying bribes (column 5).[11] In fact, the point estimate is negative, although it does not come close to becoming significant at standard levels. Another somewhat surprising result is that the number of tax inspections (a variable that can be seen as enforcement efforts by the government) does not seem to enter the bribes equation.

One natural question in this context regards whether all firms face the same incentives to engage in corrupt practices. For example, does size play a role in this context? Table 4.1 includes variables to control for size, but perhaps size is relevant for the slopes and not for the intercept of the equations. To explore this possibility, the study replicates the regressions in table 4.1, but only for small firms (those with fewer than 20 employees). Table 4.2 shows the estimation results. Comparison of this table with table 4.1 reveals that the effect of size is very modest and that most of the results in table 4.1 are maintained. For example, regulatory compliance and foreign ownership continue to enter with negative signs, as do trust in the courts' enforcement power and access to finance. Moreover, a firm with extensive dealings with the public sector is more likely to pay bribes.

Table 4.2 Determinants of Bribe Payments in Latin America: Small Firms

	(1)	(2)	(3)	(4)	(5)	(6)
Regulatory compliance	-0.002*** [5.00]	-0.002*** [4.96]	-0.002*** [4.71]	-0.002*** [4.62]	-0.002*** [4.75]	-0.002*** [4.72]
Log of capital per worker	0.003 [1.62]	0.003* [1.69]	0.003* [1.72]	0.003 [1.54]	0.003* [1.67]	0.003* [1.71]
Foreign owned	-0.184*** [2.69]	-0.183*** [2.70]	-0.185*** [2.81]	-0.190*** [2.97]	-0.184*** [2.81]	-0.185*** [2.82]
Access to finance		-0.056** [2.01]	-0.055** [1.98]	-0.061** [2.18]	-0.055** [1.96]	-0.056** [1.99]
Trust in courts' enforcement power			-0.083*** [3.32]	-0.082*** [3.28]	-0.082*** [3.31]	-0.083*** [3.31]
Requested public services				0.076*** [3.21]		
Government as main client					0.069 [1.08]	
Number of tax inspections						0.001 [0.36]

(continued)

Table 4.2 Determinants of Bribe Payments in Latin America: Small Firms *(continued)*

	(1)	*(2)*	*(3)*	*(4)*	*(5)*	*(6)*
Log of firm's age	−0.014	−0.012	−0.014	−0.004	−0.014	−0.014
	[0.85]	[0.75]	[0.86]	[0.24]	[0.89]	[0.86]
Exporter	−0.024	−0.021	−0.02	−0.03	−0.02	−0.019
	[0.71]	[0.63]	[0.59]	[0.90]	[0.58]	[0.57]
Observations	1,849	1,849	1,849	1,849	1,849	1,849

Source: Authors' calculations.

Note: * = significant at the 10 percent level; ** = significant at the 5 percent level; *** = significant at the 1 percent level. Robust z statistics are in brackets. The table reports the results of a probit regression of the frequency of bribe payments by small firms on the variables in the first column. The coefficients reported correspond to marginal effects; that is, they reflect the (percentage) change in the probability of paying bribes if there is a one (percentage) point increase in the explanatory variable. All regressions include country, industry, and region effects.

However, the installed stock capital enters the equation significantly in four of the specifications and comes close to being significant in the other two, something that would be consistent with the bargaining hypothesis (although one would need to explain the result regarding access to finance).

In short, there are three main findings from these two exercises. First, there is evidence to support the control rights hypothesis. Both the extent of regulatory compliance and the extent of dealings with the public sector enter the specification with the expected sign. Second, there is also evidence to support the grease the wheels hypothesis, as suggested by the coefficient of the variables measuring the ownership of the firm and the role of the courts. Third, there is not very robust evidence of the bargaining hypothesis. If anything, when the full sample is considered, the evidence supports the opposite situation (that is, more solvent firms paying less frequently). With the small firms sample, the evidence is somewhat mixed (access to finance lowers the probability of paying bribes, but the stock of capital increases it), perhaps reflecting that with respect to petty corruption, this specific corruption mechanism may be at work.

Robustness Checks

The next step is to test the robustness of the results. To that end, several alternative specifications must be run that intend to address, in turn, issues of parameter heterogeneity, sample size, measurement of the dependent variable, use of subjective measures for the courts' enforcement power, and endogeneity in the equation.

Country Heterogeneity

The results based on pooled data have some advantages and disadvantages. On the plus side, pooled data can capture variance in some of the variables across countries and exploit the benefits of working with a large sample. On the minus side is the problem that results from imposing homogeneity to a set of parameters likely to be heterogeneous.

To explore whether the determinants of bribe payment change significantly from country to country, table 4.3 presents the country-specific results corresponding to equation 4.2 in tables 4.1 and 4.2. Broadly speaking, the results from these regressions are consistent with the previous pooled-regression results—namely, in 7 out of 16 countries, the variable of regulatory compliance has a negative and significant coefficient. Furthermore, those seven countries compose more than 70 percent of the entire sample.[12] The analysis also finds, albeit to a lesser extent, consistency with the pooled sample results for the variables that measure access to finance and trust in the court's enforcing power. The rest of the variables tend to

Table 4.3 Country-by-Country Analysis

	Argentina	Bolivia	Brazil	Chile	Colombia	Costa Rica	Ecuador	El Salvador
Regulatory compliance	-0.003** [2.14]	-0.004*** [2.97]	-0.003*** [4.54]	-0.002*** [4.25]	-0.002*** [2.73]	-0.003*** [2.64]	-0.001 [0.62]	-0.001 [1.02]
Log capital per worker	-0.004 [1.27]	-0.001 [0.22]	-0.002 [0.63]	0.000 [0.07]	0.008 [1.45]	0.018*** [2.68]	0.013 [1.34]	0.001 [0.10]
Foreign owned	-0.001 [0.01]	-0.055 [0.37]	-0.079 [1.31]	0.019 [0.86]	-0.024 [0.18]		0.011 [0.07]	-0.110 [0.92]
Access to finance	-0.192** [2.09]	-0.133 [1.28]	-0.006 [0.15]	-0.023 [1.04]	-0.035 [0.36]	0.021 [0.30]	-0.287** [2.37]	-0.168 [1.38]
Trust in courts' enforcement power	-0.116* [1.70]	0.076 [0.79]	0.027 [1.00]	-0.060*** [4.11]	-0.015 [0.35]	-0.130** [2.21]	-0.093 [0.82]	-0.033 [0.49]
Log of firm's age	-0.054 [1.56]	-0.019 [0.39]	-0.030 [1.49]	-0.009 [0.86]	-0.014 [0.65]	0.014 [0.42]	0.063 [0.95]	-0.122** [2.09]
Exporter	0.020 [0.27]	-0.051 [0.50]	-0.013 [0.42]	-0.016 [0.89]	0.028 [0.58]	0.029 [0.46]	0.131 [1.05]	0.078 [1.04]
20–99 employees	0.043 [0.55]	0.053 [0.57]	0.010 [0.25]	-0.014 [0.87]	0.011 [0.25]	-0.127** [1.98]	-0.009 [0.08]	0.018 [0.22]
100+ employees	0.001 [0.01]	0.178 [1.23]	-0.04 [0.86]	-0.008 [0.32]	-0.015 [0.20]	-0.179* [1.76]	-0.266 [1.48]	-0.068 [0.64]
Observations	226	157	1,023	914	298	242	119	223

(continued)

156

Table 4.3 Country-by-Country Analysis (continued)

	Guatemala	Honduras	Mexico	Nicaragua	Panama	Paraguay	Peru	Uruguay
Regulatory compliance	-0.001 [0.86]	0.000 [0.44]	-0.001*** [3.71]	0.000 [0.05]	0.000 [0.08]	-0.002 [0.79]	0.000 [0.06]	-0.002 [1.05]
Log capital per worker	0.050* [1.70]	-0.004 [0.95]	0.001 [0.60]	0.002 [0.34]	-0.041 [1.37]	0.005 [1.21]	0.002 [0.34]	-0.002 [0.50]
Foreign owned		-0.242** [2.55]	0.043 [0.85]	-0.090 [0.89]	-0.128 [1.27]	-0.199 [1.27]	-0.011 [0.06]	
Access to finance	-0.008 [0.05]	-0.103 [1.29]	0.013 [0.42]	-0.123** [2.03]			-0.144 [0.92]	0.081 [0.59]
Trust in courts' enforcement power	-0.058 [0.55]	-0.163*** [2.72]	-0.054* [1.95]	-0.091 [1.61]	0.045 [0.53]	0.006 [0.06]	-0.185 [1.54]	-0.019 [0.19]
Log of firm's age	-0.030 [0.49]	0.025 [0.54]	0.020 [1.24]	0.017 [0.44]	-0.092 [1.42]	-0.114 [1.28]	-0.026 [0.47]	-0.088* [1.81]
Exporter	0.019 [0.20]	-0.028 [0.38]	0.003 [0.08]	-0.045 [0.65]	0.108 [0.74]	0.046 [0.39]	0.030 [0.31]	0.012 [0.11]
20–99 employees	0.157 [1.41]	-0.030 [0.41]	-0.013 [0.43]	-0.038 [0.61]	0.094 [0.90]	0.079 [0.72]	0.005 [0.04]	-0.001 [0.01]
100+ employees	0.162 [1.17]	-0.135 [1.43]	-0.03 [0.84]	-0.147 [1.34]	-0.118 [0.90]	0.323 [1.64]	0.121 [0.87]	
Observations	107	294	595	339	76	108	125	53

Source: Authors' calculations.

Note: * = significant at the 10 percent level; ** = significant at the 5 percent level; *** = significant at the 1 percent level. Robust z statistics are in brackets. The table reports the results of a probit regression of the frequency of bribe payments by country on the variables in the first column. The coefficients reported correspond to marginal effects; that is, they reflect the (percentage) change in the probability of paying bribes if there is a one (percentage) point increase in the explanatory variable. All regressions include industry and region effects.

carry coefficients with signs in line with those in tables 4.1 and 4.2, but in most of the cases, these coefficients are not significant.

On the one hand, the exercise is not fully successful in the sense that most of the country-specific coefficients are not significant, a problem that somewhat limits the extent of the comparison. On the other hand, the few results that can be read from table 4.3 appear to confirm the previous findings.

Sample Size

Among the explanatory variables in tables 4.1 to 4.3 is the (log) of capital per worker. When the sample of small, medium, and large firms is considered, this variable does not come close to being significant. Thus, in this exercise, the (log) capital per worker is eliminated from the regression. Because of this change, the sample size increases dramatically to more than 7,000 observations. (See also chapter 2 for a discussion on the issue.)

The results (table 4.4), however, remain strikingly similar (both quantitatively and quantitatively) to those reported in table 4.1. The only noticeable difference is that now medium firms appear to be more likely to pay bribes, even after all other firm characteristics are controlled for.

Alternative Measures for the Courts' Enforcement Power Variable

As discussed previously, the variable used to measure the extent of trust in the courts' enforcement power is based on perceptions, and this basis could lead to perception biases. After all, subjective measures are often criticized as being difficult to compare across countries, especially when countries' standards of what is acceptable differ. To assess whether this issue is important in this context, the next exercise uses an alternative, objective measure of court quality that can be computed for the countries included in the new wave of Enterprise Surveys. More specifically, the exercise takes the average of three dummy variables that measure the use and effectiveness of the court system. The first equals one if the firm answers "yes" to this question: "In the past two years, did this establishment have a dispute with clients over payments owed to it, in which the [court system was used to resolve it]?" The second equals one if (after answering "yes" to the previous question), the firm answers "yes" to the following question: "Was a court judgment made?" The last variable is equal to one if the firm answers "yes" to this question: "Was the decision of the court enforced?"

In principle, this alternative measure tries to minimize differences coming from perception. However, one should be aware that differences in how often people resort to courts could also stem from the existence of a wider range of options in countries where the legal system is more efficient. With this caveat in mind, one may now turn to table 4.5, which

Table 4.4 Determinants of Bribe Payments in Latin America: Excluding Capital

	(1)	(2)	(3)	(4)	(5)	(6)
Regulatory compliance	-0.002*** [8.46]	-0.002*** [8.41]	-0.002*** [8.23]	-0.002*** [8.12]	-0.002*** [8.20]	-0.002*** [8.23]
Foreign owned	-0.075*** [3.60]	-0.076*** [3.64]	-0.073*** [3.51]	-0.076*** [3.63]	-0.073*** [3.51]	-0.073*** [3.49]
Access to finance		-0.077*** [4.43]	-0.077*** [4.45]	-0.082*** [4.74]	-0.077*** [4.45]	-0.077*** [4.45]
Trust in courts' enforcement power			-0.067*** [5.30]	-0.066*** [5.24]	-0.067*** [5.31]	-0.067*** [5.30]
Requested public services				0.075*** [6.05]		
Government as main client					-0.029 [0.99]	
Number of tax inspections						0 [0.32]
Log of firm's age	-0.011 [1.41]	-0.01 [1.30]	-0.01 [1.28]	-0.005 [0.61]	-0.01 [1.25]	-0.01 [1.27]

(continued)

159

Table 4.4 Determinants of Bribe Payments in Latin America: Excluding Capital (*continued*)

	(1)	(2)	(3)	(4)	(5)	(6)
Exporter	-0.001	0.001	0.002	-0.005	0.001	0.002
	[0.09]	[0.05]	[0.11]	[0.33]	[0.07]	[0.11]
20–99 employees	0.024*	0.030**	0.028**	0.019	0.028**	0.029**
	[1.77]	[2.18]	[2.06]	[1.36]	[2.05]	[2.07]
100+ employees	-0.03	-0.022	-0.02	-0.037*	-0.021	-0.02
	[1.57]	[1.14]	[1.06]	[1.92]	[1.07]	[1.03]
Observations	7,273	7,273	7,273	7,273	7,273	7,272

Source: Authors' calculations.

Note: * = significant at the 10 percent level; ** = significant at the 5 percent level; *** = significant at the 1 percent level. Robust z statistics are in brackets. The table reports the results of a probit regression of the frequency of bribe payments on the variables in the first column. The coefficients reported correspond to marginal effects; that is, they reflect the (percentage) change in the probability of paying bribes if there is a one (percentage) point increase in the explanatory variable. All regressions include country, industry, and region effects.

Table 4.5 Determinants of Bribe Payments in Latin America: Objective Court Quality Measure

	(1)	(2)	(3)	(4)	(5)	(6)
Regulatory compliance	-0.002*** [2.83]	-0.002*** [2.89]	-0.002*** [2.83]	-0.002*** [2.85]	-0.002*** [2.88]	-0.002*** [2.87]
Foreign owned	-0.032 [0.64]	-0.03 [0.60]	-0.034 [0.67]	-0.035 [0.69]	-0.03 [0.60]	-0.04 [0.81]
Access to finance		-0.122** [2.15]	-0.127** [2.25]	-0.123** [2.17]	-0.122** [2.15]	
Objective court quality measure	-0.116** [2.36]	-0.112** [2.28]	-0.112** [2.27]	-0.115** [2.35]	-0.111** [2.25]	
Requested public services			0.068* [1.92]			
Government as main client				-0.105 [1.52]		
Number of tax inspections					0.001 [0.41]	
Log of firm's age	-0.005 [0.23]	-0.001 [0.07]	0.002 [0.11]	0.000 [0.00]	-0.001 [0.05]	-0.009 [0.47]

(continued)

Table 4.5 Determinants of Bribe Payments in Latin America: Objective Court Quality Measure (*continued*)

	(1)	(2)	(3)	(4)	(5)	(6)
Exporter	0.018	0.023	0.014	0.02	0.023	0.019
	[0.47]	[0.62]	[0.37]	[0.52]	[0.60]	[0.51]
20–99 employees	0.051	0.056	0.048	0.051	0.055	0.044
	[1.32]	[1.44]	[1.24]	[1.32]	[1.43]	[1.16]
100+ employees	-0.025	-0.020	-0.035	-0.024	-0.023	-0.039
	[0.50]	[0.40]	[0.70]	[0.49]	[0.46]	[0.81]
Observations	1,024	1,024	1,024	1,024	1,023	1,024

Source: Authors' calculations.

Note: * = significant at the 10 percent level; ** = significant at the 5 percent level; *** = significant at the 1 percent level. Robust z statistics are in brackets. The table reports the results of a probit regression of the frequency of bribe payments on the variables in the first column. The coefficients reported correspond to marginal effects; that is, they reflect the (percentage) change in the probability of paying bribes if there is a one (percentage) point increase in the explanatory variable. All regressions include country, industry, and region effects.

reports the results of the alternative specification. Note that the sample size is reduced dramatically, excluding Brazil, Chile, Costa Rica, Ecuador, El Salvador, Honduras, and Nicaragua.

Inspection of table 4.5 indicates that the coefficient of the quality of courts is negative and significant, suggesting that firms that report better quality of courts tend to pay bribes less frequently, a finding that also confirms the validity of the subjective measure. As for the coefficients of the other variables, table 4.5 indicates that ownership does not appear to enter into the specification, although clearly this finding could be related more to the sample than to the new variable. To explore this issue, the exercise replicates in column 6 the model in the first column but excludes the courts' enforcement power measure. The results indicate that, indeed, firm ownership does not seem to matter as a result of the sample used.

Alternative Measures for the Dependent Variable

Could the results be driven by the specific dependent variable chosen? Recall that the dependent variable equals one if the firm agrees that bribes are necessary for procurement or if the firm has been asked for informal payments whenever it requested public services. Clearly, firms that requested public services have a positive probability of having to pay bribes, so in principle one could find that, by construction, there is a positive correlation between paying bribes and the variable used to measure the dealings of the firm with the government.

Table 4.6 reports the results from those estimations. They suggest that while in principle it is possible that some of the correlation between the variable measuring whether the firm requested a public service results from data construction (this variable is not significantly different from zero in the specification where bribe payments concern only procurement activities), the rest of the results are maintained. In fact, the coefficients of regulatory compliance, trust of courts' enforcement abilities, and access to finance continue to be negative and significantly different from zero.

The coefficient of ownership continues to be significant when bribes are measured on the basis of procurement, but it is not significant when bribes are measured on the basis of public services. Although this condition can be related to sample issues affecting the econometric estimates, it is also possible that different types of corruption activities exist and that for each type a different mechanism is at work. For example, when one focuses on big projects that require procurement practices, the grease the wheels hypothesis may be particularly important because firms may have an incentive to bribe officials to get a contract. But when one focuses on services that can be provided only by the public sector, then perhaps the control rights hypothesis is more relevant. These issues will require additional attention in future work.

Table 4.6 Alternative Measures of Bribe Payments

	Reports bribes in procurement	Reports bribes to "get things done"
Regulatory compliance	-0.002*** [8.54]	-0.001*** [6.04]
Foreign owned	-0.066*** [3.37]	-0.008 [0.44]
Access to finance	-0.053*** [3.36]	-0.059*** [3.92]
Trust in courts' enforcement power	-0.048*** [4.11]	-0.086*** [7.74]
Requested public services	0.01 [0.88]	0.045*** [4.22]
Log of firm's age	-0.003 [0.45]	-0.004 [0.61]
Exporter	-0.025* [1.82]	-0.005 [0.37]
20–99 employees	0.002 [0.15]	0.025** [2.09]
100+ employees	-0.063*** [3.61]	-0.034** [2.02]
Observations	6,927	6,395

Source: Authors' calculations.

Note: * = significant at the 10 percent level; ** = significant at the 5 percent level; *** = significant at the 1 percent level. Robust z statistics are in brackets. The table reports the results of a probit regression of the frequency of bribe payments on the variables in the first column. The coefficients reported correspond to marginal effects; that is, they reflect the (percentage) change in the probability of paying bribes if there is a one (percentage) point increase in the explanatory variable. All regressions include country, industry, and region effects.

Reverse Causality

So far, this chapter has argued that the quantity and quality of regulation has a direct effect on corruption, but to the extent that the private sector pays bribes to avoid regulation, it is difficult to have a clear sense of causality. In fact, it could be the case that in a corrupt environment both public officials and firms resort to corruption rather than comply with regulation, regardless of the quantity and quality of regulation.

To address this issue, the next exercise estimates the same specifications in table 4.1, but this time it instruments compliance with a region–industry–firm size mean, as chapter 2 did for the firm performance estimations.

The results (table 4.7) provide some comfort in that they are quite similar to those in table 4.1. Moreover, the coefficient of regulatory compliance is now larger (in absolute value) than in the previous probit estimation, and it continues to be significant above 5 percent. Similarly, the variables that were significant in table 4.1 remain significant, as do coefficients with larger magnitudes.

General Environment

A final test is whether bribe payments are more frequent in countries with a wider acceptance of corrupt practices. This acceptance could be reflected in lower enforcement of corruption laws or higher social tolerance of corrupt practices. Two different measures are used to capture acceptance or prevalence of corrupt practices in the country. First is the Index of Economic Freedom from the Heritage Foundation, which measures economic freedom on a 1 to 5 scale, where 1 indicates the most economic freedom. This index combines many measures of regulation, governance, and corruption.[13] Second is the World Economic Forum's Business Costs of Corruption, which measures the extent of diversion of public funds and public trust of politicians. The scale goes from 1 to 7, where 7 reflects lower corruption levels.[14] The study also used alternative measures, such as the Corruption Perceptions Index from Transparency International, and the results were strikingly similar.[15]

Tables 4.8 and 4.9 report the results from these regressions. (Because they use countrywide measures, country effects are not included in the estimations; however, other country controls are included, specifically GDP per capita and growth of GDP per capita.) The coefficients of regulatory compliance are strikingly similar to those of previous specifications, and all other coefficients significant in other specifications remain significant here as well. This result suggests that in previous estimations the country effect was capturing mostly the environment related to corruption and governance, which is now replaced by more specific measures.

Determinants of Regulatory Compliance

This section describes the last missing link of the analysis and asks about the wider relationship between regulatory compliance and the quality of institutions in a country. Previous sections argued that regulatory compliance reflects to some extent public officials' leverage in dealing with firms. If the regulatory framework is stringent, the argument goes, public officials have more power to demand bribes from firms. At the same time, firms' costs of complying with regulations increase, thus creating incentives for firms to shun them. Hence, a negative relationship between regulatory compliance and incidence of bribe payments is observed. As stated before, empirical

Table 4.7 Determinants of Bribe Payments in Latin America: Instrumental Variable Results

	(1)	(2)	(3)	(4)	(5)	(6)
Regulatory compliance	-0.009*** [2.63]	-0.009*** [2.60]	-0.008** [2.50]	-0.008** [2.49]	-0.008** [2.49]	-0.008** [2.48]
Log of capital per worker	0.002 [0.67]	0.002 [0.70]	0.002 [0.76]	0.002 [0.57]	0.002 [0.77]	0.002 [0.76]
Foreign owned	-0.248*** [2.90]	-0.250*** [2.92]	-0.245*** [2.86]	-0.257*** [2.99]	-0.245*** [2.86]	-0.244*** [2.84]
Access to finance		-0.162*** [2.70]	-0.162*** [2.71]	-0.177*** [2.95]	-0.162*** [2.71]	-0.163*** [2.72]
Trust in courts' enforcement power			-0.136*** [2.90]	-0.132*** [2.82]	-0.136*** [2.90]	-0.137*** [2.91]
Requested public services				0.202*** [4.44]		
Government as main client					-0.032 [0.26]	
Number of tax inspections						-0.001 [0.41]
Log of firm's age	-0.052* [1.77]	-0.050* [1.69]	-0.048 [1.64]	-0.032 [1.07]	-0.048 [1.63]	-0.048 [1.64]

(continued)

Table 4.7 Determinants of Bribe Payments in Latin America: Instrumental Variable Results *(continued)*

	(1)	(2)	(3)	(4)	(5)	(6)
Exporter	-0.038	-0.033	-0.032	-0.051	-0.033	-0.032
	[0.73]	[0.63]	[0.62]	[0.97]	[0.63]	[0.62]
20–99 employees	0.057	0.069	0.064	0.039	0.064	0.065
	[1.06]	[1.29]	[1.20]	[0.72]	[1.20]	[1.21]
100+ employees	-0.061	-0.044	-0.04	-0.081	-0.041	-0.038
	[0.78]	[0.57]	[0.52]	[1.03]	[0.53]	[0.50]
Observations	4,870	4,870	4,870	4,870	4,870	4,870

Source: Authors' calculations.

Note: * = significant at the 10 percent level; ** = significant at the 5 percent level; *** = significant at the 1 percent level. Robust *z* statistics are in brackets. The table reports the results of a probit regression of the frequency of bribe payments on the variables in the first column. Regulatory compliance is instrumented with the average of the corresponding region–industry–firm size group.

Table 4.8 Including Countrywide Governance Measures: Index of Economic Freedom

	(1)	(2)	(3)	(4)	(5)	(6)
Regulatory compliance	-0.002*** [8.46]	-0.002*** [8.41]	-0.002*** [8.23]	-0.002*** [8.12]	-0.002*** [8.20]	-0.002*** [8.23]
Foreign owned	-0.075*** [3.60]	-0.076*** [3.64]	-0.073*** [3.51]	-0.076*** [3.63]	-0.073*** [3.51]	-0.073*** [3.49]
Access to finance		-0.077*** [4.43]	-0.077*** [4.45]	-0.082*** [4.74]	-0.077*** [4.45]	-0.077*** [4.45]
Trust in courts' enforcement power			-0.067*** [5.30]	-0.066*** [5.24]	-0.067*** [5.31]	-0.067*** [5.30]
Requested public services				0.075*** [6.05]		
Government as main client					-0.029 [0.99]	
Number of tax inspections						0 [0.32]
Log of firm's age	-0.011 [1.41]	-0.01 [1.30]	-0.01 [1.28]	-0.005 [0.61]	-0.01 [1.25]	-0.01 [1.27]
Exporter	-0.001 [0.09]	0.001 [0.05]	0.002 [0.11]	-0.005 [0.33]	0.001 [0.07]	0.002 [0.11]
20–99 employees	0.024* [1.77]	0.030** [2.18]	0.028** [2.06]	0.019 [1.36]	0.028** [2.05]	0.029** [2.07]

(continued)

Table 4.8 Including Countrywide Governance Measures: Index of Economic Freedom *(continued)*

	(1)	(2)	(3)	(4)	(5)	(6)
100+ employees	-0.030	-0.022	-0.020	-0.037*	-0.021	-0.020
	[1.57]	[1.14]	[1.06]	[1.92]	[1.07]	[1.03]
Index of Economic Freedom[a]	0.376***	0.373***	0.367***	0.364***	0.366***	0.367***
	[7.45]	[7.35]	[7.21]	[7.09]	[7.19]	[7.21]
GDP per capita[b]	0.000**	0.000**	0.000**	0.000**	0.000**	0.000**
	[2.33]	[2.38]	[2.38]	[2.39]	[2.38]	[2.37]
GDP per capita growth	-0.076***	-0.077***	-0.079***	-0.078***	-0.079***	-0.079***
	[4.58]	[4.60]	[4.72]	[4.61]	[4.73]	[4.71]
Pseudo R-squared	0.23	0.24	0.24	0.24	0.24	0.24
Observations	7,273	7,273	7,273	7,273	7,273	7,272

Source: Heritage Foundation Index of Economic Freedom.

Note: * = significant at the 10 percent level; ** = significant at the 5 percent level; *** = significant at the 1 percent level. Robust z statistics are in brackets. Reported coefficients are marginal effects. Region and industry dummies are included in all regressions.

a. Index is measured on 1 to 5 scale; higher values indicate a worse environment.

b. GDP per capita is purchasing power parity in constant 2000 U.S. dollars.

Table 4.9 Including Countrywide Governance Measures: Business Costs of Corruption Index

	(1)	(2)	(3)	(4)	(5)	(6)
Regulatory compliance	-0.002*** [8.46]	-0.002*** [8.41]	-0.002*** [8.23]	-0.002*** [8.12]	-0.002*** [8.20]	-0.002*** [8.23]
Foreign owned	-0.075*** [3.60]	-0.076*** [3.64]	-0.073*** [3.51]	-0.076*** [3.63]	-0.073*** [3.51]	-0.073*** [3.49]
Access to finance		-0.077*** [4.43]	-0.077*** [4.45]	-0.082*** [4.74]	-0.077*** [4.45]	-0.077*** [4.45]
Trust in courts' enforcement power			-0.067*** [5.30]	-0.066*** [5.24]	-0.067*** [5.31]	-0.067*** [5.30]
Requested public services				0.075*** [6.05]		
Government as main client					-0.029 [0.99]	
Number of tax inspections						0.000 [0.32]
Log of firm's age	-0.011 [1.41]	-0.010 [1.30]	-0.010 [1.28]	-0.005 [0.61]	-0.010 [1.25]	-0.010 [1.27]
Exporter	-0.001 [0.09]	0.001 [0.05]	0.002 [0.11]	-0.005 [0.33]	0.001 [0.07]	0.002 [0.11]
20–99 employees	0.024* [1.77]	0.030** [2.18]	0.028** [2.06]	0.019 [1.36]	0.028** [2.05]	0.029** [2.07]

(continued)

Table 4.9 Including Countrywide Governance Measures: Business Costs of Corruption Index *(continued)*

	(1)	*(2)*	*(3)*	*(4)*	*(5)*	*(6)*
100+ employees	−0.030	−0.022	−0.020	−0.037*	−0.021	−0.020
	[1.57]	[1.14]	[1.06]	[1.92]	[1.07]	[1.03]
Business Costs of Corruption Index[a]	−0.116**	−0.117**	−0.103**	−0.100**	−0.104**	−0.103**
	[2.34]	[2.36]	[2.06]	[2.01]	[2.07]	[2.07]
GDP per capita[b]	0.000	0.000	0.000	0.000	0.000	0.000
	[0.03]	[0.01]	[0.00]	[0.06]	[0.02]	[0.00]
GDP per capita growth	0.023	0.021	0.022	0.022	0.021	0.022
	[0.73]	[0.67]	[0.68]	[0.70]	[0.65]	[0.68]
Pseudo *R*-squared	0.23	0.24	0.24	0.24	0.24	0.24
Observations	7,273	7,273	7,273	7,273	7,273	7,272

Source: World Economic Forum Business Costs of Corruption Index.

Note: * = significant at the 10 percent level; ** = significant at the 5 percent level; *** = significant at the 1 percent level. Robust *z* statistics are in brackets. Reported coefficients are marginal effects. Region and industry dummies are included in all regressions.

a. Index is measured on a 1 to 7 scale; higher values indicate lower costs.

b. GDP per capita is purchasing power parity in constant 2000 U.S. dollars.

evidence in other countries, particularly in the United States, suggests that the quantity and quality of regulation is indeed associated with differences in compliance across sectors of economic activity (Olson 1999).

This section investigates how other institutional aspects affect regulatory compliance. It explores the possibility that not only regulation, but also the general institutional environment affects the behavior of firms when they decide the extent to which they should comply with existing regulations. In particular, it looks at how the quality of the judicial system affect firms' compliance incentives, as well as how firms with different characteristics behave. Note that if the quality of the judicial system does affect compliance, there would be a double payoff in terms of corruption from improving the system. The first payoff would work directly on corruption, as evidenced by the discussion in previous sections. The second payoff would come through some determinants of corruption themselves.

Table 4.10 reports results from a number of regressions that look at how the quality of courts, as measured by the trust in the power of courts to enforce property rights, and how other firm characteristics affect regulatory compliance.[16]

The first column shows a basic specification that suggests that better courts significantly increase the rate of compliance. This result is largely maintained when included among the regressors are the variables indicating whether firms that request public services tend to also comply less (which they do) or whether firms that provide services mostly to the government tend to comply less (which they do not). Somewhat surprisingly, the number of tax inspections, a measure of enforcement, is not significant. As for the control variables in the equation, older, medium and large, foreign-owned, and exporting firms have higher compliance rates than small, domestic, or nonexporting firms. These results suggest that small firms are not necessarily in a worse position when it comes to bribe payments (see tables 4.1 and 4.2), but they do circumvent regulations more successfully than larger firms.

Conclusions

Chapter 2 identified corruption as one of the main issues affecting firm performance in Latin America. This chapter has asked, what drives corruption? To answer that question, the chapter has discussed three hypotheses that may explain the mechanism operating behind corruption and has estimated an encompassing econometric model that allows the capture of aspects related to the control rights hypothesis (where regulations give public officials extensive discretionary power to extract bribes from firms), the bargaining hypothesis (where more profitable firms have more incentive to pay bribes), and the grease the wheels hypothesis (where firms have incentives to bribe officials perhaps to skip regulation or to secure a contract).

Table 4.10 Determinants of Regulatory Compliance

	(1)	(2)	(3)	(4)	(5)
Trust in courts' enforcement power	1.436** [2.43]	1.415** [2.39]	1.450** [2.45]	1.450** [2.45]	1.444** [2.44]
Requested public services		-1.774*** [3.05]			-1.811*** [3.11]
Government as main client			3.886** [2.49]		3.990** [2.56]
Number of tax inspections				0.039 [1.40]	0.04 [1.42]
Foreign owned	3.449*** [3.59]	3.479*** [3.63]	3.465*** [3.61]	3.405*** [3.55]	3.453*** [3.60]
Log of firm's age	0.805** [2.20]	0.722** [1.97]	0.789** [2.16]	0.787** [2.15]	0.686* [1.87]
Exporter	1.601** [2.34]	1.739** [2.54]	1.634** [2.39]	1.609** [2.35]	1.784*** [2.60]
20–99 employees	3.049*** [4.68]	3.248*** [4.97]	3.046*** [4.68]	3.031*** [4.66]	3.231*** [4.94]

(continued)

Table 4.10 Determinants of Regulatory Compliance (continued)

	(1)	(2)	(3)	(4)	(5)
100+ employees	5.870***	6.244***	5.868***	5.771***	6.150***
	[6.62]	[6.98]	[6.62]	[6.49]	[6.86]
Constant	73.032***	74.028***	73.079***	72.867***	73.928***
	[38.27]	[38.25]	[38.30]	[38.05]	[38.08]
Observations	10,123	10,123	10,123	10,119	10,119
R-squared	0.13	0.13	0.13	0.13	0.13

Source: Authors' calculations.

Note: * = significant at the 10 percent level; ** = significant at the 5 percent level; *** = significant at the 1 percent level. Absolute value of t statistics is in brackets.

The analysis finds evidence for the first and the third of these hypotheses but much less for the second, with the possible exception of small firms. Also, evidence supports the hypothesis that the country's general attitude toward corruption is a strong determinant of the incidence of bribes.

What should be done from a policy perspective? To address the control rights hypothesis corroborated in the analysis, policy makers should simplify the regulatory framework and improve it from an administrative point of view. Critical elements and instruments to simplify the regulatory framework are

- Creating a unit with the mandate to simplify and eliminate unnecessary procedures
- Limiting discretionary powers of public servants as much as possible
- Developing e-government to place as many procedures, permits, licenses, and payments online as possible
- Implementing administrative silence procedures
- Passing freedom of information rights
- Mandating that all public procurement contracts be put online
- Having sequential (multiple) approvals of major public contracts (at least two different persons approving contracts)
- Setting up whistle-blower hotlines
- Imposing exemplary sanctions against public servants and firms caught in corruption acts

Similarly, to the extent that some firms may have incentives to grease the wheels and gain advantage over other firms, policy makers may consider reducing those incentives by increasing the costs of corruption both for public officials who accept graft and for firms that provide it. Reducing discretionary powers, requiring multiple approvals and transparent contracts, implementing systemic random audits, and imposing sizable sanctions on both parties could have significant deterrent effects. An efficient judiciary branch seems particularly relevant in this context.

Notes

1. This brief review is based on Lambsdorff (1999). Refer to that paper for details.

2. In addition to the variables reviewed here, many others have been considered in the literature, but they are less suggestive of policy interventions. Among these variables are population density, geography, mineral wealth, state formations, colonial legacies, social heterogeneity, and religion.

3. More important, the results found by Recanatini, Prati, and Tabellini (2005) indicate that agencies with politically appointed leaders are less corrupt than those in which leaders are elected by the people, and agencies that have externally audited, transparent, and open processes are less corrupt. Agencies with meritocratic promotion systems are also less corrupt.

4. One counterargument is that more solvent firms might have better political connections to bypass the bribe game and that any form of compensation to the connections is not perceived as a bribe. In other words, large firms do not necessarily have more bargaining power, but they are less likely altogether to be involved in negotiations with corrupt public officials. Furthermore, because the analysis uses a composite measure of bribe payments, data on the amount of the bribe is unavailable, thereby making it impossible to properly test the bargaining hypothesis that more solvent firms pay larger bribes (even if a smaller fraction of them pay bribes).

5. As noted by Svensson (2003), exit can, in this context, be thought of as changing sector or location or as reorganizing business.

6. The equation assumes that the firm has full information regarding the gross profit and the associated bribe.

7. However, that a firm pays bribes to reduce its operating costs does not imply that corruption is optimal at the aggregate level.

8. Clearly, one would prefer an objective measure of the courts' enforcement power, and to some extent such a measure is possible for the new wave of Enterprise Surveys. Unfortunately, to work with the sample of 16 countries used in chapter 2, the analysis here had to settle for a subjective measure. Later, the chapter explores whether this measure affected the results.

9. It is worth noting other unobserved firm characteristics may affect the results. For example, some firms may have managers who are good at obtaining finance and at the same time are reluctant to pay bribes. The empirical analysis would show a negative relationship between the two when they are in fact related to a third, unobserved, factor. Unfortunately, the lack of panel data does not allow control of these types of unobservables—that is, the study cannot control for managers' fixed effects.

10. The "dprobit" command in the Stata software package was used. For continuous variables, the reported coefficients correspond to marginal effects; that is, they reflect the (percentage) change in the probability of paying bribes if there is a one (percentage) point increase in the explanatory variable. For dummy variables, the discrete change in the probability of paying bribes is reported for a discrete change in the dummy variable from 0 to 1.

11. This result is also found by Svensson (2003).

12. The seven countries are Argentina, Bolivia, Brazil, Chile, Colombia, Costa Rica, and Mexico.

13. For a detailed description of the methodology, see http://www.heritage.org/Index/.

14. For more information about the index, see http://www.weforum.org/en/initiatives/gcp/index.htm.

15. These results are not reported here, but they can be provided upon request.

16. Because most firms have a high compliance rate (the median firm reports 95 percent of its sales, and the 25th percentile is at 60 percent), robust regressions are also performed so as to give relatively less weight to firms that report a very low percentage of their sales. Results are very similar to the ordinary least squares results reported here.

References

Ades, A., and R. Di Tella. 1995. "Competition and Corruption." Applied Economics Discussion Paper 169, Oxford, U.K.: Oxford University Press.

———. 1996. "The New Economics of Corruption: A Survey and Some New Results." In *Liberalization and the New Corruption*, ed. B. Harris and G. White, *IDS Bulletin* 27 (2): 6–12.

———. 1997. "National Champions and Corruption: Some Unpleasant Interventionist Arithmetic." *Economic Journal* 107 (443): 1023–43.

Brunetti, A., and B. Weder. 2003. "A Free Press Is Bad News for Corruption." *Journal of Public Economics* 87 (7): 1801–24.

Goel, R., and M. Nelson. 1998. "Corruption and Government Size: A Disaggregated Analysis." *Public Choice* 97 (1–2): 107–20.

Hellman J., G. Jones, and D. Kaufmann. 2000. "Seize the State, Seize the Day: State Capture, Corruption, and Influence in Transition Economies." Policy Research Working Paper 2444, World Bank, Washington, DC.

Kaufmann, D., A. Kraay, and P. Zoido-Lobatón. 1999. "Governance Matters." Policy Research Working Paper 2196, World Bank, Washington, DC.

Kaufmann, D., and S. Wei. 1999. "Does 'Grease Money' Speed Up the Wheels of Commerce?" NBER Working Paper 7093, National Bureau of Economic Research, Cambridge, MA.

Lambsdorff, J. G. 1999. "Corruption in Empirical Research: A Review." Working Paper, Transparency International, Berlin.

LaPalombara, J. 1994. "Structural and Institutional Aspects of Corruption." *Social Research* 61 (2): 325–50.

Leite, C., and J. Weidmann. 1999. "Does Mother Nature Corrupt? Natural Resources, Corruption, and Economic Growth." IMF Working Paper 99/85, International Monetary Fund, Washington, DC.

Loayza, N., A. M. Oviedo, and L. Servén. 2004. "Regulation and Macroeconomic Performance." Policy Research Working Paper 3469, World Bank, Washington, DC.

———. 2005. "The Impact of Regulation on Growth and Informality: Cross-Country Evidence." Policy Research Working Paper 3623, World Bank, Washington, DC.

Mauro, P. 1995. "Corruption and Growth." *Quarterly Journal of Economics* 110 (3): 681–712.

Montinola, G., and R. Jackman. 2002. "Source of Corruption: A Cross-Country Study." *British Journal of Political Science* 32 (1): 147–70.

Olson, M. K. 1999. "Agency Rulemaking, Political Influences, Regulation, and Industry Compliance." *Journal of Law, Economics, and Organization* 15 (3): 573–601.

Paldam, M. 1999. "The Big Pattern of Corruption, Economics, Culture, and the Seesaw Dynamics." Economics Working Paper 1999-11, University of Aarhus, Aarhus, Denmark.

Rauch, J., and P. Evans. 2000. "Bureaucratic Structure and Bureaucratic Performance in Less Developed Countries." *Journal of Public Economics* 75 (1): 49–71.

Recanatini, F., A. Prati, and G. Tabellini. 2005. "Why Are Some Public Agencies Less Corrupt Than Others? Lessons for Institutional Reform from Survey Data." Paper presented at the Sixth Jacques Polak Annual Research Conference, International Monetary Fund, Washington, DC, November 3–4.

Seligson, M. 2006. "The Measurement and Impact of Corruption Victimization: Survey Evidence from Latin America." *World Development* 34 (2): 381–404.

Svensson, J. 2003. "Who Must Pay Bribes and How Much? Evidence from a Cross-Section of Firms." *Quarterly Journal of Economics* 118 (1): 207–30.

Treisman, D. 1999. *After the Deluge*. Ann Arbor: University of Michigan Press.

World Bank. 1997. *World Development Report 1997: The State in a Changing World*. World Bank, Washington, DC.

5

What Are the Determinants of Financial Access in Latin America?

Inessa Love

A well-functioning financial system is an important component of the investment climate and hence of a growth and development strategy. Yet very few studies have looked at financial sector development from the perspective of access to financial services—something that has left many questions unanswered. What are the determinants of access to credit? Which firms tend to lack access and hence would benefit from targeted policies? What is the role played by the legal system in this context? How does financial deepening affect access to financial services?

Well-functioning financial systems ameliorate the problems created by information and transaction costs and help allocate resources across space and time. Not surprisingly, a large number of studies have found a robust relationship between the level of financial development and long-run growth (Beck, Levine, and Loayza 2000; Loayza, Fajnzylber, and Calderón 2005). Financial development affects capital accumulation and technological innovation through at least five channels: by facilitating risk management, by reducing the costs of acquiring information about new investment opportunities, by simplifying corporate control over managers, by mobilizing savings, and by facilitating exchanges and thus promoting specialization and innovation (Levine 1997).

Figure 1.16 in chapter 1 presents regional ratios of domestic credit to the private sector as a percentage of gross domestic product (GDP) in

1990 and 2004. Credit is an important link in the monetary transmission process because it finances production, consumption, and capital formation, which in turn affect the overall level of economic activity. Figure 1.16 indicates (a) that Latin America is well behind, not only with respect to high-income countries but also in comparison to all other regions of the developing world, and (b) that unlike in other regions of the world, over the past one and one-half decades, credit to the private sector has declined in Latin America (as a percentage of GDP).

Another financial indicator that suggests the region has significant progress to make is the interest rate spread (that is, the margin between rates paid on liabilities and those received on assets). This spread is usually taken as a measure of the efficiency of the financial sector. Recall from chapter 1 that in terms of financial deepening, Latin America was well behind other developing regions. This situation is also evident from figure 5.1, which presents another financial indicator: the difference between lending and deposit interest rates. This figure indicates that only Sub-Saharan Africa has spreads above those found in Latin America, which are close to 8 percent.

This chapter provides new evidence on the extent of firms' access to financial services in the Latin America and Caribbean region and the relationships between access and selected policy-relevant variables. First, it explores the determinants of access by firms in the Enterprise Surveys sample, with a special focus on differences in access by small and medium enterprises. This section helps to explain which types of firms lack access to financial services and thus might benefit from specially designed policies.

Second, the chapter studies the relationship between quality of courts and access to financial services. The effectiveness of courts is an important ingredient in the functioning of the legal system. It has been proven to have a crucial effect on the level of financial development and financial access (see Beck, Demirgüç-Kunt, and Levine 2003, 2005; La Porta and others 1997, 1998). This chapter assumes that courts within the region have a similar level of quality and that the effectiveness of the regional courts is most relevant for firms located in that region. The Enterprise Surveys data are used to construct several indicators of court effectiveness at the regional level; these include objective indicators of court quality (percentage of disputes that use courts, percentage of judgments made, and percentage of resolutions enforced) and subjective measures based on respondents' perceptions of court quality (such as whether courts are quick, fair, affordable, and enforceable).

Third, this chapter studies how changes in aggregate measures of financial sector development affect firms' access to finance and how that effect varies with firm size and other firm characteristics. Knowing whether aggregate financial development translates into improved firm access and whether these improvements are equally available to firms of different sizes is important. From Enterprise Surveys data, a country-year panel of

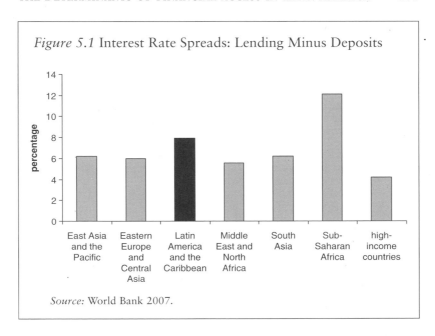

Figure 5.1 Interest Rate Spreads: Lending Minus Deposits

Source: World Bank 2007.

loan characteristics (such as maturity of the loan, percentage "overcollat-eralization," type of collateral used, type of institution granting the loan, and value of the loan) can be constructed as well as a similar panel with percentage of enterprise start-up funds coming from commercial and state banks. Then, the chapter relates aggregate measures of financial develop-ment (as measured by standard indicators, such as domestic credit as a percentage of GDP) to specific loan characteristics and start-up funds and tests whether that effect varies according to firm size.

Because of a lack of available data, no prior study seems to have looked at the relationship between aggregate level of financial development as measured by standard indicators of financial development (such as ratio of private credit to GDP) and the loan characteristics. The data set used here contains data on loan characteristics for the most recent loan, including the year of the loan. This information allows construction of a panel of loan characteristics and its correlation with aggregate measures of finan-cial development.

Finally, the chapter considers a relationship between informality and access to finance. The study tests whether those firms that are formally registered when they start doing business are more likely to have higher percentages of bank finance coming from commercial or state banks and whether this effect varies with the size of the firm at the start of its business.

Data

Unless otherwise specified, all data used in this chapter are obtained from the latest wave of Enterprise Surveys. Several groups of variables used for analysis in this chapter are described in the following sections.

Access Variables for Cross-Sectional Analysis

The analysis of access focuses on the following six principal measures:

- *Checking.* An indicator variable that equals 1 if the enterprise has a checking account.
- *Credit.* An indicator variable that equals 1 if the enterprise has over-draft, loan, line of credit, or any bank financing for working capital or investment. This measure indicates whether the firm has *any* credit products. It is complemented by the *depth* measure, described below, which indicates *how many* different credit products a firm has.
- *Unconstrained.* An indicator variable for those enterprises that are not constrained (that is, the reverse of being credit constrained), where *constrained* is defined as an indicator variable that equals 1 if one of the following two conditions is satisfied: (a) the firm has applied for a loan but has been rejected,[1] or (b) the firm has not applied for a loan for reasons other than "do not need a loan." In other words, firms that need a loan and do not apply are considered to be constrained.
- *Access index.* A categorical variable equal to the sum of *checking, credit,* and *unconstrained.* This variable captures a combination of the three measures of access, and it ranges from 0 for those with no checking account, no credit, and a 0 value for unconstrained, to a value of 3 for those with a checking account, that have some credit, and that report being unconstrained. Higher numbers indicate more access.
- *Depth.* A categorical variable that contains a count of how many credit products a firm reports. One point is added for each of the following: overdraft, loan or line of credit,[2] bank financing for working capital, bank financing for investment, and issuance of stock. The *depth* variable complements the *credit* variable because the latter measures whether there is any access and the former measures the depth of access—that is, how many different financial products the firm uses. The *depth* measure ranges from 0 to 5.
- *Access obstacle.* An indicator variable that equals 1 if the firm reports access to finance as one of the three major obstacles to doing business. This measure of access is subjective in that it reports respondents' perceptions of the severity of access obstacle, whereas previously discussed measures capture a more objective dimension of access.

As with any study of access, the *use* of financial products and the *access* to financial products must be distinguished. Use shows whether the enterprises use any of the financial products. Use is easy to measure, and three of the variables described above capture the use of financial products—*checking*, *credit*, and *depth*. Use is a useful measure because it can serve as a proxy for how much access to finance a firm has.

Nevertheless, use measures have an important drawback: they present the equilibrium outcome of the supply and demand for funds. Often, lack of use for financial products is assumed to signify problems with supply of finance. However, firms may not use financial products because they do not need them; that is, they have no demand for financial products. This situation may occur for several reasons. One is lack of profitable growth opportunities that would require additional financing; another may be unwillingness to grow, as could be the case for subsistence-type enterprises that choose to stay small and self-financed. Another reason could be lack of financial literacy. Thus, a number of reasons may exist for lack of use, and each reason would imply a different policy intervention.

Access, in contrast, should measure whether firms that have a demand for financial products are able to obtain them. This definition is simplified because it abstracts from the pricing of financial products, which would require a structural model to estimate. Firms that have a demand for financing but that are not able to obtain it should be considered financially constrained, which would point to problems with credit supply.

The data allow two crude measures of *access* to be constructed. The first one is the measure of whether the firm is *constrained* or *unconstrained*. These measures capture whether the firms that have demand are able to obtain loans. It is crude because it is an indicator variable and therefore does not distinguish between the degrees of being constrained (that is, the severity of financial constraints). In addition, this measure uses self-reported reasons for lack of loan applications, classifying as unconstrained all those firms that say they do not need a loan. The demand is not based on sound financial calculations of whether the firm indeed has profitable growth opportunities that would deliver a rate of return over and above the costs of financing.

Another measure of access used is the *access obstacle*—the self-reported measure of the severity of access obstacles. In evaluating the obstacle, the respondents are likely to consider their demand for funds and match it against their supply of funds. So this measure is likely to take the demand side into consideration. Self-reported measures have a different problem, however, because they clearly are perceptions of the person answering the questions. Even if the respondent is the right person, well versed in the financial status of the firm, the respondent's incentives and even mood on the day of the survey can affect the reported answers. For example, more pessimistic respondents would report higher obstacles, and respondents who imagine that their self-reported constraints may lead to favored access (such as directed credit) in the future are likely to overstate their constraints. Among several possible measures of the *access obstacle* available, this study selected the one that may be least affected by the pessimism of the respondent—that is, pessimism is less likely to play into the measure that captures the top three obstacles.[3]

Finally, the aggregated *access index* collates elements of use and access into one variable. Although this index is also a crude measure (subject to all the caveats discussed previously), it may be a useful summary for the extent of access. This summary measure is the focus of attention in this chapter.

For readability, all measures described in this section are often referred to in the rest of the chapter as access indicators, but the caveats discussed here should be kept in mind while interpreting the results.

Court-Quality Measures

Several court-quality measures were created to study the relationship between access and court quality. They are grouped into objective and subjective court measures. The *objective court* measure is a simple average of the following three variables:

- *Court use.* Percentage of firms that used the courts to resolve conflict, of those that had any payment disputes in the past two years
- *Court judgment made.* Percentage of firms (of those that used courts) that received a judgment on their case
- *Court enforced.* Percentage of firms (of those for which judgment was made) that got their judgment enforced

Higher numbers for the *objective court* index would indicate that courts are more likely to be used for resolving conflicts, courts are more likely to reach a decision, and decisions are more likely to be enforced. These qualities are expected from a well-functioning court system.[4]

These measures are not without their drawbacks. For example, the fact that the courts are widely used for dispute resolution may imply that courts are cost-effective in resolving these types of conflicts. Presumably, if the courts are ineffective, nobody would use them; so in this case, higher use would proxy for higher quality of the courts. Note that the percentage of court use is constructed only for those firms that indicated they have had a dispute with their client over payments owed.[5] Alternatively, higher court use for dispute resolution may indicate lack of alternative formal resolution mechanisms (for example, out-of-court mediation or arbitration). Similarly, the question on judgment reached is limited in the sense that one does not know if the judgment was fair and impartial. For example, high enforcement rates of ineffective or unfair judgments are not necessarily a good thing. Despite these potential drawbacks, these measures are still useful as a first approximation of court quality relevant to the firms in the study's sample.

Subjective assessments of court quality are also used. In the survey, the respondents were asked to rate court quality on the basis of several dimensions, using categorical ratings that ranged from 1 to 4, with higher measures indicating better quality. To increase the validity of an individual's court-quality assessments, the study uses only data from respondents who used the courts to resolve a dispute in the past two years. Assessments from people with actual experience with the courts are assumed to have less noise; however, the results are very similar if all respondents are used in the analysis. The *subjective court* measure is an average of the measures for the following four variables (the titles are self-explanatory): *court fair*, *court quick*, *court affordable*, and *court enforceable*.

To increase the degrees of freedom, these measures are averaged for each country-region pair.[6] Only 8 countries (but 28 country-region pairs) have available data. To reduce noise, the study does not use data from country-region pairs that have less than five observations for each variable. Court quality in the region where the firm is located may be more relevant to the firm than the overall court quality in the country. In addition, a country-regional measure, which combines the answers from a number of firms, is unlikely to be endogenous to each firm (the issue of endogeneity is discussed in more depth in the relevant regression analysis section).

Time-Varying Loan Characteristics, Start-up Capital, and Registration

Several time-varying measures of access are created to study the relationship between the aggregate level of financial development and firm access. The survey asked for a number of characteristics of the most recent loan, including the date of the loan. This set of questions allows the loan characteristics to be aggregated across time, according to the date of the loan. Thus, a short time-varying panel of loan characteristics is created, even though the original data are cross-sectional. The following loan characteristics are available:

- *Maturity* (mean and median) is the loan maturity, in months.
- *Loan to sales* (mean and median) is the ratio of loan amount to firm's sales. However, sales data are not available for the same year as the year of the loan, so this measure is very noisy.[7]
- *Collateral dummy* is an indicator variable for whether or not collateral was required.
- *Percent collateral* (mean and median) is percentage of collateral to loan amount.

- *Type of collateral* consists of indicator variables for whether or not each type of collateral was used by the firm (more than one type is frequently used):
  - Land and buildings
  - Machinery and equipment
  - Receivables and inventory
  - Personal assets of the owner
  - Movable assets (a dummy that equals 1 if either the machinery and equipment dummy or the receivables and inventory dummy is equal to 1)
- *Type of bank* that issued the loan. Three types are distinguished:
  - Commercial bank
  - State bank
  - Nonbank financial institution (NBFI)

These data are limited in their scope because they give only a few selected measures of loan characteristics for the subsmall sample of firms that have a loan at the time of the survey. Unfortunately, no data are available on the use of or access to financial services over time (for example, the number of firms with access to finance in each year). However, these data are unique in that they produce time-varying measures of loan characteristics for each country, which have not been explored in the past. The panel, however, is relatively short, with only about five years of data per country.

Two additional time-varying financial indicators are based on the questions that refer to firm financing at the start of the business: *start commercial* measures the percentage of start-up funds that came from a commercial bank, and *start state* measures the percentage of start-up funds that came from a state bank. These are the only two financial indicators available at firm start-up. These percentages are averaged across country and time to obtain a fairly long panel, often going back 30 years or more.

Finally, to study the relationship between access and informality, *start registered* indicates the proportion of firms that were registered at business start-up. The date of the business registration is known, which allows creation of a time-varying panel of the percentage of firms that were registered at the start of their business in each country and in each year. For comparison, an indicator of whether the firm is currently registered, called *registered*, is also created. This measure does not have time variation.

Only country-year averages that use at least five observations to construct the average are used for all the time-varying measures in an effort to reduce noisiness. This limitation reduces the length of the panel; however, it still remains quite substantial for start-up measures, with at least 10 or more years per country.

One obvious problem with these time-aggregated measures is that in each year a different sample of firms is used to construct the country-year average. Because this study's interest is in constructing country-varying averages of firm-specific loan characteristics, the averages need to be representative of the country's population.[8] Because the sample is not purely random, but was stratified, weights are used in generating country-year averages of firm characteristics. The results are qualitatively similar if weights are not used.

Other Controls

The following firm controls are used in the cross-sectional regressions:

- *Size dummies. Small* is defined as firms with fewer than 20 employees, *medium* as those with between 20 and 99 employees, and *large* as those with 100 or more employees.
- *Start-size dummies.* These dummies, using the same cutoffs as size dummies, define the size of a firm at the start of the business.
- *Firm age.* Three categories are defined: 0 to 5 years old (very young firms), 6 to 10 years old (medium age group), and more than 10 years old (mature firms).
- *Exporter.* This dummy equals 1 if the firm exports at least 5 percent of its output directly or indirectly.
- *Foreign ownership.* This dummy equals 1 if the firm has any foreign ownership.
- *State ownership.* This dummy equals 1 if the firm has any government ownership.
- *Female.* This dummy equals 1 if the main owner is a female.[9]
- *LLC.* This dummy equals 1 if the firm has limited liability (it includes publicly listed and privately held shareholding companies, limited liability companies, and limited partnerships) and 0 for sole proprietorships and partnerships with unlimited liability.
- *Certified.* This dummy equals 1 if the firm has any certification.
- *Subsidiary.* This dummy equals 1 if the establishment is a subsidiary of a larger corporation.
- *Own land.* This dummy equals 1 if the firm owns land.
- *Industry dummies.* The following industry dummies are defined: food, garments, textiles, chemicals, other manufacturing, retail, other services, and construction and transport (which is omitted in regressions).
- *Sales.* Amounts are in thousands of U.S. dollars.

In court-quality regressions, some additional country-regional controls are used:

- *Internet use.* Country-regional average of percentage of people who have e-mail or a Web site (c22).
- *Wait for government service.* Country-regional average of (standardized) wait for electrical connection (c4), phone connection (c20), and land-use permit (g3).

- *Number of power outages.* Country-regional average of the number of power outages in a year (c7).
- *Government obstacle.* Country-regional average of the average of six obstacles of government functions: tax rates, tax administration, business licensing and permits, macroeconomic instability, political instability, and corruption (j30).
- *Time spent with the government.* Country-regional average of the average of (standardized) management time spent dealing with government regulations (j2) and number of visits by tax officials (j4).
- *Percent of sales or workforce reported.* Country-regional average of the average percentage of sales reported (j8) and average percentage of workers reported (j9).
- *Average corruption obstacle.* Country-regional average of corruption obstacle (j30f).
- *Index of bribes.* Country-regional average of the index of bribery, constructed as the average (standardized) of the number of bribes (count of the number of positive responses to questions c5, c21, g, j5, j12, j15); perception whether bribes are common (j1b); and whether the expected amount of bribe is known (j7a).

In time-series regressions, several country-time controls are used:

- *Financial development* is defined as the ratio of private credit to GDP and is the main measure of the overall level of financial development.
- *GDP per capita* controls for the overall level of economic development.
- *GDP* is the level of GDP in real U.S. dollars, which controls for the overall macroeconomic conditions in a country in each given year.

These measures are obtained from the World Bank's (2007) *World Development Indicators.*

Descriptive Statistics

This section presents descriptive statistics for the variables of interest.

Access Variables for Cross-Sectional Analysis

Table 5.1 summarizes descriptive statistics of the main measures of access, and figure 5.2 presents these data in graphical form. All measures show a monotonic increase in use and access with size. Medium firms have more access than small firms, and large firms are better off than medium firms. Only 60 percent of small firms have any *credit* products, whereas 80 percent of large firms do. The measure of *depth* is also higher for large

Table 5.1 Descriptive Statistics for Cross-Sectional Access Measures

a. By firm size

Variable	All firms	Small	Medium	Large
Checking (%)	85	80	90	92
Credit (%)	68	60	75	80
Unconstrained (%)	72	68	74	80
Access obstacle (%)	25	27	24	19
Access index (index number)	2.2	2.1	2.4	2.5
Depth (number of credit products)	1.5	1.2	1.8	1.9
Overdraft (%)	58	48	66	71
Line of credit or loan (%)	47	37	55	59
Bank finance for working capital (%)	14	11	16	17
Bank finance for investment (%)	19	15	23	21
Issued stock (%)	1	1	2	2
Applied for a loan (%)	37	31	42	46
Did not need a loan (%)	65	63	65	74
Rejected (%)	15	18	12	11

(continued)

Table 5.1 Descriptive Statistics for Cross-Sectional Access Measures *(continued)*

b. By country

Variable	All	Argentina	Bolivia	Colombia	Mexico	Panama	Paraguay	Peru	Uruguay
Checking (%)	85	98	92	97	55	98	86	94	87
Credit (%)	68	76	72	90	27	79	77	88	70
Unconstrained (%)	72	63	68	78	71	84	75	79	64
Access obstacle (%)	25	32	27	32	17	10	35	20	25
Access index (index number)	2.2	2.4	2.3	2.6	1.5	2.6	2.4	2.6	2.2
Depth (number of credit products)	1.5	1.5	1.6	2.4	0.4	1.8	1.5	2.4	1.4
Overdraft (%)	58	71	44	86	19	64	64	73	59
Line of credit or loan (%)	47	42	55	68	12	57	47	70	53
Bank finance for working capital (%)	14	9	19	23	3	23	9	28	8
Bank finance for investment (%)	19	5	21	34	8	29	9	41	14
Issued stock (%)	1	2	2	1	1	2	2	1	1
Applied for a loan (%)	37	36	41	62	11	33	39	63	31
Did not need a loan (%)	65	53	59	67	71	80	65	61	55
Rejected (%)	15	18	18	15	29	7	7	10	14

Source: Author's calculations based on Enterprise Surveys data.

firms. Small firms have on average about one credit product, and large firms have close to two products. Most firms in the sample have *checking* accounts: 80 percent of small firms and 92 percent of large firms. Surprisingly, most firms are *unconstrained*; 68 percent of small firms report being unconstrained, as do 80 percent of large firms.

The aggregate *access index* equals 2.1 for small firms and 2.5 for large firms. The magnitude of the difference for different size groups is relatively

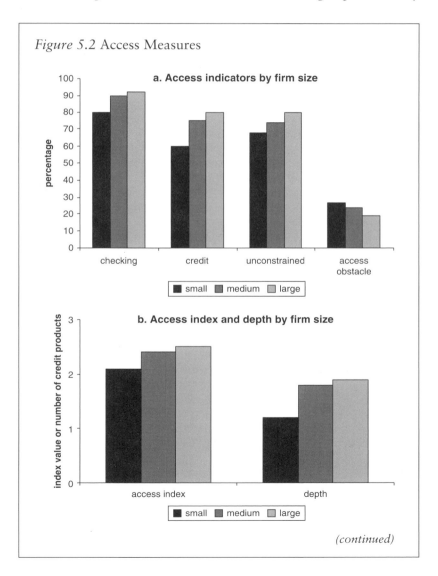

Figure 5.2 Access Measures

a. Access indicators by firm size

b. Access index and depth by firm size

(continued)

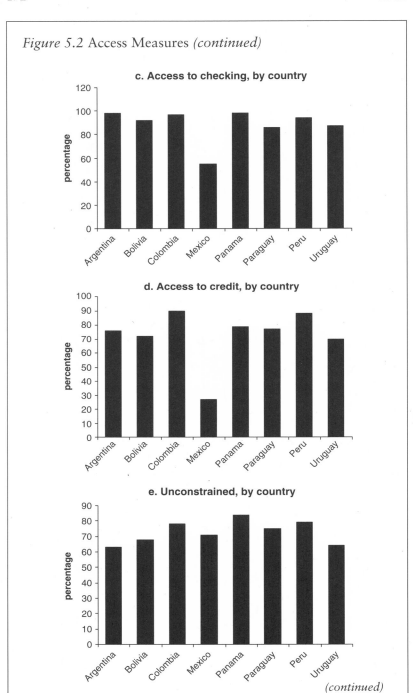

Figure 5.2 Access Measures *(continued)*

c. Access to checking, by country

d. Access to credit, by country

e. Unconstrained, by country

(continued)

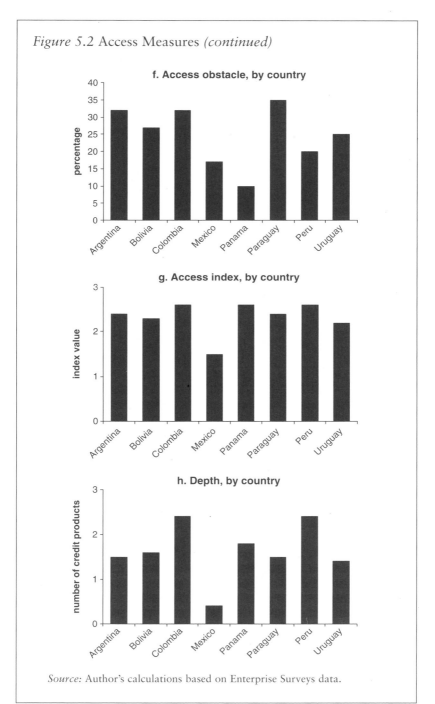

Figure 5.2 Access Measures *(continued)*

f. Access obstacle, by country

g. Access index, by country

h. Depth, by country

Source: Author's calculations based on Enterprise Surveys data.

small; however, the difference between small firms and medium or large firms is statistically significant (at 1 percent). In terms of subjective access obstacles, only about 27 percent of small firms and 19 percent of large firms report access as one of the top three obstacles to the operation and growth of their business.

These results present a picture of relatively good access to financial products in the sample. For this sample of firms, other obstacles are likely to be more binding than access to finance. In addition, the differences between small, medium, and large firms are not very large, even though a monotonic relationship clearly exists between size and access.

Among different countries, Mexico scores low on all the objective indicators of access (*checking*, *credit*, *access index*, and *depth*), but surprisingly, firms in Mexico also report fairly low *access obstacle*. Uruguay is often second to Mexico on the low end, whereas Colombia and Peru score higher than their peers on *access index* and *depth*.

Table 5.2 reports correlations of these main access measures. The correlations are quite intuitive and not surprising. Firms that have a *checking* account are also more likely to have *credit*. Firms are more likely to be classified as *unconstrained* if they have *checking* or *credit* or higher *depth*. Interestingly, the *access obstacle* indicator is related only to the *unconstrained* measure—those firms that are classified as unconstrained report lower access obstacle. However, subjective access obstacles are not related to *checking* or *credit*, and the correlation is even reverse (but quite small) with *depth*.

Time-Varying Loan Characteristics, Start-up Capital, and Registration

Table 5.3 presents descriptive statistics for time-varying measures. On average, all types of firms have loans of about the same maturity, but the

Table 5.2 Correlations of Cross-Sectional Access Measures

Variable	Checking	Credit	Unconstrained	Access obstacle	Access index	Depth
Checking	1.00					
Credit	0.42*	1.00				
Unconstrained	0.04*	0.17*	1.00			
Access obstacle	0.01	0.02	−0.26*	1.00		
Access index	0.65*	0.79*	0.62*	−0.12*	1.00	
Depth	0.35*	0.76*	0.22*	0.04*	0.66*	1.00

Source: Author's calculations based on Enterprise Surveys data.
Note: * = significant at the 5 percent level.

Table 5.3 Descriptive Statistics for Time-Varying Measures

Variable	All firms	Small	Medium	Large	Argentina	Bolivia	Colombia	Mexico	Panama	Paraguay	Peru	Uruguay
Maturity (mean) (month)	31	33	29	32	31	46	29	23	45	21	23	34
Maturity (median) (month)	24	24	18	12	18	36	24	18	24	12	12	18
Loan-to-sales ratio (mean) (%)	14	17	12	10	7	31	9	13	24	12	13	15
Loan-to-sales ratio (median) (%)	6	8	5	4	3	18	5	6	13	6	5	7
Collateral dummy (%)	66	66	66	64	57	95	51	65	84	56	63	72
Percentage of collateral to loan (mean)	136	135	139	130	130	190	118	169	88	116	113	180
Percentage of collateral to loan (median)	100	100	100	100	100	200	100	150	100	100	100	127
Collateral types												
Land and buildings (%)	48	44	50	49	37	74	26	45	57	49	56	33
Machinery and equipment (%)	24	19	23	38	17	43	13	41	18	17	24	25

(continued)

Table 5.3 Descriptive Statistics for Time-Varying Measures *(continued)*

Variable	All firms	Small	Medium	Large	Argentina	Bolivia	Colombia	Mexico	Panama	Paraguay	Peru	Uruguay
Receivables and inventory (%)	10	7	11	14	12	11	8	11	6	9	14	9
Personal assets of owner (%)	33	38	32	25	29	32	35	27	30	46	25	40
Movable assets (%)	34	26	34	52	30	54	22	52	24	26	38	34
Bank types												
Commercial, (%)	87	84	88	90	81	90	93	90	97	66	97	70
State (%)	3	3	4	4	7	0	2	1	1	2	0	13
NBFI (%)	5	8	4	3	2	8	3	4	0	28	1	4
Start-up finance and registration												
Start commercial	12	11	13	13	5	24	13	6	29	14	14	6
Start state	2	1	2	3	3	1	1	1	3	3	1	4
Start registered (%)	93	92	94	96	93	86	89	95	98	94	97	98

Source: Author calculations based on Enterprise Surveys data.

median maturity is much longer for smaller firms. Loans-to-sales ratios are also larger for small firms. This finding could be because large firms have more than one loan (and the data on loan characteristics refer to the most recent loan). Thus, the latest loan for a large firm could be relatively small (because it is incrementally adding to the existing stock of loans) and of shorter maturity. For smaller firms, the most recent loan is more likely to be the only loan; hence, it has longer maturity and larger size, relative to sales. Unfortunately, no data are available to confirm or dispute this argument. This finding is revisited in the regression analysis.

About 66 percent of all firms are asked to post collateral, and this variable shows no variation by firm size. Banks appear to have the same collateral rules for firms of different sizes. Not much variation occurs in amount of collateral relative to loan either, although small and medium firms post slightly more collateral on average than large firms do, and the median for all firm sizes is 100 percent, as it should be.

In terms of types of collateral, smaller firms are less likely to use machinery and equipment or inventory and receivables as collateral than are larger firms; therefore, the use of movable assets, which represents the sum of these two categories, varies significantly by size. Smaller firms are slightly more likely to use personal assets as collateral.

Most loans in the sample are issued by commercial banks; state banks capture on average only about 3 percent of total loans, and NBFIs capture about 5 percent. Notice that small firms are more likely to have loans issued by NBFIs: close to 8 percent of the small firms report a loan by an NBFI, whereas only 2.5 percent of large firms do. This finding is not surprising because many of the NBFIs are special-purpose organizations, often with mandates to serve smaller firms. Surprisingly, no large differences occur in state bank loans by size. If anything, larger firms are more likely to have state loans than are smaller firms (but the difference is minor). Commercial banks provide on average 12 percent of start-up finance, whereas state banks provide only about 2 percent. Smaller firms receive less start-up capital from commercial and state banks alike.

Figure 5.3 presents start-up registrations by size and country along with the current registration. Somewhat surprisingly, most firms in the sample registered when they started business. Bolivia has the lowest percentage of start-up registrations, and even there 85 percent of all firms register at the start, followed by Colombia with 89 percent. In the rest of the countries, more than 90 percent of enterprises register at the start of their business. Almost all enterprises in the sample are currently registered; only in Bolivia and Mexico are a few enterprises currently unregistered.

As discussed in the data section, these measures are constructed on country-time level and country-time-size level. Figure 5.4 presents a few selected graphs of the evolution of these measures over time, along with the aggregate financial development measure. The time-series measures are clearly very noisy by construction; for each point on the graph, different

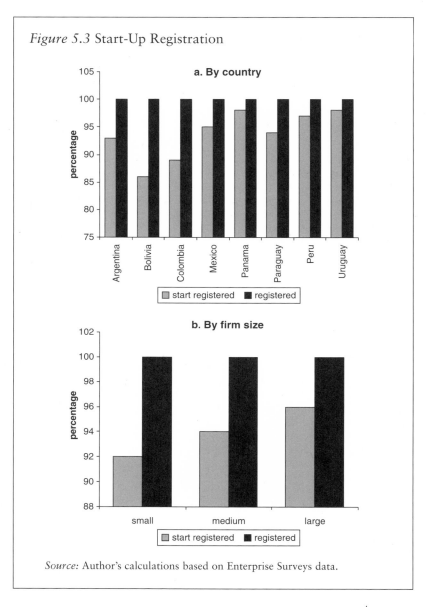

Figure 5.3 Start-Up Registration

a. By country

b. By firm size

Source: Author's calculations based on Enterprise Surveys data.

firms are used to construct the country-year average. However, some patterns can be seen, especially on the graphs for maturity, which seems to follow financial development. Other measures appear to be quite noisy without clear patterns. *Start state* is most often 0 (remember that this is the average of firms that started in that country-year), and *start commercial* does not seem to exhibit any clear patterns. Finally, *start registered* is most

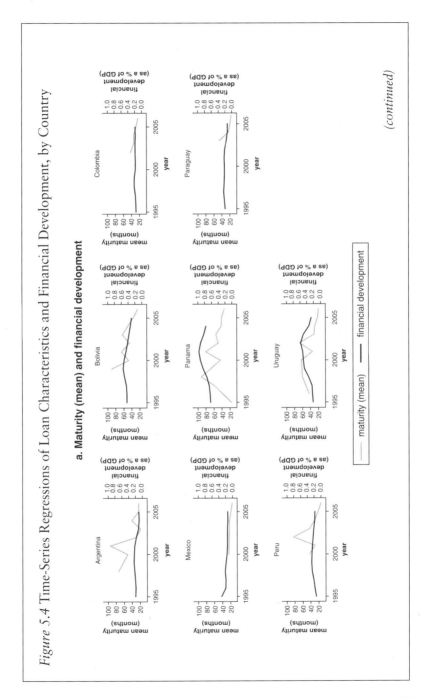

Figure 5.4 Time-Series Regressions of Loan Characteristics and Financial Development, by Country

a. Maturity (mean) and financial development

(continued)

199

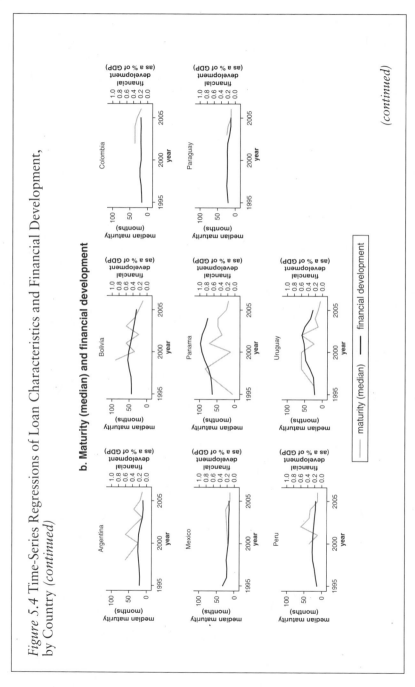

Figure 5.4 Time-Series Regressions of Loan Characteristics and Financial Development, by Country *(continued)*

b. Maturity (median) and financial development

— maturity (median) — financial development

(continued)

Figure 5.4 Time-Series Regressions of Loan Characteristics and Financial Development, by Country *(continued)*

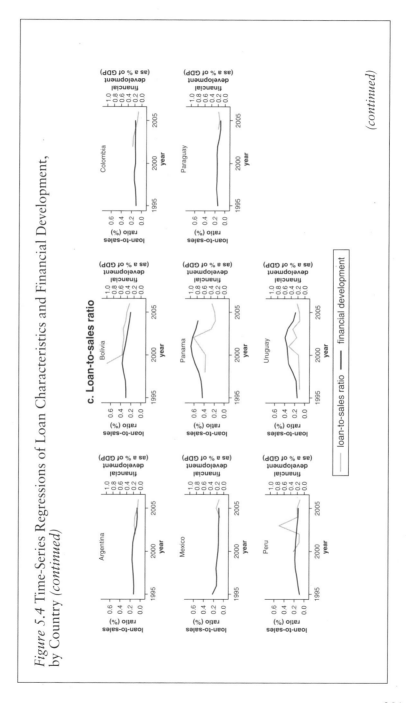

c. Loan-to-sales ratio

loan-to-sales ratio —— financial development

(continued)

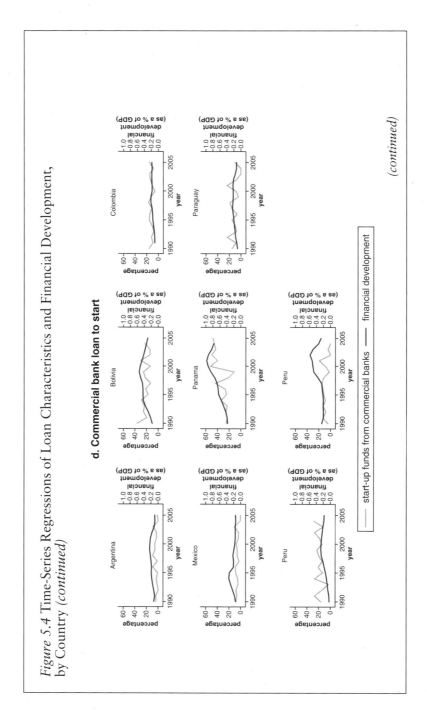

Figure 5.4 Time-Series Regressions of Loan Characteristics and Financial Development, by Country *(continued)*

d. Commercial bank loan to start

——— start-up funds from commercial banks ——— financial development

(continued)

Figure 5.4 Time-Series Regressions of Loan Characteristics and Financial Development, by Country *(continued)*

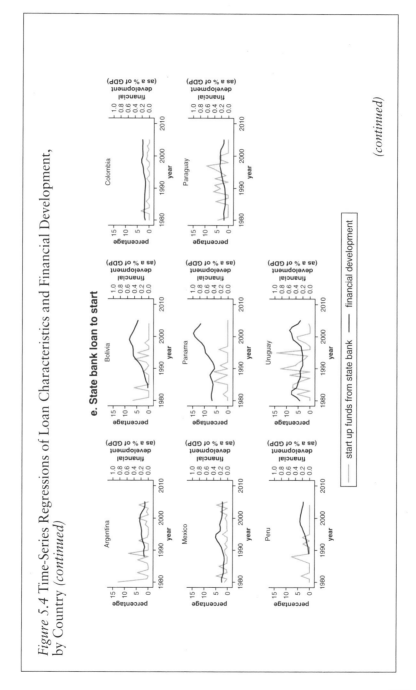

e. State bank loan to start

start up funds from state bank —— financial development

(continued)

Figure 5.4 Time-Series Regressions of Loan Characteristics and Financial Development, by Country *(continued)*

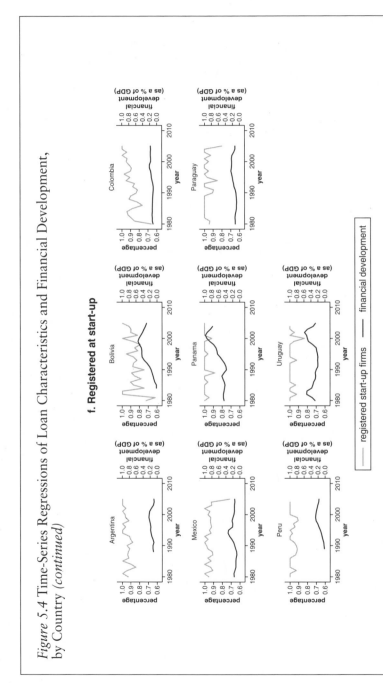

f. Registered at start-up

Source: Author's calculations based on Enterprise Surveys data.

often 1, except for Bolivia and Colombia, which show an increasing trend with more registrations in later years.

Court-Quality Measures

Quite a bit of variation exists in objective court-quality measures across the regions in each country; however, substantially less variation occurs in subjective measures (see table 5.4 and figure 5.5). Mexico appears to be on the low side of the scale for both objective and subjective indicators. There is a relatively low correlation between objective and subjective measures of court quality (only about 0.16—see panel b in table 5.4). This finding is attributable to the measure *court quick*, which is negatively correlated with objective court quality, whereas other subjective measures are positively correlated with objective court quality.

Figure 5.6 presents the cross-sectional access measures plotted against categories of court-quality indicators. For these figures, the regions were grouped into high court quality (above the median) and low court quality (below the median). Most of the access measures are higher in regions with higher objective court quality. In these regions, firms are more likely to have a *checking* account, to have any *credit*, and to have more *depth* (that is, a larger number of credit accounts); they are more likely to be *unconstrained* and therefore have a higher *access index*. However, no difference exists in subjective measures of *access obstacle* when it is plotted against objective court quality, and there is no difference for the measure *unconstrained*.

Interestingly, the difference in objective indicators of access when the sample is split on subjective court indicators is very small—almost not visible. The direction is the same as before, with higher subjective court quality indicating better access, but the magnitude is negligible.

Other Controls

Table 5.5 presents descriptive statistics for firm-level controls, country-regional controls, and country-year controls. Panel a presents firm-level controls broken down by size, and panel b presents the same controls by country. Because all controls (except sales in U.S. dollars) are binary variables, the percentage of each type of firm in the sample is reported. Most of the firms in the sample are classified as mature: 74 percent are more than 10 years old, and larger firms are older. Only 10 percent of all firms have any foreign ownership, and 20 percent are exporters. Large firms are more likely to have foreign ownership and to be exporters. Most of the firms have limited liability, which is also related to size, and about 40 percent have females as the main owner (this number is slightly higher for small firms). Small firms are less likely to be a subsidiary of a large corporation, to have certification, or to own land. Within each industry,

Table 5.4 Descriptive Statistics for Court-Quality Measures

a. Average court quality by country-region

Country and region	Court objective	Court subjective	Court use	Court judgment made	Court enforced	Court fair	Court quick	Court affordable	Court enforceable
			Court objective					Court subjective	
Argentina									
Buenos Aires	0.64	1.9	0.77	0.42	0.73	1.8	1.22	2.34	2.17
Córdoba	0.54	1.9	0.71	0.3	0.6	2.04	1.25	1.92	2.23
Mendoza	0.67	1.9	0.65	0.38	1	2	1.32	2	2.21
Rosario	0.56	1.8	0.81	0.29	0.57	2	1.13	1.97	2.17
Bolivia									
Cochabamba	0.49	1.9	0.65	0.33	—	1.58	1.29	2.63	2.08
La Paz	0.61	1.7	0.78	0.38	0.67	1.53	1.18	2.08	2.02
Santa Cruz	0.63	1.8	0.74	0.33	0.83	1.91	1.31	1.98	2.09
Colombia									
Barranquilla	0.61	2.2	0.85	0.43	0.56	2.14	1.57	2.57	2.39
Bogotá	0.63	2.1	0.62	0.49	0.78	2.08	1.46	2.33	2.49
Cali	0.73	2	0.64	0.55	1	2.08	1.28	2.32	2.4
Medellín	0.55	2.2	0.63	0.35	0.68	2.42	1.57	2.33	2.58

(continued)

Table 5.4 Descriptive Statistics for Court-Quality Measures (continued)

a. Average court quality by country-region

Country and region	Court objective	Court subjective	Court objective			Court subjective			
			Court use	Court judgment made	Court enforced	Court fair	Court quick	Court affordable	Court enforceable
Mexico									
Chihuahua	0.35	—	0.38	0.33	—	—	—	—	—
Coahuila	0.8	—	0.6	1	—	—	—	—	—
Estado	0.48	1.8	0.67	0.3	—	1.94	1.44	1.56	2.06
Jalisco	0.32	1.8	0.48	0.17	—	1.82	1.73	1.73	1.91
Mexico	0.45	1.9	0.37	0.41	0.57	2.05	1.45	2.11	2
Nuevo León	0.64	1.9	0.58	0.35	1	2.12	1.5	1.83	2.28
Puebla	0.45	—	0.4	0.5	—	—	—	—	—
Veracruz	—	—	—	—	—	—	—	—	—
Panama									
Colón	0.42	1.8	0.33	0.5	—	1.6	1	2.2	2.4
Panama City	0.71	2	0.58	0.63	0.91	1.97	1.63	2.16	2.31

(continued)

Table 5.4 Descriptive Statistics for Court-Quality Measures *(continued)*

a. Average court quality by country-region

Country and region	Court objective	Court subjective	Court objective			Court fair	Court subjective		
			Court use	Court judgment made	Court enforced		Court quick	Court affordable	Court enforceable
Paraguay									
Asunción	0.66	1.5	0.72	0.46	0.8	1.4	1.19	1.88	1.64
Central	0.7	1.7	0.73	0.47	0.89	1.67	1.32	1.67	2.08
Peru									
Arequipa	0.62	1.9	0.63	0.58	0.64	1.75	1.33	2.25	2.13
Chiclayo	0.64	1.9	0.28	1	—	1.6	1	2.8	2.2
Lima	0.66	1.7	0.73	0.62	0.64	1.59	1.21	2.16	1.84
Uruguay									
Canelones	0.68	2.3	0.7	0.67	—	3.17	1.25	2.38	2.43
Montevideo	0.71	2.2	0.73	0.63	0.78	2.6	1.24	2.34	2.5
Mean	0.59	1.9	0.62	0.48	0.76	1.95	1.33	2.15	2.19
Median	0.63	1.9	0.65	0.43	0.75	1.96	1.3	2.16	2.19
Standard deviation	0.12	0.2	0.15	0.19	0.15	0.38	0.18	0.3	0.23

(continued)

Table 5.4 Descriptive Statistics for Court-Quality Measures *(continued)*

b. Correlations for court-quality measures

	Court objective	Court subjective	Court objective			Court subjective			
			Court use	Court judgment made	Court enforced	Court fair	Court quick	Court affordable	Court enforceable
Court objective	1.00								
Court subjective	0.16*	1.00							
Court use	0.59*	−0.13*	1.00						
Court judgment made	0.67*	0.26*	0.04*	1.00					
Court enforced	0.71*	0.10*	0.03*	0.23*	1.00				
Court fair	0.10*	0.88*	−0.11*	0.19*	0.07*	1.00			
Court quick	−0.30*	0.38*	−0.49*	−0.21*	0.25*	0.26*	1.00		
Court affordable	0.28*	0.61*	0.07*	0.46*	−0.24*	0.31*	−0.15*	1.00	
Court enforceable	0.24*	0.92*	−0.01*	0.21*	0.25*	0.77*	0.28*	0.51*	1.00

Source: Author's calculations based on Enterprise Surveys data.

Note: — = not available; * = significant at the 5 percent level or better.

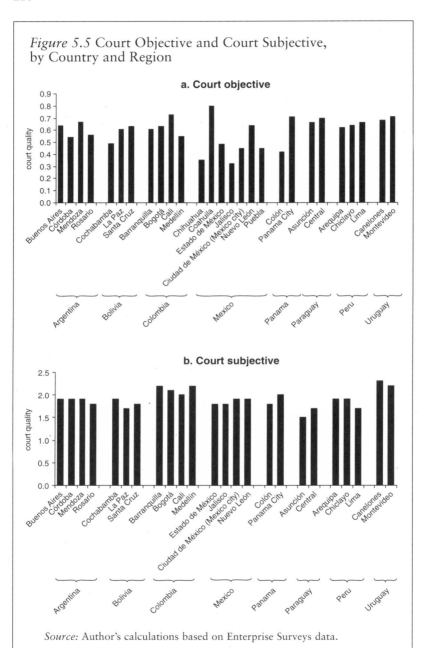

Figure 5.5 Court Objective and Court Subjective, by Country and Region

Source: Author's calculations based on Enterprise Surveys data.

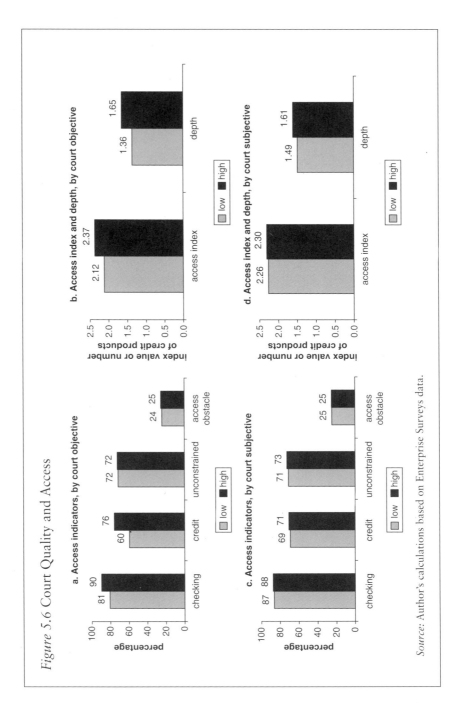

Figure 5.6 Court Quality and Access

a. Access indicators, by court objective

b. Access index and depth, by court objective

c. Access indicators, by court subjective

d. Access index and depth, by court subjective

Source: Author's calculations based on Enterprise Surveys data.

Table 5.5 Descriptive Statistics for Other Controls

a. By size

(percentage unless otherwise noted)

Variable	All firms	Small	Medium	Large
Firm characteristics				
Firm age: Young	11	15	9	5
Firm age: Medium	15	18	13	11
Firm age: Mature	74	67	78	84
Exporter	20	11	25	40
Foreign ownership	10	5	11	26
State ownership	0	0	0	1
Female	37	39	36	31
LLC	82	70	91	97
Certified	17	7	19	45
Subsidiary	15	8	16	35
Own land	62	54	65	77
Audited	48	37	52	73
Sales (mean; US$ thousands)	11,500	788	5,046	57,100
Sales (median; US$ thousands)	551	186	1,033	8,717

(continued)

Table 5.5 Descriptive Statistics for Other Controls *(continued)*

a. By size
(percentage unless otherwise noted)

Variable	All firms	Small	Medium	Large
Industry				
Food	15	14	15	19
Garment	13	13	13	10
Textile	8	7	8	8
Chemicals	12	11	13	12
Other manufacturing	19	19	20	20
Retail	15	18	13	10
Other service	13	13	13	12
Construction and transportation	6	5	6	9

b. By country
(percentage unless otherwise noted)

Variable	All	Argentina	Bolivia	Colombia	Mexico	Panama	Paraguay	Peru	Uruguay
Firm characteristics									
Size: small	50	39	53	56	50	59	54	46	49
Size: medium	34	37	34	34	30	30	37	38	37
Size: large	16	24	13	10	20	11	9	16	14

(continued)

Table 5.5 Descriptive Statistics for Other Controls *(continued)*

b. By country

(percentage unless otherwise noted)

Variable	All	Argentina	Bolivia	Colombia	Mexico	Panama	Paraguay	Peru	Uruguay
Firm age: young	11	10	13	20	10	4	9	10	13
Firm age: medium	15	12	11	18	19	11	15	19	11
Firm age: mature	73	78	75	62	71	85	77	71	76
Exporter	20	33	17	19	11	18	17	27	24
Foreign ownership	10	14	14	3	9	12	11	12	13
State ownership	0	0	1	1	0	0	0	0	0
Female	37	31	44	47	24	39	45	34	44
LLC	82	88	65	85	69	90	87	89	91
Certified	17	25	19	12	24	13	7	15	11
Subsidiary	15	26	21	3	15	20	8	9	16
Own land	62	66	76	42	65	54	71	65	58
Sales (mean; US$ thousands)	11,500	22,400	3,029	3,057	18,400	4,566	12,200	7,154	6,179
Sales (median; US$ thousands)	551	1,213	298	388	443	563	243	1,312	817

(continued)

Table 5.5 Descriptive Statistics for Other Controls *(continued)*

b. By country

(percentage unless otherwise noted)

Variable	All	Argentina	Bolivia	Colombia	Mexico	Panama	Paraguay	Peru	Uruguay
Industry									
Food	15	16	20	15	11	11	15	19	19
Garment	13	11	20	17	11	3	9	19	12
Textile	8	11	0	15	10	0	1	6	7
Chemicals	12	6	10	16	11	2	18	13	20
Other manufacturing	19	26	17	2	35	23	29	0	6
Retail	15	12	20	12	8	20	21	19	20
Other service	13	16	6	15	11	21	3	20	9
Construction and transportation	6	2	8	8	2	19	5	3	7
Country-year controls									
Financial development	23	10	30	19	15	77	12	18	27
GDP per capita (US$)	4,442	8,096	1,061	2,174	6,172	4,408	1,377	2,319	6,269
GDP level (US$ billion)	146	314	10	99	636	14	8	65	22

(continued)

Table 5.5 Descriptive Statistics for Other Controls *(continued)*

b. By country

(percentage unless otherwise noted)

Variable	All	Argentina	Bolivia	Colombia	Mexico	Panama	Paraguay	Peru	Uruguay
Country-region controls									
Internet use (%)	0.82	0.97	0.88	0.88	0.64	0.8	0.79	0.92	0.81
Wait for government service[a]	-0.11	-0.01	-0.08	-0.11	-0.23	-0.23	0.02	0.01	-0.12
Number of power outages[a]	0	-0.09	-0.11	-0.18	0	0.74	0.42	-0.29	-0.28
Government obstacle (scale of 1–4)	1.94	2.38	2.01	1.89	1.88	1.35	1.78	2.12	1.94
Time spent with the government[a]	-0.01	0.06	0.06	0.05	0.14	-0.08	-0.29	-0.02	-0.31
Percentage of sales or workforce reported (%)	80.15	83.31	76.74	83.73	77.33	67	78.45	87.64	85.92
Average corruption obstacle (scale of 1–4)	2.29	2.61	2.72	2.19	2.16	1.6	2.75	2.59	1.71
Index of bribes[a]	-0.01	0.22	0.59	-0.6	-0.49	-0.31	2.26	-0.07	-0.76

Sources: Author's calculations based on Enterprise Surveys data and World Bank 2007.

Note: a. Standardized to have a mean of zero and standard deviation of one.

however, the proportion of small, medium, and large firms is about equal (because of the stratified sampling design).

Panel b in table 5.5 presents a breakdown of types of firms by country. In all countries, small and medium firms are overrepresented, and on average, small firms represent 50 percent of the sample and large firms represent only 16 percent. The opposite is true for firm ages: the sample contains mostly mature firms. Some variation occurs among countries by the type of firms in the sample.

Panama appears to have the highest level of financial development (measured as ratio of private credit to GDP), whereas Argentina has the highest level of GDP per capita.

Regression Results

Next, regression analysis is performed for each of the three sets of indicators.

Access Indicators

Cross-sectional analysis of access indicators is conducted using the following simple model:

$$Y_{icr} = \alpha_c + \beta X_i + \varepsilon_{icr}. \tag{5.1}$$

Here, Y_i stands for the six main access measures described in the section "Access Variables for Cross-Sectional Analysis," X_i represents the firm controls described in the section "Other Controls," α_c is country fixed effects, i indexes individual firm observations, c indexes countries, and r indexes regions. Because this model is used later to estimate the effect of court quality, which is measured on the country-regional level, the errors are allowed to have an unspecified correlation within each country-region. The results for this model are similar if they are clustered on country level.

Table 5.6 reports these baseline results. One of the most significant and consistent findings is that small firms use fewer financial products and have less access to finance than do large firms. Note that large firms are the omitted category here. Small firms are less likely to have a *checking* account and any *credit*, and they are more likely to be *constrained* and have fewer credit products (that is, less *depth*). The aggregate *access index* is significantly lower for smaller firms, and they are more likely to say access is one of the top four obstacles for their business (that is, higher *access obstacle*).

Medium firms are also different from large firms, but the differences are less pronounced than those observed for small firms. For several indexes, the significance is lower, and the magnitude is half of the magnitude observed

Table 5.6 Baseline Regressions of Cross-Sectional Access Measures

	Checking	Credit	Unconstrained	Access index	Depth	Access obstacle
Size: small	-0.41	-0.72	-0.36	-0.6	-0.7	0.11
	[0.00]***	[0.00]***	[0.00]***	[0.00]***	[0.00]***	[0.07]*
Size: medium	-0.05	-0.31	-0.17	-0.23	-0.25	0.03
	[0.48]	[0.00]***	[0.02]**	[0.00]***	[0.00]***	[0.55]
Age: 0–5 years	-0.05	-0.2	-0.04	-0.12	-0.05	0.13
	[0.63]	[0.00]***	[0.57]	[0.03]**	[0.27]	[0.01]***
Age: 6–9 years	-0.2	-0.11	-0.1	-0.15	-0.07	0.18
	[0.01]**	[0.03]**	[0.12]	[0.00]***	[0.08]*	[0.00]***
Subsidiary	0.22	0.07	0.15	0.16	0.06	-0.17
	[0.03]**	[0.32]	[0.00]***	[0.00]***	[0.15]	[0.00]***
Foreign ownership	0.28	-0.07	0.05	0.07	-0.21	-0.32
	[0.19]	[0.36]	[0.55]	[0.26]	[0.00]***	[0.00]***
Female owned	0.01	0.05	0.03	0.04	0.03	-0.02
	[0.90]	[0.20]	[0.47]	[0.30]	[0.25]	[0.63]
Certified	0.43	0.04	0.08	0.16	0.07	-0.06
	[0.01]***	[0.59]	[0.25]	[0.02]**	[0.27]	[0.26]

(continued)

Table 5.6 Baseline Regressions of Cross-Sectional Access Measures (continued)

	Checking	Credit	Unconstrained	Access index	Depth	Access obstacle
Exporter	0.29	0.23	-0.09	0.09	0.2	0.1
	[0.00]***	[0.00]***	[0.15]	[0.09]*	[0.00]***	[0.00]***
Own land	0.18	0.17	0.06	0.14	0.15	-0.07
	[0.00]***	[0.00]***	[0.16]	[0.00]***	[0.00]***	[0.17]
Audited	0.14	0.26	0.1	0.19	0.27	0.04
	[0.19]	[0.00]***	[0.12]	[0.00]***	[0.00]***	[0.50]
LLC	0.3	0.07	0.04	0.15	0.08	-0.04
	[0.00]***	[0.20]	[0.39]	[0.00]***	[0.16]	[0.60]
Argentina	0.65	-0.02	-0.17	-0.05	-0.2	0.13
	[0.00]***	[0.71]	[0.04]**	[0.48]	[0.00]***	[0.04]**
Colombia	0.68	0.84	0.38	0.71	0.76	0.05
	[0.00]***	[0.00]***	[0.00]***	[0.00]***	[0.00]***	[0.52]
Mexico	-1.33	-1.21	0.18	-0.93	-1.27	-0.39
	[0.00]***	[0.00]***	[0.12]	[0.00]***	[0.00]***	[0.00]***
Panama	0.67	0.23	0.5	0.46	0.15	-0.64
	[0.00]***	[0.00]***	[0.00]***	[0.00]***	[0.00]***	[0.00]***

(continued)

Table 5.6 Baseline Regressions of Cross-Sectional Access Measures *(continued)*

	Checking	Credit	Unconstrained	Access index	Depth	Access obstacle
Paraguay	-0.26	0.29	0.31	0.21	0.03	0.23
	[0.00]***	[0.00]***	[0.00]***	[0.00]***	[0.27]	[0.00]***
Peru	0.16	0.62	0.38	0.52	0.7	-0.23
	[0.02]**	[0.00]***	[0.00]***	[0.00]***	[0.00]***	[0.00]***
Uruguay	-0.21	0	-0.07	-0.11	-0.1	-0.05
	[0.00]***	[0.95]	[0.40]	[0.07]*	[0.03]**	[0.48]
Observations	6,005	6,025	5,873	5,853	6,025	5,947
Pseudo R-squared	0.32	0.25	0.04	0.14	0.14	0.05
N clusters	28	28	28	28	28	28

Source: Author's calculations.

Note: * = significant at the 10 percent level; ** = significant at the 5 percent level; *** = significant at the 1 percent level. Robust *p*-values are in brackets. Industry dummies are included.

for small firms. Younger firms have less access to financial services and report higher access obstacles.

Among other controls, some findings follow:

- Subsidiaries of larger corporations have more access and report lower access obstacles.
- Foreign firms have fewer credit accounts, but they report lower obstacles.
- Firms owned by females demonstrate no difference in access indicators.
- Firms with certified products have more checking accounts but no significant difference for other access characteristics.
- Exporters are more likely to have a checking account and any credit, but they are also slightly likely to be more constrained (significant only at 15 percent), and they report higher *access obstacles*. Perhaps their need for finance exceeds their use of funds.[10]
- Firms with owned land, audited financial statements, and limited liability (that is, *LLC*) have more access to finance (although some variation exists for individual indexes, the results for *access index* and *depth* are all significant).
- Among different industries, firms in the garment and food product sectors have less access to finance (the results for garments are more significant), while not much consistent difference is observed for other industries.
- Among different countries, Colombia, Panama, and Peru score highest: that is, they have most access to finance. Bolivia (the omitted category) falls in the middle, and Mexico is on the lower end for objective measures of access, but scores lower on *access obstacles*.

Court Quality and Access

To study the relationship between court quality and access, indicators of court quality are appended to model 5.1:

$$Y_{icr} = \alpha + \beta X_i + \gamma Court_{cr} + \varepsilon_{icr}. \tag{5.2}$$

As before, Y_i represents the six main access measures described in the section "Access Variables for Cross-Sectional Analysis," X_i is a vector of firm controls described in the section "Other Controls," and $Court_{cr}$ is one of the court-quality indicators described in the section "Time-Varying Loan Characteristics, Start-up Capital, and Registration." Because the main variable of interest is measured on country-region level, country dummies are not included in this model (to preserve the degrees of freedom). However, to reduce the likelihood that the court measures simply proxy for the overall level of development, GDP per capita is included as a control. Unfortunately, GDP per capita data are available only on the country level, whereas the court-quality data are on the country-region level, so GDP per capita is not a perfect control. Therefore, the robustness of the results is also tested using a variety of country-regional measures constructed from the Enterprise Surveys. As before, the errors are allowed to have an unspecified correlation within each country-region.

The country-regional court-quality variables represent the court quality in the country-region estimated using the firms in the sample. Therefore, they are a relevant measure of the court quality faced by firms in the sample. Thus, even though the sample is not purely random (that is, it is stratified), weights were not used for calculating country-regional averages of court quality, because weights would make the measures representative of the population, whereas the regression would be representative of the sample. In this approach, both the regression and the country-regional averages are unweighted and thus represent the sample results.

Table 5.7 presents the results from estimating this model separately for each of the court-quality measures. Note that each cell in the table corresponds to one regression. Similar to results obtained in the descriptive analysis, objective measures of court quality are strongly correlated with access indicators. All access indicators respond to court quality except the measure of *unconstrained*, which is a weak measure to start with and is marginally negative. Among the individual indicators, *court use* and *court judgment made* have a significant positive influence on access indicators (again, except *unconstrained*); however, the percentage of judgments enforced, *court enforced*, does not seem to matter. This result could be attributable to lower variation in the enforcement rates and some missing data, because not all regions have enforcement data. Note that enforcement rate is observed only if the respondent says it has used the court and the court has made a judgment. This restriction explains a significant number of missing data for *court enforced*. The average enforcement rate is about 75 percent, the average judgment made rate is only about 50 percent, and the average court use rate is only 25 percent.

The subjective measures of court-quality perceptions are also positively related to access, especially the measures of *court affordable* and *court enforceable*. *Court fair* is not significant and *court quick* is even negative (expect for *unconstrained*). The aggregate *subjective court* index is significantly related to access as well.

For comparison purposes, all court measures in table 5.7 are standardized to have a mean of zero and a standard deviation of one, which makes the magnitude comparison much simpler. The *court objective* index has about twice as large an effect in magnitude as *court subjective*. For example, one standard deviation improvement in *court objective* increases the *access index* by about 0.30, whereas the same increase in *court subjective* increases the *access index* by only 0.15.

Table 5.7 Access and Court Quality

	Checking	Credit	Unconstrained	Access index	Depth	Access obstacle
Court objective	0.38 [0.01]***	0.46 [0.00]***	-0.1 [0.11]a	0.29 [0.00]***	0.34 [0.01]***	0.13 [0.12]a
Court use	0.37 [0.00]***	0.34 [0.00]***	-0.14 [0.00]***	0.21 [0.00]***	0.24 [0.00]***	0.15 [0.00]***
Court judgment made	0.19 [0.03]**	0.25 [0.00]***	0.04 [0.49]	0.18 [0.00]***	0.24 [0.00]***	-0.01 [0.87]
Court enforced	-0.02 [0.94]	0.07 [0.64]	0.01 [0.77]	0.04 [0.76]	0 [0.97]	-0.01 [0.92]
Court subjective	0.18 [0.01]**	0.19 [0.00]***	0.05 [0.15]a	0.15 [0.00]***	0.19 [0.00]***	-0.03 [0.59]
Court fair	0.02 [0.89]	0.1 [0.37]	0.05 [0.29]	0.08 [0.32]	0.12 [0.15]	-0.03 [0.69]
Court quick	-0.19 [0.12]a	-0.18 [0.11]a	0.13 [0.00]***	-0.07 [0.46]	-0.09 [0.32]	-0.17 [0.00]***
Court affordable	0.33 [0.00]***	0.28 [0.00]***	0.01 [0.90]	0.22 [0.00]***	0.3 [0.00]***	0.06 [0.31]
Court enforceable	0.26 [0.01]**	0.26 [0.01]***	0.03 [0.41]	0.2 [0.00]***	0.22 [0.01]***	0 [0.95]

Source: Author's calculations.
Note: * = significant at the 10 percent level; ** = significant at the 5 percent level; *** = significant at the 1 percent level; a = significant at the 15 percent level. Robust p-values are in brackets. Each cell reports the results from a separate regression with the same controls as in table 5.6, except country dummies, which are replaced with GDP per capita (country level) as a control.

As in any study of access, using care is important in assigning the causality of the relationship between court quality and access. The reversed causality problem is more likely to affect the subjective measures of access. For example, firms with better access to finance are likely to give higher ratings on subjective court quality (because they are more optimistic overall, or because they may infer that since they have access, the courts are functioning well). The potential for reverse causality is less obvious in the objective court indicators. For example, the reason firms with access to finance would be more likely to use courts for resolving disputes over payments with their clients is not obvious.[11] In any case, because country-regional averages of court quality are used, the endogeneity problem should be mitigated somewhat. For each individual firm, the country-regional average is unlikely to bias the coefficients. Although the approach was to use country-regional averages of court quality as regressors, this approach is numerically equivalent to using country-regional averages as instruments in a two-stage least squares framework (see chapter 2 for details and calculations).

Table 5.8 reports a number of robustness tests for *objective court* and *subjective court* indexes. Only the *access index* is reported as an aggregate measure of access, because it represents an aggregate of the three other measures (*checking*, *credit*, and *unconstrained*). The results are similar for individual measures. The *court objective* index is robust to inclusion of a number of country-regional control variables, which are described in the section "Other Controls." The only variable that has some effect on the *court objective* index is average use of the Internet. The *court objective* index loses some of its significance—it is significant only at 13 percent when Internet use is added to the regression. The *court subjective* index remains significant with inclusion of any of the control variables. The Internet use measure is likely to capture the quality of the telecommunications network, which is clearly an important ingredient for financial access. Note that country-level GDP per capita is included in all of these regressions.[12]

It is not self-evident whether court quality would have the same effect on financial access for firms of different sizes. On one side, larger firms are more stable, more transparent, and more likely to have a history and a reputation at stake. For these firms, court quality may be less important as a determinant of their access because they are less likely to fail and require court intervention. On the other side, smaller firms may incur significant fixed costs in using courts; thus, small firms are less likely to rely on courts for dispute resolution. The relationship between court quality and size of firms can be explored by adding interactions of dummies for small and medium enterprises with a court-quality indicator to model 5.2.

Table 5.9 presents the results. Some evidence indicates that smaller firms derive less benefit from court quality than larger firms; the interaction of court objective and small dummy is negative for *credit*, *access*

Table 5.8 Access and Court-Quality Robustness Checks

a. Court objective

	Dependent variable: Access index							
Court objective	0.29 [0.00]***	0.3 [0.00]***	0.28 [0.00]***	0.26 [0.01]**	0.32 [0.00]***	0.3 [0.00]***	0.24 [0.02]**	0.14 [0.13]a
Internet use								2.23 [0.00]***
Wait for government service							0.9 [0.16]	
Power outages						-0.02 [0.80]		
Government obstacle					0.44 [0.13]			
Time spent with the government				0.01 [0.97]				
Percentage of sales or workforce reported			0.01 [0.45]					
Average corruption obstacle		0.1 [0.58]						

(continued)

Table 5.8 Access and Court-Quality Robustness Checks (continued)

a. Court objective

				Dependent variable: Access index				
	1	2	3	4	5	6	7	8
Index of bribes	-0.04 [0.65]							
Observations	5,832	5,832	5,832	5,717	5,779	5,779	5,832	5,717

b. Court subjective

				Dependent variable: Access index				
	1	2	3	4	5	6	7	8
Court subjective	0.29 [0.03]**	0.18 [0.04]**	0.14 [0.02]**	0.15 [0.00]***	0.17 [0.00]***	0.16 [0.01]**	0.23 [0.00]***	0.14 [0.00]***
Internet use								2.48 [0.00]***
Wait for government service							1.92 [0.00]***	
Power outages						0 [0.96]		
Government obstacle					0.21 [0.56]			

(continued)

Table 5.8 Access and Court-Quality Robustness Checks *(continued)*

b. Court subjective

	Dependent variable: Access index							
	1	2	3	4	5	6	7	8
Time spent with the government				-0.03 [0.91]				
Percentage of sales or workforce reported			0.01 [0.35]					
Average corruption obstacle		0.09 [0.75]						
Index of bribes	0.21 [0.19]							
Observations	5,621	5,621	5,621	5,621	5,568	5,568	5,621	5,621

Source: Author's calculations.

Note: * = significant at the 10 percent level; ** = significant at the 5 percent level; *** = significant at the 1 percent level, a = significant at the 15 percent level. Robust *p*-values are in brackets.

Table 5.9 Access, Court Quality, and Size

	Checking	Credit	Unconstrained	Access index	Depth	Access obstacle
Court objective	0.46	0.70	-0.11	0.38	0.59	0.25
	[0.05]*	[0.00]***	[0.27]	[0.00]***	[0.00]***	[0.00]***
Court objective × small dummy	-0.12	-0.34	0.00	-0.14	-0.36	-0.16
	[0.52]	[0.00]***	[1.00]	[0.07]*	[0.00]***	[0.01]***
Court objective × medium dummy	0.00	-0.13	0.03	-0.03	-0.19	-0.07
	[0.98]	[0.26]	[0.71]	[0.70]	[0.06]*	[0.36]
Court subjective	0.11	0.13	0.16	0.15	0.14	-0.03
	[0.46]	[0.16]	[0.01]***	[0.01]**	[0.08]*	[0.44]
Court subjective × small dummy	0.10	0.04	-0.13	0.00	0.04	-0.02
	[0.52]	[0.56]	[0.02]**	[1.00]	[0.59]	[0.76]
Court subjective × medium dummy	0.04	0.10	-0.09	0.00	0.08	0.03
	[0.72]	[0.09]*	[0.01]**	[0.98]	[0.13]	[0.44]

Source: Author's calculations.
Note: * = significant at the 10 percent level; ** = significant at the 5 percent level; *** = significant at the 1 percent level. Robust p-values are in brackets.

index, and *depth*. The coefficient magnitude implies that the benefit of court quality for small firms is half the benefit for large firms because the interaction is about half the size of the coefficient on court objective. For example, for *credit*, the court objective coefficient is 0.7 whereas the interaction with small dummy equals –0.34, or about half the coefficient level. However, the results seem the opposite for a subjective measure of *access obstacle*—in country-regions with higher court quality, larger firms complain more of subjective access obstacles, and smaller firms complain less than large firms. This finding is somewhat puzzling.

The relationship between the objective court measures and financial access is largely unrelated to size. The interactions of the *court objective* index and size dummies are insignificant for objective measures of access. The only significant interaction is with *access obstacle*, which is a perception of access. In country-regions with better court quality, smaller firms report lower *access obstacles*, while large firms report higher *access obstacles* (even though the subjective indicators of access have improved). Because court quality shows no difference on objective measures of access, this study does not put much emphasis on that result.

The subjective measures of court quality are largely insignificant, except a surprising result for the measure of *unconstrained*: it is positive for *court subjective* and negative for interactions of small and medium firms. So in country-regions with high ratings for *court subjective*, only large firms appear to report being less constrained (that is, the coefficient on *court subjective* captures the effect of courts on large firms and is positive), and whether or not small and medium firms are constrained is unrelated to subjective measure of court quality (that is, the interaction coefficients on small and medium dummies almost exactly offset the positive effect of *court subjective* on large firms).

In sum, objective measures of court quality have a consistent positive effect on objective measures of access, that is, *checking* account, *credit* use, and *depth*. Some evidence suggests that court quality is more important for objective measures of access for large firms. The subjective measures of court quality are also positively related to access, but not all subjective measures perform the same. Some measures (*court affordable* and *court enforceable*) indicate improved access, and others (*court quick*) indicate reduced access, whereas *court fair* is not significant.

Time-Series Analysis of Loan Characteristics

This section studies the relationship between loan characteristics and the aggregate level of financial development over time, using the following model:

$$Y_{ct} = \alpha_c + \beta_1 Fin.Dev_{ct} + \gamma GDP_{ct} + Trend_t + \varepsilon_{ct}. \qquad (5.3)$$

In this model, Y_{ct} is one of the time-varying loan characteristic variables described in the section "Court-Quality Measures," $Fin.Dev_{ct}$ is a measure of financial development, and GDP_{ct} is the log level of GDP (in real U.S. dollars), which captures the overall macroeconomic conditions in country c at time t. *Trend* is a linear trend included to ensure that the results are not spuriously driven by a common trend. This model is estimated with country fixed effects, α_c, and with country clusters, which correct for any possible unspecified correlation of errors within each country.

The results of estimating model 5.3 are presented in table 5.10. Despite controlling for the overall macroeconomic conditions (measured by the log level of GDP) and a linear time trend, *financial development* is significant for several of the measures used. Specifically, a higher level of financial development is associated with increased mean and median maturity of loans and larger size of loans relative to sales (both mean and median are increasing). There is no relationship with the likelihood of using collateral or percentage of collateral relative to the loan amount.

In terms of types of collateral, the use of land and buildings increases with higher levels of financial development. Surprisingly, no relationship exists between financial development and other types of collateral used. One would expect the use of movable assets (especially receivables and inventories) to increase with the overall level of financial development, but this is not the case in the study's sample.[13]

The next consideration is how the effect of financial development varies by firm size. Aggregate measures of loan characteristics Y_{ctj} are created separately for three size categories: small, medium, and large firms. In other words, average loan characteristics are created for each country-year-size combination. So the modified model becomes the following:

$$Y_{ctj} = \alpha_c + \beta_1 Fin.Dev_{ct} + \gamma GDPPC_{ct} + Trend_t + \beta_2 Small_{ctj}$$
$$+ \beta_3 Medium_{ctj} + \beta_4 Small_{ctj} * Fin.Dev_{ct} + \beta_5 Medium_{ctj}$$
$$* Fin.Dev_{ct} + \varepsilon_{ctj}. \tag{5.4}$$

Here j indicates the firm size, and *Small* and *Medium* capture two size categories (while *Large* is omitted). The coefficients of interest are β_4 and β_5—the interaction of financial development and size. They capture the differential effect of financial development on loan characteristics of small and medium firms, while β_1 captures the effect of financial development on loan characteristics of large firms.

The results of estimating model 5.4 are presented in table 5.11. Although the interactions of size and mean maturity are not significant, interaction with the median maturity is positive for small and medium firms. This finding suggests that the benefit of longer maturity is accruing mainly to small and medium firms. It is plausible that in country-years with lower levels of financial development, large firms are able to obtain loans with disproportionably longer maturity (relative to those obtained by small and

Table 5.10 Time-Series Loan Characteristics and Financial Development

	Maturity (mean)	Maturity (median)	Loan-to-sales ratio (mean)	Loan-to-sales ratio (median)	Collateral dummy	Percent collateral	Collateral: land and buildings	Collateral: machinery and equipment	Collateral: receivables and inventory	Collateral: personal assets
Financial development	85.35	102.12	0.51	0.51	0.14	-46.61	0.67	-0.08	0.02	0.14
	[0.01]***	[0.03]**	[0.00]***	[0.00]***	[0.31]	[0.31]	[0.01]***	[0.75]	[0.88]	[0.80]
GDP	39.87	10.56	-0.33	-0.15	0.34	33.19	0.25	0.69	-0.03	-0.27
	[0.16]	[0.61]	[0.33]	[0.37]	[0.40]	[0.73]	[0.74]	[0.32]	[0.78]	[0.24]
Trend	-3.25	-1.99	0.00	0.00	-0.03	0.84	-0.02	-0.03	0.01	0.01
	[0.02]**	[0.23]	[0.54]	[0.16]	[0.09]*	[0.85]	[0.43]	[0.36]	[0.28]	[0.39]
Observations	45	44	37	37	52	44	46	46	46	46
Groups (countries)	8	8	8	8	8	8	8	8	8	8
R-squared	0.12	0.14	0.18	0.27	0.08	0.04	0.13	0.06	0.05	0.02

Source: Author's calculations.

Note: * = significant at the 10 percent level; ** = significant at the 5 percent level; *** = significant at the 1 percent level. Robust p-values are in brackets.

Table 5.11 Time-Series Loan Characteristics, Financial Development, and Size

	Maturity (mean)	Maturity (median)	Loan-to-sales ratio (mean)	Loan-to-sales ratio (median)	Collateral dummy	Percent collateral	Collateral: land and buildings	Collateral: machinery and equipment	Collateral: receivables and inventory	Collateral: personal assets
Financial development	-5.3	-155.97	0.25	-0.51	-0.21	48.64	1.7	0.27	-0.16	-0.81
	[0.91]	[0.04]**	[0.65]	[0.38]	[0.63]	[0.78]	[0.18]	[0.59]	[0.49]	[0.68]
Small	-6.4	-28.6	-0.08	-0.12	0.06	23.53	0.05	-0.12	-0.11	-0.17
	[0.47]	[0.04]**	[0.14]	[0.15]	[0.80]	[0.47]	[0.88]	[0.15]	[0.08]*	[0.48]
Medium	-5.29	-19.26	-0.1	-0.13	0.02	8.58	0.17	-0.05	-0.09	-0.34
	[0.48]	[0.16]	[0.14]	[0.15]	[0.93]	[0.86]	[0.65]	[0.71]	[0.29]	[0.09]*
Small × financial development	26.79	133.24	0.76	0.97	0.07	-84	-1.37	-0.42	0.25	1.06
	[0.28]	[0.00]***	[0.04]**	[0.06]*	[0.86]	[0.60]	[0.24]	[0.24]	[0.32]	[0.46]
Medium × financial development	7.53	85.2	0.77	0.96	0.21	-68.28	-1.38	-0.25	0.22	1.08
	[0.76]	[0.03]**	[0.02]**	[0.05]**	[0.55]	[0.70]	[0.26]	[0.53]	[0.39]	[0.47]
GDP	-30.89	-43.54	0.74	-0.43	-0.24	-21.18	-0.27	0.78	-0.11	-0.65
	[0.00]***	[0.10]*	[0.38]	[0.23]	[0.49]	[0.78]	[0.43]	[0.16]	[0.48]	[0.28]
Trend	-1.82	-1.31	-0.02	0.01	-0.02	1.17	-0.01	-0.05	0.01	0.02
	[0.07]*	[0.38]	[0.66]	[0.59]	[0.15]	[0.46]	[0.26]	[0.00]***	[0.27]	[0.41]
Observations	73	73	56	56	81	60	69	69	69	69
Groups (countries)	8	8	8	8	8	8	8	8	8	8
R-squared	0.14	0.18	0.27	0.19	0.07	0.02	0.16	0.16	0.03	0.14

Source: Author's calculations.

Note: * = significant at the 10 percent level; ** = significant at the 5 percent level; *** = significant at the 1 percent level. Robust p-values are in brackets.

medium firms). As financial development improves, the small and medium firms can extend the maturity of their loans.

Some evidence indicates that higher financial development results in larger amounts of loans for small and medium firms, significant for both the mean and median loan-to-sales ratios. No differences exist in collateral use, percentage of collateral, and types of collateral for firms of different sizes.

In sum, a higher level of financial development is associated with increased loan maturity, larger size of loans relative to sales, and more likely use of land and buildings as collateral. In addition, the majority of small and medium firms benefit from increased maturity of loans (that is, median maturity is increasing for small and median firms). Small and medium firms also benefit from increasing loan sizes (as a result of financial development) more than large firms do.

Time-Series Analysis of Start-up Financing and Registrations

This section studies the relationship between financial development, start-up financing, and registrations at the start of the business. The country-year framework is used for this analysis with the same models used to study loan characteristics.

Table 5.12 presents the baseline results for start-up financing. No significant relationship is found between the aggregate level of financial development and start-up capital. The coefficient on commercial bank is positive but not significant, whereas the coefficient on state bank is negative and is also not significant. In model 5.3, some positive correlation is seen between start-up registrations and percentage of start-up capital from commercial banks.[14] This correlation becomes insignificant in model 5.2, however, when the overall level of financial development is added to the model. Given the low variation in start-up registrations over time, this finding is not considered robust.

Table 5.13 presents the interaction of financial development with size and the interaction of registrations with size. For the purpose of these regressions, size is measured at the start of the business. No significant interactions are found of small and medium dummies and financial development (model 5.1) and percentage of start-up funds from commercial banks as a result of improving financial development.

The results on state bank start-up financing are somewhat surprising. Improvements in financial development lead to an increasing proportion of state bank finance for large firms but not for small and medium firms. Note that coefficients on small and medium interactions show the difference with the large firms, and the effect of financial development on large firms is shown by the coefficient on the level of financial development. So the magnitude of coefficients on small and medium

Table 5.12 Start-Up Capital and Registrations

	Start commercial	Start commercial	Start commercial	Start state	Start state	Start state
Financial development	7.01 [0.62]	7.35 [0.63]		-1.95 [0.48]	-1.93 [0.50]	
GDP	5.06 [0.63]	2.75 [0.79]	-3.57 [0.71]	0.58 [0.71]	0.68 [0.67]	-0.11 [0.95]
Trend	-0.28 [0.48]	-0.25 [0.52]	0.12 [0.66]	-0.06 [0.44]	-0.06 [0.44]	-0.03 [0.57]
Start registered		23.70 [0.23]	21.24 [0.03]**		-2.40 [0.56]	-4.57 [0.29]
Constant	-103.45 [0.68]	-70.78 [0.77]	78.21 [0.73]	-10.84 [0.77]	-10.93 [0.77]	8.80 [0.81]
Observations	212	210	263	211	209	261
Groups (countries)	8	8	8	8	8	8
R-squared	0.01	0.02	0.01	0.02	0.02	0.02

Source: Author's calculations.
Note: * = significant at the 10 percent level; ** = significant at the 5 percent level; *** = significant at the 1 percent level. Robust p-values are in brackets.

Table 5.13 Start-Up Capital, Registrations, and Size

	Start commercial	Start commercial	Start dommercial	Start state	Start state	Start state
Financial development	9.06	6.07	2	17.9	-2.4	18.53
	[0.09]*	[0.67]	[0.77]	[0.00]***	[0.47]	[0.00]***
Small	2.66	4.06	3.17	3.62	2.71	6.93
	[0.59]	[0.44]	[0.63]	[0.00]***	[0.55]	[0.11]
Medium	7.52	38.98	46.72	3.86	17.48	22.78
	[0.27]	[0.20]	[0.20]	[0.01]***	[0.23]	[0.17]
Small × financial development	-3.27		6	-21.72		-21.82
	[0.74]		[0.66]	[0.00]***		[0.00]***
Medium × financial development	-11.26		-6.28	-20.29		-23.24
	[0.62]		[0.80]	[0.00]***		[0.01]***
GDP	-2.77	-4.98	-5.8	1.73	1.56	2
	[0.78]	[0.59]	[0.52]	[0.36]	[0.52]	[0.39]
Trend	-0.11	-0.11	-0.09	-0.09	-0.1	-0.11
	[0.77]	[0.76]	[0.80]	[0.17]	[0.20]	[0.17]
Start registered		17.19	17.79		1.05	0.62
		[0.32]	[0.31]		[0.69]	[0.81]

(continued)

Table 5.13 Start-Up Capital, Registrations, and Size *(continued)*

	Start commercial	Start commercial	Start dommercial	Start state	Start state	Start state
Small × start registered		−0.73	−1.16		−3.58	−3.5
		[0.91]	[0.87]		[0.36]	[0.35]
Medium × start registered		−34.11	−40.41		−17.86	−18.5
		[0.29]	[0.28]		[0.24]	[0.25]
Observations	267	261	261	266	260	260
Groups (countries)	8	8	8	8	8	8
R-squared	0.02	0.03	0.03	0.03	0.03	0.04

Source: Author's calculations.

Note: * = significant at the 10 percent level; ** = significant at the 5 percent level; *** = significant at the 1 percent level. Robust *p*-values are in brackets.

interactions almost exactly offsets the increase observed for large firms. Possibly, in earlier years state banks had a mandate to offer directed credit, which was targeting small and medium firms, but in more recent years, as directed credit became unpopular, they started acting more like commercial banks and, hence, disproportionately increased the financing provided to larger firms.

Not much effect on the registration results was found, which is not surprising given the high proportion of firms in the sample that are registered when they start doing business. Only 4 percent of large firms and 8 percent of small firms are not registered at start-up. As a result, a fairly flat line is observed on the country-year average *percent registered* for most countries (except Bolivia and Colombia). This lack of variation is likely to explain the insignificant results. Clearly, this study's data set is not well suited to study the effect of registrations on access to finance.

In sum, the study finds that improvements in financial development lead to an increasing proportion of state bank financing for large firms but not for small and medium firms. No significant relationship exists between registration status at the start of the business and sources of start-up capital.

Summary and Conclusions

In this chapter, evidence is provided on the extent of firms' access to financial services in the Latin American and Caribbean region and the relationships between access and selected policy-relevant variables. A special focus is financial access of small and medium firms, which have been noted to suffer more from lack of access in previous studies. This study confirms those findings: small and medium firms have consistently lower use of financial products and lower access to finance than large firms do.

The objective measures of court quality exhibit a consistently positive correlation with objective measures of access—that is, checking account, credit use, and depth (number of credit products). There is some suggestive evidence that court quality is more important for objective measures of access for large firms. The subjective measures of court quality are also positively related to access, but not all subjective measures perform the same. Some measures (*court affordable* and *court enforceable*) indicate improved access, and others (*court quick*) indicate reduced access, whereas *court fair* is not significant.

Higher level of financial development is associated with increased loan maturity, larger size of loans relative to sales, and more likely use of land and buildings as collateral. In addition, the majority of small and medium firms benefit from increased maturity of loans (that is, median maturity is increasing for small and median firms). Small and medium firms also benefit from larger loan sizes more than large firms do.

Finally, improvements in financial development are correlated with an increasing proportion of state bank start-up financing for large firms but not for small and medium firms. Not much of a correlation is found between firms' registration status at the start of the business and sources of start-up capital. As was clear from the descriptive analysis, the data set is not well suited to study start-up registrations because a high proportion of firms are registered at start-up.

The results highlight the importance of court quality in improving financial access. Specifically, court reform should promote wider court use for dispute resolution and improve court outcomes in terms of percentage of cases that result in court judgments.

Notes

1. A firm is considered to be constrained if it has been rejected at least once.

2. The data do not allow loans to be separated from lines of credit because they are grouped in the same question.

3. Although the access measure reported is preferred, the results on other access measures are qualitatively similar.

4. The length of time the court takes to reach and enforce decisions is also a useful measure of court quality. However, in this study's data set, the length of time is observed only for those cases that actually included a judgment and for those cases that are actually enforced. Thus, this measure is conditional on a court making a judgment, and if the courts are not used or have not made a judgment, the data are missing. Because it is not clear how to impute the length (for judgment and its enforcement) for those cases that have not used courts, have not received a judgment, or have not enforced it, these aggregates are not created for the country-region sample.

5. The exact survey question is worded as follows: "In the past two years, did this establishment have a dispute with clients over payments owed to it in which the establishment had to engage a third party, such as arbiters, collecting agency, or judicial system?" The indicator of court use comes from the following survey question: "In reference to this payment dispute, was the court system used to resolve it?" The wording of the survey questionnaire assumes only one dispute; how a firm would reply if it had more than one dispute and some of them were resolved in court and some were not is not clear.

6. In the case of courts, weights are not used. Instead, the analysis uses sample averages. Recall from chapter 2 that this method is equivalent to the instrumental variable estimation using the regional average as the instrument.

7. In an attempt to improve this measure, adjusted sales were constructed as follows: for loans issued three or more years in the past, sales from three years ago were used; for loans issued two years in the past, the average sales (that is, the average of current sales and sales three years ago) were used; and for loans issued in the current year or the previous year, current sales were used. This measure has more missing data relative to using current sales. Both measures (using the adjusted sales or current sales) produce similar results.

8. Recall from chapter 2 that if the sample is stratified, the sample average will provide an inconsistent estimate of the mean.

9. The literature studying whether entrepreneurs' financial constraints vary across demographic groups, such as race, ethnicity, and gender, has been growing.

Overall, the results for gender discrimination in access to finance are mixed, but the evidence suggests that women are relatively more credit constrained than men in developing countries. For a review of this literature, see Muravyev, Schäfer, and Talavera (2007), who use Enterprise Survey data to show a gender gap in a sample of Western European countries and transition economies of Eastern Europe.

10. A possible caveat is that the variables that measure firm size and export status could also be capturing firm productivity, which is likely to be correlated with access to credit.

11. Firms with access to finance could potentially have more disputes with their clients because they are more likely to extend trade credit to their clients (that is, accounts receivable). However, here the measures of court use are calculated among only the firms that have had a dispute with their clients. Among those firms, it is not clear why access to finance might lead to a higher proportion of court use.

12. Surprisingly, no correlation exists on the country level of GDP per capita and Internet use, so this measure does not seem to capture the overall level of development.

13. Note, however, that the lack of significance could be attributable to the small size of the sample.

14. This finding is simply a correlation. One can argue that firms that need to obtain bank financing are more likely to register, and the converse argument is also possible—those that are registered may have an easier time accessing finance. These data do not allow the correlation to be disentangled. However, lack of correlation suggests that no relationship exists.

References

Beck, T., A. Demirgüç-Kunt, and R. Levine. 2003. "Law, Endowments, and Finance." *Journal of Financial Economics* 70 (2): 137–81.

———. 2005. "Law and Firms' Access to Finance." *American Law and Economics Review* 7 (1): 211–52.

Beck, T., R. Levine, and N. Loayza. 2000. "Finance and the Sources of Growth." *Journal of Financial Economics* 58 (1–2): 261–300.

La Porta, R., F. Lopez-de-Silanes, A. Shleifer, and R. Vishny. 1997. "Legal Determinants of External Finance." *Journal of Finance* 52 (3): 1131–50.

———. 1998. "Law and Finance." *Journal of Political Economy* 106 (6): 1113–55.

Laeven, L. and C. Woodruff. 2007. "The Quality of the Legal System, Firm Ownership, and Firm Size." Review of Economics and Statistics, forthcoming.

Loayza, N., P. Fajnzylber, and C. Calderón. 2005. *Economic Growth in Latin America and the Caribbean: Stylized Facts, Explanations, and Forecasts.* Washington, DC: World Bank.

Muravyev, A., D. Schäfer, and O. Talavera. 2007. "Entrepreneurs' Gender and Financial Constraints: Evidence from International Data." Discussion Paper 706, DIW Berlin, German Institute for Economic Research, Berlin. http://www.diw.de/documents/publikationen/73/60165/dp706.pdf.

World Bank. 2007. *World Development Indicators 2007.* Washington, DC: World Bank.

6

Product Innovation: The Roles of Research and Development Expenditures and the Investment Climate

Daniel Lederman

A model of firm innovation illustrates the effects of the threat of imitation and product varieties on a representative firm's decision to spend resources to produce new product varieties. The model motivates two empirical questions: Is research and development (R&D) partially correlated with firms' propensity to introduce new products or product innovation in developing countries? Do the national investment climate and trade policies affect firms' propensity for product innovation? Although the study does not identify causal effects from R&D (or other firm-level characteristics such as export status) and product innovation, the econometric evidence suggests that the answer is yes to both questions, but the investment climate affects product innovation in a manner that is consistent with the presence of market failures and state capture. Also, national trade policy distortions appear to reduce the probability of product innovation.

The author gratefully acknowledges the impeccable research assistance provided by Daniel Chodos and Javier Cravino. Two anonymous referees provided insightful comments on an earlier version of this chapter. I had numerous helpful discussions with Pablo Fajnzylber, J. Luis Guasch, J. Humberto López, and Verónica Alaimo. Mary Hayworth and Alvaro González also provided important written comments on a preliminary draft.

Innovation is so widely recognized as a key driver of economic growth that it is almost a cliché to say so.[1] In spite of the extensive literature on the importance of expenditures in research and development and science and technology policy to innovation, the distinction between adoption and invention in developing countries should lead us to explore numerous other areas that may pose barriers to the emergence of innovative firms. Emerging literature on what can be called *product innovation* focuses on the introduction of new products by firms. Hausmann and Rodrik (2003), for example, present a theoretical framework where market failures affecting the introduction of new export products in developing countries might be more severe than those affecting innovation in developed countries, because in the latter most innovations can be patented, thus providing at least a partial institutional solution to the appropriability problem that inhibits private sector innovation. In developing countries, where most innovations are probably not patentable, other policy instruments would need to be devised to stimulate private sector investments in product innovation. Related theoretical literature has emphasized the role of entrepreneurship in commercializing research outputs, which are then reflected in the introduction of new products (Michelacci 2003).

Even in the context of high-income countries, the determinants of product innovation across firms might be different from those of patentable innovation. Criscuolo, Haskel, and Slaughter (2005) find in a panel of firms from the United Kingdom that the correlates of patents and product innovation are different, particularly with respect to the role played by links between firms and universities, the latter being more important for patentable innovations. Another example is the study by Aghion and others (2006) that found that the response of U.K. firms (measured by productivity changes and patenting) to increased competition caused by the regulatory reforms of the Thatcher government was different across firms, depending on their distance to the technological frontier (proxied by the productivity gap with respect to the most product firms in each industry). Yet much is left to learn about the empirical correlates of product innovation in developing countries.

This chapter examines the empirical determinants of firm-level innovation in a large sample of manufacturing firms, covering 36 to 60 developing countries and eight manufacturing industries and totaling thousands of firms, depending on the empirical model. More specifically, the chapter addresses two questions: First, is there evidence of market failures that would justify government involvement to raise private sector investments in product innovation? In the presence of market failures, aspects of the investment climate associated with the extent of market competition can have unexpected effects on the private firms' propensity to innovate, especially among firms that are farthest from the global technological frontier. For instance, regulatory reforms, as in the United Kingdom during the Thatcher era, might reduce private sector innovation as the enhanced entry of firms raises the prospects of imitation, thus leading entrepreneurs to reduce their innovation expenditures. Second, is R&D investment correlated with product innovation in firms in developing countries? If so, the *D* in R&D—investments in product development—might be an important correlate of the propensity to innovate by firms in developing countries even when such innovations are not patentable.

The evidence discussed herein, which is motivated by a simple model of firm behavior with respect to product innovation, suggests that market failures are empirically noticeable. Thus, regulatory reforms can be beneficial for enhancing the diffusion of ideas and technology across firms and therefore for enhancing productivity growth, but they are not enough to stimulate product innovation. Also, the study finds that R&D expenditures, which are mismeasured in the firm data, are highly correlated with the propensity for product innovation by firms in developing countries, although the estimates do not prove that there is a causal effect. Nevertheless, the main policy implication from these findings is that in the context of reforms that improve the investment climate, the public sector plays an important role in stimulating private R&D expenditures associated with product innovation, even in poor developing countries.

The rest of the chapter is organized as follows. The next section briefly presents a model of a representative firm's decision to spend resources for product innovation. The section that follows presents the data. The chapter then focuses on the partial correlation between firm-level R&D expenditures and product innovation. The penultimate section discusses the econometric strategy and presents the results concerning the role of the investment climate in determining firms' propensity for product innovation. The final section summarizes the main findings.

A Model of Product Innovation

A broad literature depicts structural models that link market structure and competition to agents' decisions to invest in products and product innovation. A fully developed structural dynamic model goes beyond the scope of this chapter. Instead it follows Klette and Kortum (2004) by modeling firms' innovation behavior in terms of an innovation production function with product varieties, with dynamics modeled explicitly only by analyzing the present value of profits derived from a representative firm's product varieties. A discussion of the model follows its presentation.

The Model

Let the innovation production function $I(.)$ depend on R&D expenditures, R, and knowledge capital embodied in the number of product varieties, n, produced by a representative firm:

$$I = g(R, n) \tag{6.1}$$

If both research expenditures and product varieties (current and in the past) were observed, one could estimate an empirical counterpart of this equation directly. These variables are usually not observed in firm data.

The corresponding research cost function, $C(.)$, can be written as follows:

$$R = C(I,n) = n \bullet c\left(\frac{I}{n}\right) \tag{6.2}$$

This equation can be interpreted as the reverse function of equation 6.1. Again, it could be estimated only if product varieties were observed, and additional assumptions are thus required to find an empirical counterpart. Standard assumptions about diminishing returns to scale in the form of $g(.)$ and $c(.)$ can be used, but they are irrelevant for the present discussion. This finding is interesting as one does not need to rely on increasing returns to analyze the determinants of product innovation. Equation 6.2 simply states that the total cost of research for product innovation is the product of the number of varieties times the research cost intensity function, $c(.)$, of each product variety.[2] But one does need to introduce mechanisms through which a firm interacts with the market and competitors.

Under the assumptions that the price of each variety is exogenous and that each firm faces an exogenous probability that one of its product varieties will become obsolete or be replaced in the market by a competitor's newer or superior substitute product, the firm's *expected present value* of the firm's profit streams at any point in time, $E(\pi)$ can be written as follows:

$$E(\pi) = \frac{n}{1+r} \bullet \left[(1-\delta) \bullet \bar{P} - c\left(\frac{I}{n}\right)\right], \tag{6.3}$$

where $\bar{P}$ is *current operating profits* per product.[3] Also, $0 \le \delta \le 1$ represents the permanent hazard rate associated with losing any number of product varieties at any point in time, which would be associated with an expected loss of operating profits. Note that expected costs of research or research intensity per product is unaffected by the hazard rate.[4] The discount rate is represented by r. For the firm to incur further research costs, the expected present value of profits would have to be larger than zero, and the corresponding research cost intensity of the firm in the positive present value of profits state is

$$c\left(\frac{I}{n}\right) \le (1-\delta) \bullet \bar{P}. \tag{6.4}$$

Market prices for the firm's varieties are consequently expected to be positively correlated with research cost intensity, as current operating profits rise with the average price of a firm's varieties. But prices of inputs implicit in current operating profits per variety would obviously reduce the incentives to invest in product innovation. Unlike Hausmann and Rodrik (2003), the appropriability problem does not affect prices, but rather the probability of losing varieties through the instantaneous hazard rate. To the extent that the discount rate is common to the current profits per variety and research investments, it becomes immaterial and it is not present in equation 6.4.

If exogenous demand shifts or policy changes affect prices, innovation expenditures of firms as a share of sales would also depend on the probability of future imitation and on the number of varieties currently produced by the firm. R&D is observed as a share of sales in firm data, but probably with some measurement error. Proxies for market conditions that are likely to be correlated with the average (relative) price of the firm's varieties, such as the growth of manufacturing value added, can also be used to capture the effect of market prices. The probability of entry can be thought to be affected by policies, especially the regulatory environment, as suggested by Aghion and others (2006).

Discussion

The model is quite tractable and intuitive, but it does open the door to many questions of relevance for the empirical work. Before discussing the empirical strategy, it is worth highlighting that the positive-profit condition in equation 6.4 does not imply any particular direction of causality. It is nothing more than an accounting identity. To the extent that the investment climate and policies are beyond the control of any given firm, these types of factors could influence the arguments in the model and thus exogenously affect product innovation decisions by firms. This issue will be discussed further later.

Although the empirics discussed in the following sections are done with cross-sections of firms, most of the interesting questions are related to dynamics. First, it has already shown that the predictions of the model are unaffected by the discount rate, as long as the rate is the same for current operating profits and for research costs, and as long as all firms face the same opportunity costs of research capital investments. Thus, one potential weakness of the model is that if there is uncertainty about a firm's research cost intensity function, then a risk premium could apply to that portion of the expected present value of profits function. This risk premium would inevitably lead to a discussion about the role of risk capital markets and other interesting policy issues related to financial markets and their potentially differential effects on the present value of current operating profits and innovation decisions for producing new varieties in the future. This discussion is an area for future research.

Second, how would the firm respond when market demand for (and the relative price of) its product varieties fall? One response would be to reduce research cost intensity, but another would be to increase research so as to enhance the chances of raising the number of varieties. The latter would be a retooling strategy, whereas the former could be called a cost-reduction strategy. Neither strategy is analyzed here, but the point is that either option could be viable depending on an unspecified production function. One need only assume that firms' overall production function (as opposed to the innovation function analyzed here) is positive with respect to $I(.)$.

Third, would the predictions of the model change if the probability of imitation is endogenous with respect to firms' number of varieties or research costs? Probably not, because any plausible strategic game among firms that would need to be modeled would not change the signs of the predictions. What would result from such a modeling approach is an optimal dynamic path for the firm in terms of different combinations of research cost intensity changes and number of varieties, rather than the effect of the probability of imitation imposed by other firms' strategic behavior.

Thus far, the discussion has been interpreting research cost intensity as referring strictly to R&D expenditures. Because there is substantial literature on international technology diffusion (for example, Keller 2004), it is worth asking whether this model would apply to other forms of innovation expenditures. The answer is yes, as the model does not have sufficient structure to distinguish between innovation expenditures to import capital goods or licensing payments to use foreign technologies. Some of the empirical exercises presented later in this chapter use data on R&D as well as licensing payments as proxies for research effort.

The simplicity of this setup, however, is attractive for empirical analysis in spite of the open questions already discussed or many others.[5] An important advantage is that it explicitly models the direct (equation 6.1) and the reverse (equation 6.4) models of innovation expenditures. The following section presents the data that are used to explore the partial correlation between firms' R&D as a share of sales—a proxy for research cost intensity when product prices are exogenous—and firms' propensity to introduce a new product in developing countries, as well as to assess the role of the investment climate. The reverse model turns out to be an important tool to estimate the true partial correlation between product innovation and research cost intensity.

Data

This section first discusses the data sources and definitions. Then it presents some descriptive statistics of relevance for the empirical analyses that follow.

Data Definitions and Sources

The present study characterizes the role of the investment climate within which firms operate and the ways this climate affects product innovation.

It uses data from the World Bank's numerous Enterprise Surveys (ESs) and Business Environment and Enterprise Performance Surveys (BEEPSs). There is substantial overlap between the ES and BEEPS questionnaires, but some differences do exist in their sampling approaches. The ESs tend to focus on manufacturing firms; the BEEPSs are drawn from a broad range of economic activities, including services (actually the BEEPS database is slightly skewed toward services firms). In this study, the coverage of the BEEPS data is restricted to firms in the manufacturing sectors.

Three sets of variables are used in the regression analyses that follow—namely, firm-, sector-, and country-level variables. The first set includes a product innovation proxy that is also a dependent variable: the introduction of a new product. The surveys asked managers whether the firm had introduced a new product during the past two years. Hence, the dependent variable is dichotomous.

Regarding explanatory variables, firm characteristics that may affect a firm's proclivity to innovate include firm size, measured by the natural logarithm of the average number of permanent and temporary workers and its squared term (to test for a nonlinear relationship); a firm's exporter status, measured by a dummy variable equal to 1 when a firm exports at least 10 percent of its sales; firm ownership, measured by a dummy variable equal to 1 for foreign ownership (when more than 1 percent of assets of the firm are owned by foreigners); and capacity utilization, measured as the average utilization of the firm's productive capacity over the year preceding the survey. The surveys also provide information about the value of R&D expenditures and firm sales. From those data, the share of R&D in sales is calculated. Because the literature on innovation has paid much attention to the adoption of foreign technologies, the study also uses data derived from a question in the surveys that asked managers whether the firm had paid licensing fees during the past two years. This variable is also dichotomous.

Sector-level variables include information on trade policies—namely, a composite index of the average applied tariffs and its standard deviation. The index was estimated as the first principal component derived from factor analysis. The other trade policy indicator measure at the industry level is the share of tariff lines within each industry that faces one of the so-called core nontariff barriers. These data were taken from Nicita and Olarreaga (2006).

Country-level explanatory variables capture various aspects of the investment climate besides trade policies. They include an index of infrastructure coverage from World Bank (2007), institutional quality (from Kaufmann, Kraay, and Mastruzzi 2005), and real manufacturing gross domestic product (GDP) growth (also from World Bank 2007). Some models also include the level of development (GDP per capita from the Center for International Comparisons of Production, Income, and Prices 2007). An important explanatory variable for the analysis is a regulatory index capturing the ease of entry, which was calculated from data from the World Bank's Doing Business database.[6] Principal components analysis is used to calculate a composite index on infrastructure coverage (including paved roads per square kilometer and telephone lines per capita); the institutional index (including corruption, political stability, and rule of law); and the regulatory index (including difficulty of firing index, difficulty of hiring index, and days for starting a business). The analysis also uses patent-counts data from Lederman and Saenz (2005)—namely, the sum (stock) of utility patents granted to researchers in each country from 1963 to 2000 by the U.S. Patent and Trademark Office per person. The latter provides a measure of the density of innovative ideas available to firms operating in each country.

Some studies, including Criscuolo, Haskel, and Slaughter (2005) and other chapters in this volume also treat explanatory variables measured at a higher level of aggregation than the firm level as exogenous factors, but these variables are measured with data from the firm surveys themselves. The approach here is different in this regard, because objective data from other sources are used. As discussed elsewhere in this volume, the use of aggregate variables derived from the same data set as the firm data can be assumed to be exogenous only under certain conditions; namely, firms' deviations from the average must be orthogonal to the average and normally distributed with an expected value of zero. One need not make any assumptions in this regard because the data are objectively measured at the country level from data from other sources. The disadvantage of this approach is that there are fewer degrees of freedom to estimate the relevant coefficients of the variables measure at the national level, which is limited by the number of countries.

Missing data inevitably introduce ambiguity into the inferences that can be drawn from a study, so another caveat is in order. This section, as well as the regression analyses, relies on variables that were taken from firm survey questions that are straightforward and unambiguous. That is, the question of whether a firm introduced a new product in the previous two years is straightforward. Therefore, it is safe to assume that firms that did not answer this question had not, in fact, introduced a new product. Although this change in the data is marginal, more realistic estimates of the share of firms by country that introduced new products are obtained. For example, the percentage of firms reporting a new product in China changes from 25 percent to 15 percent for all firms, which is a more reasonable share. In other countries, such as Turkey, there are no missing values. The data from the Latin American and Caribbean countries are a mixed bag, but the same procedure was applied to all. R&D/sales and licensing payments are likely to be measured with error, and this issue is discussed in the context of the econometric methodology in the section titled "Is R&D Related to Product Innovation?"

Descriptive Statistics

Table 6.1 presents some descriptive statistics for a sample of 36 countries, which covers the sample of countries used in the econometric analysis discussed in the section titled "The Role of the Investment Climate." The sample used for the analyses of the section titled "Is R&D Related to Product Innovation?" is larger, because estimations of the partial correlation between R&D and product innovation use country dummies to control for any country-level characteristic rather than specific aspects of the business environment. Hence, the sample was restricted because of the availability of data on the other country-level determinants of product innovation discussed previously. The following paragraphs focus on the restricted sample because it poses some issues about the representativeness of the sample of firms among developing countries.

The sample includes six countries that are high-income countries: Germany (including the territory of the German Democratic Republic after reunification), Greece, Ireland, the Republic of Korea, Portugal, and Spain. It includes 13 countries from Latin America and the Caribbean, 9 from Eastern Europe and Central Asia, 4 from East Asia and the Pacific (including China), and 3 from Sub-Saharan Africa, plus the Arab Republic of Egypt. Clearly, this sample, which is used for econometric analysis, is not representative across all regions of the world. However, the sample of firms might be representative of manufacturing firms from around the world, especially from developing countries. Because this assumption might not be true, some of the relevant regressions use weights that are based on each country's labor force (that is, the population age 15 to 64 years). This approach is reasonable if the number of firms from each country is proportional to the labor force in each.

Regarding the incidence of firms innovating through the introduction of a new product, the data show a wide range of country experiences, ranging from 15 percent of firms in the Arab Republic of Egypt and China to 75 percent in Argentina. It is noteworthy that the percentages for the richer countries in the sample are not above the overall sample average of 43 percent. But the average for Latin America and the Caribbean is above the sample average.

In most countries, a large share of firms that reported new products also report R&D expenditures. In the total sample, 60 percent of firms with product innovation also report R&D, whereas only 15 percent of noninnovative firms report some R&D expenditures. This pattern holds for most countries individually for R&D, licensing, export status, and foreign ownership. China is the only exception: there, the percentage of noninnovative firms that report R&D expenditures, licensing payments, exporting, and foreign ownership is higher than among the innovative firms.[7] Although the high correlation between innovation and the other

Table 6.1 New Product versus Noninnovative Firms (Percentage of Firms with Key Characteristics) and Trade Indicators

Country	Percentage of firms reporting a new product (%)	Made R&D expenditures		Paid for licensed technology from foreign firms		Exported in previous years		Foreign ownership		Trade variables		
		Firms with a new product (%)	Other firms (%)	Firms with a new product (%)	Other firms (%)	Firms with a new product (%)	Other firms (%)	Firms with a new product (%)	Other firms (%)	Weighted average applied tariff rate (%)	Mean standard deviation of the applied tariff (%)	Mean of percentage of tariff lines with core NTBs (%)
Argentina	75	88	17	83	10	86	19	78	9	15.1	5.4	29.47
Bolivia	43	73	7	85	1	83	16	49	7	9.4	1.3	2.64
Brazil	68	76	33	76	5	68	18	76	4	16.1	4.8	14.87
Chile	45	65	11	56	14	55	25	51	14	8.8	0.6	5.67
China	15	22	38	0	6	11	27	11	24	15.0	7.3	9.93
Colombia	69	81	26	76	5	77	17	79	2	16.0	3.6	28.63
Costa Rica	53	70	7	65	24	71	15	67	6	8.9	6.3	0.57
Czech Republic	42	59	14	—	—	59	38	68	9	8.0	4.8	2.13
Ecuador	52	60	33	51	24	60	71	50	13	14.5	3.7	16.70

(continued)

Table 6.1 New Product versus Noninnovative Firms (Percentage of Firms with Key Characteristics) and Trade Indicators (continued)

| Country | Percentage of firms reporting a new product (%) | Made R&D expenditures | | Paid for licensed technology from foreign firms | | Exported in previous years | | Foreign ownership | | Trade variables | | |
		Firms with a new product (%)	Other firms (%)	Firms with a new product (%)	Other firms (%)	Firms with a new product (%)	Other firms (%)	Firms with a new product (%)	Other firms (%)	Weighted average applied tariff rate (%)	Mean standard deviation of the applied tariff (%)	Mean of percentage of tariff lines with core NTBs (%)
Egypt, Arab Rep. of	15	35	6	37	7	35	15	26	3	32.2	41.8	6.37
El Salvador	62	78	10	69	11	65	34	68	7	11.8	6.6	19.81
Germany	35	51	35	—	—	47	39	55	13	4.7	5.2	14.59
Greece	43	81	7	—	—	65	20	17	9	5.2	5.6	18.28
Guatemala	54	66	27	62	16	59	30	50	10	13.4	5.8	0.20
Honduras	47	69	7	62	11	48	33	45	16	13.0	6.4	0.09
Hungary	34	55	8	—	—	44	35	42	19	15.1	5.7	14.11
Indonesia	37	—	—	57	12	46	33	53	12	12.7	9.4	4.29
Ireland	50	73	21	—	—	68	29	68	11	3.2	3.6	10.35

(continued)

Table 6.1 New Product versus Noninnovative Firms (Percentage of Firms with Key Characteristics) and Trade Indicators (continued)

Country	Percentage of firms reporting a new product (%)	Made R&D expenditures		Paid for licensed technology from foreign firms		Exported in previous years		Foreign ownership		Trade variables		
		Firms with a new product (%)	Other firms (%)	Firms with a new product (%)	Other firms (%)	Firms with a new product (%)	Other firms (%)	Firms with a new product (%)	Other firms (%)	Weighted average applied tariff rate (%)	Mean standard deviation of the applied tariff (%)	Mean of percentage of tariff lines with core NTBs (%)
Korea, Rep. of	**46**	**72**	**18**	—	—	**56**	**31**	**72**	**8**	**8.3**	**3.4**	**0.06**
Latvia	47	33	6	—	—	55	45	50	39	5.5	4.2	6.10
Lithuania	46	90	1	45	14	59	35	54	14	6.3	6.9	1.91
Mauritius	49	61	28	64	15	52	53	33	13	30.1	22.7	3.15
Mexico	34	76	6	85	2	68	6	53	6	16.5	8.2	23.92
Peru	31	93	2	95	0	80	36	38	9	15.2	1.8	8.73
Philippines	47	61	15	63	11	46	36	57	19	14.9	5.4	0.61
Poland	45	57	10	—	—	57	23	67	4	26.0	16.6	10.78
Portugal	**28**	**51**	**18**	—	—	**35**	**43**	**43**	**13**	**4.1**	**4.1**	**21.58**

(continued)

Table 6.1 New Product versus Noninnovative Firms (Percentage of Firms with Key Characteristics) and Trade Indicators (continued)

Country	Percentage of firms reporting a new product (%)	Made R&D expenditures		Paid for licensed technology from foreign firms		Exported in previous years		Foreign ownership		Trade variables		
		Firms with a new product (%)	Other firms (%)	Firms with a new product (%)	Other firms (%)	Firms with a new product (%)	Other firms (%)	Firms with a new product (%)	Other firms (%)	Weighted average applied tariff rate (%)	Mean standard deviation of the applied tariff (%)	Mean of percentage of tariff lines with core NTBs (%)
Romania	37	48	7	—	—	47	23	48	12	22.7	12.5	17.64
Slovenia	38	41	34	—	—	41	78	36	28	7.3	5.4	5.03
South Africa	68	81	30	76	17	71	41	65	20	9.5	9.1	4.78
Spain	**43**	**64**	**18**	—	—	**65**	**21**	**60**	**8**	**3.5**	**3.9**	**12.56**
Tanzania	34	76	6	46	11	50	8	52	12	18.7	8.9	0.12
Thailand	50	62	17	—	—	55	51	64	19	19.3	11.5	0.47
Turkey	36	51	12	48	11	43	49	47	5	10.0	9.1	1.04
Ukraine	65	94	1	—	—	80	17	71	13	11.2	5.0	0.01
Uruguay	67	86	12	90	3	65	34	71	10	13.3	4.9	9.56

(continued)

Table 6.1 New Product versus Noninnovative Firms (Percentage of Firms with Key Characteristics) and Trade Indicators *(continued)*

Country	Percentage of firms reporting a new product (%)	Made R&D expenditures		Paid for licensed technology from foreign firms		Exported in previous years		Foreign ownership		Trade variables		
		Firms with a new product (%)	Other firms (%)	Firms with a new product (%)	Other firms (%)	Firms with a new product (%)	Other firms (%)	Firms with a new product (%)	Other firms (%)	Weighted average applied tariff rate (%)	Mean standard deviation of the applied tariff (%)	Mean of percentage of tariff lines with core NTBs (%)
Latin American and the Caribbean average[a]	54	75	15	73	10	68	27	59	9	13.2	4.6	12.37
Total	43	60	17	60	6	52	29	47	12	14.9	8.4	9.26

Source: World Bank Investment Climate surveys; Business Environment and Enterprise Performance surveys; Nicita and Olarreaga 2006.
Note: — = not available.
a. Average of percentages of Argentina, Bolivia, Brazil, Chile, Colombia, Costa Rica, Ecuador, El Salvador, Guatemala, Honduras, Mexico, Peru, and Uruguay.

firm characteristics is expected, it is clear that identifying the partial cor-relations between the propensity to introduce a new product and the other firm characteristics is important because high correlations among all the firm-level characteristics are also expected.

There is no clear relationship between trade policies and the share of innovative firms across countries, however. For example, Argentina appears with 75 percent of firms being innovative, but it also uses numer-ous nontariff barriers (NTBs) covering, on average across the eight manu-facturing sectors, slightly more than 29 percent of its tariff lines. In con-trast, Bolivia has a low NTB coverage rate of about 3 percent, but only 43 percent of firms reported a product innovation. Hence, it is possible that trade policy has little to do with product innovation, but econometric estimations might help to clarify this potential link between innovation and trade policy by controlling for other factors that might be correlated with both sets of variables.

Is R&D Related to Product Innovation?

To answer this question, the study estimated reduced-form models of product innovation but also considered the possibility that R&D expendi-tures and perhaps the sales variables that were recorded in the firm surveys are measured with error. If they are, the standard direct regression model with product innovation as the dependent variable and the R&D/sales variable (the proxy for research cost intensity derived from the theoretical model) might be biased, possibly suffering from attenuation bias if the measurement error is random.

Econometric Strategy

Because of the dichotomous nature of the variable of interest, the direct empirical model of product innovation can be written as:

$$P(y_{isc} = 1 \mid X_{isc}, X_{sc}, X_c) = \Phi(\beta' X_{ics} + \alpha' X_{sc} + \delta' X_c + \varepsilon_{isc} + \varepsilon_c), \qquad (6.5)$$

where P is the probability of observing a value of one for product inno-vation, y. Subscript i represents firms, s represents manufacturing sec-tors, and c represents countries. Xs represent matrices of the relevant explanatory variables measured at the three levels of aggregation (firms, sectors, and countries). The βs, αs, and δs are the parameters to be estimated with a probit estimator, which assumes a standard normal dis-tribution of the relevant parameters with respect to the latent threshold variable. Therefore, ε_{isc} is the standard white noise error. The results reported are robust to heteroskedasticity of regression errors clustered around the observations of each country, ε_c. This correction becomes particularly important for the estimation of the δ parameters associated with industry and country variables when the dependent variable is a microunit (see Moulton 1990).

In this case, the variable of interest is R&D/sales measured at the level of the firm. Because this exercise is not focused on uncovering industry- and country-level characteristics that might affect a firm's propensity to innovate, one can safely control for both by including industry/country dummy variables. Because the ESs for all countries were not implemented in the same year and global economic conditions might affect firm behavior, the study also controls for survey-year dummies.

To assess the influence of measurement, errors follow Leamer (1978, chapter 8) by estimating the reverse regression model. In this approach the dependent variable becomes R&D/sales and the dummy variable for product innovation becomes an explanatory variable. If the innovation variable is measured accurately, whereas the R&D/sales is measured with error, then the inverse of the estimated coefficient from the reverse regression is the true partial correlation between product innovation and R&D/sales.

A word of caution is required here.[8] The best firms are expected to have higher factor productivities and also other potentially positive attributes that are all potentially correlated with product innovation. Hence, one reasonable empirical strategy would be to control for total factor productivity in the estimation of the product innovation function. However, the study already deals with measurement error in one key variable, R&D/sales, and including estimates of firm productivity could add more noise than signaling to the estimated parameters of interest. Nevertheless, it is important to keep in mind that many of the firm-level variables included in the empirical models might reflect the quality and productivity of firms.

The same strategy can be followed for assessing the partial correlation between product innovations and licensing payments. In this case, however, the licensing variable is also dichotomous, but that does not mean that all firms accurately report whether they made some licensing payments.

Results

The results from the estimation of equation 6.5 with the appropriate set of dummy variables are presented under the first column of table 6.2. The table reports the marginal coefficients, or the elasticities calculated at the sample mean. The R&D/sales variable is not statistically significant, and the point estimate of the elasticity is negligible. Is this unsatisfactory result due to measurement errors?

The results from the reverse regression model are presented under the second column. In this case, the estimated tobit coefficient is highly significant. Furthermore, its inverse implies a rather large partial correlation between R&D/sales and product innovation. The elasticity of the probability of introducing a new product with respect to R&D/sales would be

Table 6.2 Are R&D Expenditures Related to Productive Innovation? Direct versus Reverse Regressions

	(1)	(2)	(3)	(4)	(5)	(6)	(7)
Dependent variables	New product	R&D/sales	R&D/sales	R&D/sales	New product	New product	Licensing
Estimation method	dprobit	tobit	dtobit	tobit	dprobit	dprobit	dprobit
R&D/sales	0.019 [0.71]						
Licensing					0.127 [3.41]**	0.124 [3.43]**	
New product		0.354 [2.32]*	0.202 [2.32]*	0.330 [2.34]*			0.038 [3.64]**
Employees (log) (firm-level)	0.084 [4.30]**	0.286 [2.62]**	1.404 [2.62]**	0.316 [2.76]**	0.085 [3.66]**	0.087 [5.35]**	0.05 [3.44]**
Employees^2 (log) (firm-level)	-0.003 [1.25]	-0.014 [2.50]*	-0.295 [2.50]*	-0.016 [.]	-0.005 [1.80]	-0.005 [2.00]*	-0.002 [1.40]
Foreign ownership (firm-level) (d)	0.002 [0.12]	0.005 [0.17]	0.003 [0.17]	0.022 [0.94]	-0.009 [0.54]	-0.016 [1.45]	0.124 [9.31]**
Capacity utilization (firm-level)	0.001 [1.74]	-0.002 [.]	-0.171 [.]	-0.002 [.]	0.001 [1.56]	0.001 [1.79]	0 [0.85]
Export status (dummy) (firm-level) (d)	0.081 [3.87]**	0.145 [2.01]*	0.032 [2.01]*	0.089 [1.78]	0.082 [3.74]**	0.078 [4.52]**	0.012 [1.70]

(continued)

Table 6.2 Are R&D Expenditures Related to Productive Innovation? Direct versus Reverse Regressions *(continued)*

	(1)	(2)	(3)	(4)	(5)	(6)	(7)
Dependent variables	New product	R&D/sales	R&D/sales	R&D/sales	New product	New product	Licensing
Estimation method	dprobit	tobit	dtobit	tobit	dprobit	dprobit	dprobit
Average years of education of employees (log)	0.025 [1.86]	0.004 [0.20]	0.005 [0.20]	0.002 [.]	0.03 [1.76]	0.024 [1.56]	0.014 [2.66]**
Observations	11,924	11,924	11,924	11,924	18,587	18,587	10,898
Countries	59	59	59	59	60	60	60
Censored observations	n.a.	3,876	3,876	3,876	n.a.	n.a.	n.a.
Industry and survey-year dummies	Yes	Yes	Yes	Yes	Yes	Yes	Yes
Country dummies	Yes	No	No	Yes	No	Yes	Yes

Source: Author's calculations.

Note: n.a. = not applicable; * = significant at the 5 percent level; ** = significant at the 1 percent level. Robust z statistics are in brackets; standard errors are clustered around countries. Country, industry, and survey-year dummies are not reported. Columns 1, 3, and 4 through 7 report marginal-effects coefficients (elasticities) calculated at the sample mean.

258

around 5, which is the inverse of the reverse regression elasticity shown in column 3. And the inclusion of country dummies (in column 4) does not affect the tobit coefficient.

Columns 5 through 7 report the corresponding estimates for the licensing variable. In this case, the direct regression results suggest that licensing is positively correlated with product innovation, with and without country dummies. Nevertheless, the implied marginal effect estimated with the reverse regression model (column 7) is significantly larger, thus suggesting that there might be measurement errors in the licensing variable as well. The next section turns to the analysis of the role of the investment climate. Because the evidence suggests that R&D/sales and the dichotomous licensing variable are both measured with error, these variables are not included in the analysis. The underlying assumption is that the introduction of a new product by firms reflects past research expenditures, as in Klette and Kortum (2004).

The Role of the Investment Climate

The estimation strategy is similar to the one pursued in the previous section, but there are additional complications.

Estimation Strategy

As mentioned, the study estimates partial correlations to help characterize the relationship between firm-level probabilities of introducing a new product (that is, a nonpatentable innovation) and firm, sector, and country characteristics. Although the estimated partial correlations among the firm-level variables could be due to endogeneity, the results concerning the sector- and country-level variables are less likely to be contaminated by this problem. That is, if each firm is too small to determine the level of a country's trade protection or its aggregate level of patents accumulated since 1963, then the corresponding empirical relationships are likely to be due to causal effects.

Within this framework, one may estimate the stylized model of the probability of introducing a new product by firms in equation 6.5. To deal with the issue of the sample, the study presents both nonweighted and weighted regressions.

To deal with one potential source of joint endogeneity of the firm- and sector-level variables and the probability of observing a product innovation, the study controls for correlated country effects. Woolridge (2005) proposed modeling fixed effects in panel data by including the over-time averages of the unit of analysis as additional explanatory variables.[9] In this case, there is no time dimension, but there is a country dimension. Hence, one can control for correlated country-specific effects by including the country averages of the variables that are measured at the firm and sector levels. These estimations are termed *quasi country fixed effects*.

Finally, it is worth noting that identifying the effects on firms' product innovation of the country-level variables that capture different aspects of the national investment climate might be difficult because of the expected correlation among the relevant variables. For example, countries with good infrastructure coverage can also be expected to have higher incomes per capita, higher innovation densities, and so forth. If the point estimates seem to be stable across various specifications and the country-level variables of interest are jointly statistically significant, one can find some comfort in these estimates. Hence, *F*-tests for the joint significance of the firm-, sector-, and country-level variables are also reported.

Results

Table 6.3 presents the regression results of the determinants of the probability of product innovation by incumbent firms. The first two columns contain the results from the baseline models. The first shows the results from the nonweighted model; the second has the weighted-regression results. The last four columns show the results with quasi country fixed effects, which, as mentioned above, are captured by the country-level averages of the firm- and sector-level variables. This approach allows distinction between variables that are associated with product innovation at the various levels of aggregation. The *p*-values of specification tests for the joint endogeneity of the three sets of variables (measured at the level of firm, sector, and country) appear in the bottom three rows.

Among the firm-level variables, the most robust results are associated with the size of the firm as captured by the number of employees (but not its squared term). This variable is highly significant and positive across all specifications. The magnitude of the coefficient is slightly lower in the weighted regressions, thus suggesting that scale is less important among the countries with the largest populations (for example, Brazil, China, and Indonesia). Interestingly, foreign ownership is always negative and significant in the weighted regressions, but it is also negative in all nonweighted estimations. This finding indicates that foreign-owned firms might not settle in developing countries to undertake product innovations, although it is likely that multinational corporations can produce goods that local firms do not produce. Export status is always statistically significant and positive in the nonweighted regressions, but not in the weighted estimates with quasi country fixed effects. In those estimations, however, the national share of exporting firms does appear positive and significant, thus suggesting the firms that operate in countries with numerous exporters tend to have a higher propensity to undertake product innovations.

Regarding the trade policy variables measured at the sector level, the import tariff index is negative and significant in the baseline regressions,

Table 6.3 The Role of the Investment Climate: Marginal Effects from Probit Estimations

	Baseline regressions			Quasi country fixed effects		
	(1)	(2)	(3)	(4)	(5)	(6)
	Nonweighted	Weighted	Nonweighted	Weighted	Nonweighted	Weighted
Employees (log) (firm-level)	0.085 [0.000]***	0.056 [0.002]***	0.084 [0.000]***	0.053 [0.000]***	0.085 [0.000]***	0.053 [0.000]***
Employees^2 (log) (firm-level)	-0.004 [0.016]**	0.000 [0.916]	-0.003 [0.041]**	0.001 [0.605]	-0.003 [0.038]**	0.001 [0.619]
Foreign ownership (firm-level)	-0.007 [0.719]	-0.022 [0.016]**	-0.014 [0.393]	-0.021 [0.008]***	-0.014 [0.397]	-0.021 [0.008]***
Capacity utilization (firm-level)	0.000 [0.442]	0.000 [0.001]***	0.000 [0.175]	0.000 [0.000]***	0.000 [0.170]	0.000 [0.000]***
Export status (dummy) (firm-level)	0.096 [0.000]***	0.021 [0.458]	0.057 [0.005]***	0.004 [0.827]	0.057 [0.005]***	0.004 [0.827]
Import tariff index (by sector)	-0.047 [0.094]*	-0.059 [0.043]**	0.005 [0.629]	0.011 [0.394]	0.004 [0.674]	0.011 [0.391]
NTB coverage (by sector)	-0.141 [0.176]	-0.093 [0.406]	-0.041 [0.506]	-0.045 [0.548]	-0.043 [0.491]	-0.045 [0.549]
GDP per capita in 2000 (log, PPP) (by country)					0.065 [0.477]	0.137 [0.395]

(continued)

261

Table 6.3 The Role of the Investment Climate: Marginal Effects from Probit Estimations (continued)

	Baseline regressions			Quasi country fixed effects		
	(1)	(2)	(3)	(4)	(5)	(6)
	Nonweighted	Weighted	Nonweighted	Weighted	Nonweighted	Weighted
Manufacturing GDP growth, 1998–2003 (by country)	-0.472 [0.272]	-1.019 [0.027]**	-0.376 [0.269]	-0.681 [0.177]	-0.398 [0.256]	-0.781 [0.109]
Stock of patents per worker, 1960–2000 (log) (by country)	0.051 [0.015]**	0.077 [0.001]***	0.026 [0.145]	0.018 [0.481]	0.022 [0.256]	0.007 [0.801]
Regulation index (by country)	0.114 [0.071]*	0.155 [0.000]***	0.111 [0.026]**	0.037 [0.411]	0.106 [0.035]**	0.035 [0.446]
Infrastructure index (by country)	-0.080 [0.376]	0.031 [0.886]	-0.086 [0.345]	-0.156 [0.203]	-0.128 [0.218]	-0.276 [0.179]
Institutional index (by country)	-0.023 [0.510]	-0.089 [0.094]*	-0.016 [0.583]	-0.066 [0.172]	-0.029 [0.452]	-0.075 [0.126]
Quasi country fixed effects						
Employees (log) (firm-level, country average)			0.219 [0.501]	0.150 [0.699]	0.187 [0.557]	0.074 [0.853]
Employees^2 (log) (firm-level, country average)			-0.048 [0.232]	-0.057 [0.224]	-0.046 [0.239]	-0.053 [0.260]
Foreign ownership (firm-level, country average)			0.098 [0.809]	0.410 [0.402]	0.283 [0.587]	0.939 [0.253]

(continued)

Table 6.3 The Role of the Investment Climate: Marginal Effects from Probit Estimations *(continued)*

| | Baseline regressions | | Quasi country fixed effects | | | |
	(1) Nonweighted	(2) Weighted	(3) Nonweighted	(4) Weighted	(5) Nonweighted	(6) Weighted
Capital utilization (firm-level, country average)	0.068		0.005 [0.481]	0.011 [0.170]	0.003 [0.645]	0.006 [0.484]
Export status (dummy) (firm-level, country average)			0.518 [0.042]**	0.934 [0.001]***	0.478 [0.078]*	0.938 [0.001]***
Import tariff index (by sector, country average)			−0.145 [0.061]*	−0.292 [0.007]***	−0.149 [0.054]*	−0.277 [0.019]**
NTB coverage (by sector, country average)			−0.262 [0.497]	0.615 [0.400]	−0.211 [0.584]	0.817 [0.276]
R-squared		0.096	0.086	0.110	0.087	0.110
Firms	18,390	18,390	18,390	18,390	18,390	18,390
Sectors	8	8	8	8	8	8
Countries	36	36	36	36	36	36
p-value: joint significance of firm-level variables	0.000	0.000	0.000	0.000	0.000	0.000

(continued)

Table 6.3 The Role of the Investment Climate: Marginal Effects from Probit Estimations *(continued)*

	Baseline regressions			Quasi country fixed effects		
	(1)	*(2)*	*(3)*	*(4)*	*(5)*	*(6)*
	Nonweighted	*Weighted*	*Nonweighted*	*Weighted*	*Nonweighted*	*Weighted*
p-value: joint significance of trade variables	0.092	0.054	0.681	0.662	0.705	0.66
p-value: joint significance of country-level variables	0.051	0.000	0.052	0.008	0.082	0.001

Source: Author's calculations.

Note: * = significant at the 10 percent level; ** = significant at the 5 percent level; *** = significant at the 1 percent level. Industry and survey-year dummies are not reported. Test of joint significance of country variables excludes GDP per capita and the quasi country fixed effects variables.

but it becomes nonsignificant and changes sign when the quasi country fixed effects are controlled for. But the country-average import tariff index is negative and significant. These results suggest that it is not the cross-sector variation in tariff policies that affects product innovation, but rather it is the cross-country variance that matters. The NTB coverage rate always appears with a negative sign, but it is never statistically different from zero. The test for joint significance of the trade policy variables does suggest that they are highly significant determinants of product innovation. Thus, one can conclude that trade policy distortions matter for product innovation in general, but the most relevant aspect is probably the use of tariffs, and countries (not sectors) with high import tariffs and tariff dispersion tend to have firms with lower propensities to undertake product innovations.

The country-level variables supposedly capture each country's investment climate. Unfortunately, very few variables appear to be statistically significant. The most robust result concerns the regulatory index. It appears with a positive sign and is statistically significant in all specifications except in the two weighted regressions with quasi country fixed effects. This result is consistent with the view that market failures affect the propensity of firms to invest in product innovation: As entry becomes more restricted by regulatory policies, the propensity of firms to introduce new products tends to rise. In terms of the theoretical model, the regulatory environment seems to affect the probability of imitation, thus reducing incentives for product innovation. The lack of significance of this variable in the weighted estimations with quasi country fixed effects is less worrisome when one looks at the test for the joint significance of the country-level variables. They are always jointly highly significant, as reflected in the low p-values of the test of the null of lack of significance at the bottom of table 6.3. Because one expects that all country variables are correlated, it is actually striking that the regulatory index appears significant in some specifications and consistently with a positive sign in all regressions.

Regarding the other national variables, manufacturing GDP growth, the density of patenting activity, and the institutional index always appear with the same signs. The infrastructure variable changes sign in one specification. The positive effect of patent density could be interpreted as indicating the presence of knowledge spillovers, whereby firms that have access to a higher density of commercial ideas tend to have higher propensities to innovate than firms in countries with lower innovation densities. The negative coefficient of manufacturing GDP growth might suggest that product innovation is countercyclical, thus supporting the view that firms tend to choose the retooling strategy during downturns, which is consistent with the Schumpeterian view of creative destruction. Finally, the negative coefficients on the institutional quality variable can be interpreted as an indication that firms that reside in countries where governance is dysfunctional can find mechanisms to capture the state in order to impose barriers to competition that might not be reflected in the trade and regulatory policy variables. Again, the discussion of the results pertaining to the national variables is worthwhile because they do seem to be jointly significant, even after controlling for quasi country fixed effects and the level of development. It is actually surprising that the investment climate variables appeared with consistently estimated signs, even when they do not appear to be individually statistically significant. These symptoms are typical of collinearity among the explanatory variables.

Conclusions

The theoretical model presented motivated empirical analyses of the determinants of product innovation by firms. Both market conditions and the threat of entry by competitors were shown to be theoretical predictors of the research cost intensity of firms, even when prices were exogenously determined by market or public policies conditions (including price distortions).

The empirical analyses of "Is R&D Related to Product Innovation?" suggested that in fact data from 60 countries, covering thousands of firms, supports the main prediction of the model: research cost intensity tends to be significantly associated with product innovation. The analysis also highlighted a potential pitfall in the firm data, as both R&D/sales and licensing seem to be measured with error, thus shedding some doubt on the usefulness of direct regression estimates of the innovation function.

The investment climate also seems to play an important role for product innovation, although this finding is quite clear only for the whole set of variables measured at the national level, and the partial coefficients of each variable did not appear to be particularly robust. Trade policy distortions seem to hamper product innovation. But the evidence also highlights market failures that hamper innovation. Of particular relevance in this regard were the results concerning the regulatory barriers to firm entry. Whereas deregulation is desirable to increase competition and knowledge diffusion, the results suggest that other policy instruments might be needed to stimulate product innovation, especially after deregulation and trade liberalization. Also, the results concerning the density of patent counts suggest that knowledge spillovers might also be important, and this variable is the least feeble of the country-level variables in terms of robustness.

From a policy perspective, it is also worth noting that product innovation seems to be countercyclical with respect to manufacturing GDP growth in a period of time that predates the implementation of the firm surveys. It might not be a stretch to put on the policy table that budgets of programs to stimulate product innovation need to be protected during downturns so as to prevent the demise of firms that could have survived through retooling in terms of product innovation. The latter might have social benefits that greatly exceed the private returns, because private agents can benefit from the knowledge embodied in the product innovations of their competitors.

Notes

1. Some studies reveal that much of the gap between rich and poor countries is caused not by differences in capital investment, but by technological progress. For example, according to Dollar and Wolff (1997) and Hall and Jones (1999), roughly half of cross-country differences in per capita income and growth are driven by differences in total factor productivity generally associated with technological progress. Easterly and Levine (2003) also argue that productivity differences explain the lion's share of global income differentials. To the extent that productivity is driven by both patentable and nonpatentable innovation, one can then infer that innovation has become an important component of the new growth agenda. Furthermore, empirical evidence shows that the rates of return to investments in R&D can be high (Jones and Williams 1998). At the firm level, Klette and Kortum (2004) provide an analytical framework for understanding widely recognized stylized facts linking productivity, firm size, R&D, and patenting across firms. The empirical literature on firm-level R&D, patenting, and productivity is enormous.

2. Klette and Kortum (2004) use the term *innovation intensity* for $I(n)/n$, where $I(.)$ is the innovation production function.

3. We are indebted to an insightful anonymous referee for suggesting this modeling approach.

4. It is tempting to model the hazard rate as $E(\pi) = n/(\delta + r) \bullet \left[\bar{P} - c(I/n) \right]$ but this approach would render both the discount rate and the hazard rate irrelevant in the firm's innovation decisions.

5. One such additional question is whether the average price index in the model should be a relative price, for example, with respect to the price of alternative varieties not produced by the firm. Working with relative prices that are also exogenously given does not change the analysis.

6. The World Bank's Doing Business database can be accessed at http://www.doingbusiness.org/.

7. The data for China is consistent with product-level export data that suggests that mainland China introduced comparatively few new export products from 1994 to 2003 (Klinger and Lederman 2006).

8. The author is grateful to an anonymous referee for highlighting this point about firm productivity and the endogeneity of our firm-level characteristics.

9. Besides being concerned about unobserved unit heterogeneity, Woolridge (2005) is also concerned about dynamics; the article is about dynamic probit models with fixed effects. The case here is simpler because it does not include dynamics. If it had dynamics to deal with the endogeneity of the lagged dependent variable, it would need to control for the initial value of the dependent variable.

References

Aghion, P., R. Blundell, R. Griffith, P. Howitt, and S. Prantl. 2006. "The Effects of Entry on Incumbent Innovation and Productivity." NBER Working Paper 12027, National Bureau of Economic Research, Cambridge, MA.

Center for International Comparisons of Production, Income, and Prices. 2007. *Penn World Table*. Philadelphia: University of Pennsylvania. http://pwt.econ. upenn.edu/.

Criscuolo, C., J. Haskel, and M. Slaughter. 2005. "Global Engagement and the Innovation Activities of Firms." NBER Working Paper 11479, National Bureau of Economic Research, Cambridge, MA.

Dollar, D., and E. N. Wolff. 1997. "Convergence of Industry Labor Productivity among Advanced Economies, 1963–1982." In *The Economics of Productivity*, ed. E. N. Wolff, vol.2, 39–48. Cheltenham, U.K.: Edward Elgar.

Easterly, W., and R. Levine. 2003. "Tropics, Germs, and Crops: How Endowment Influenced Economic Development." *Journal of Monetary Economics* 50 (1): 3–39.

Hall, R., and C. Jones. 1999. "Why Do Some Countries Produce So Much More Output per Worker Than Others?" *Quarterly Journal of Economics* 114 (1): 83–116.

Hausmann, R., and D. Rodrik. 2003. "Economic Development as Self-Discovery." *Journal of Development Economics* 72 (2): 603–33.

Jones, C., and J. Williams. 1998. "Measuring the Social Return to R&D." *Quarterly Journal of Economics* 113 (4): 1119–35.

Kaufmann, D., A. Kraay, and M. Mastruzzi. 2005. "Governance Matters IV: Governance Indicators for 1996–2004." World Bank, Washington, DC.

Keller, W. 2004. "International Technology Diffusion." *Journal of Economic Literature* 42 (3): 752–82,

Klette, T., and S. Kortum. 2004. "Innovating Firms and Aggregate Innovation." *Journal of Political Economy* 112 (5): 986–1018.

Klinger, B., and D. Lederman. 2006. "Diversification, Innovation, and Imitation inside the Global Technological Frontier," Policy Research Working Paper 3872, World Bank, Washington, DC.

Leamer, E. 1978. *Specification Searches: Ad Hoc Inference with Nonexperimental Data*. New York: John Wiley & Sons.

Lederman, D., and L. Saenz. 2005. "Innovation around the World, 1960–2000." Policy Research Working Paper 3774, World Bank, Washington, DC.

Michelacci, C. 2003. "Low Returns in R&D Due to the Lack of Entrepreneurial Skills." *Economic Journal* 113 (484): 207–25.

Moulton, B. 1990. "An Illustration of a Pitfall in Estimating the Effects of Aggregate Variables on Micro Units." *Review of Economics and Statistics* 72 (2): 334–38.

Nicita, A., and M. Olarreaga. 2006. "Trade, Production, and Protection 1976–2004." Policy Research Working Paper 2701, World Bank, Washington, DC.

Woolridge, J. 2005. "Simple Solutions to the Initial Conditions Problem in Dynamic, Nonlinear Panel Data Models with Unobserved Heterogeneity." *Journal of Applied Econometrics* 20 (1): 39–54.

World Bank. 2007. *World Development Indicators*. Washington, DC: World Bank.

7

Exporter Premiums

Carlos Casacuberta, Nestor Gandelman, Marcelo Olarreaga, Guido Porto, and Eliana Rubiano

Export firms are better: they are more productive and pay higher wages. These exporter premiums have two nonmutually exclusive explanations: either better firms become exporters (self-selection), or firms become better as they engage in exporting (learning by exporting). Regardless of whether exporter premiums are attributable to self-selection or learning by exporting, reorientation of economic activity toward the export sector will lead to higher growth. If such redirection is due to self-selection, reallocation of economic activity toward better firms will make the aggregate economy more productive. If learning by exporting is the main explanation for exporter premiums, then firms will become better the more they export. The policy implications are different depending on which channel is more relevant. The evidence surveyed in this chapter suggests that learning by exporting may be more likely in economies with a small domestic market, reinforcing the importance of unexploited economies of scales. Self-selection is much more generally observed.

Early empirical literature, starting in the 1970s, argues that exports lead to higher growth. Whether bivariate studies (Bhagwati 1978; Krueger 1978) or cross-country studies (Balassa 1985; Feder 1983), such literature generally concludes that a positive relationship exists between exports and growth. The more recent country case studies, which use modern time-series analysis to address some of the methodological problems associated with bivariate or cross-country analyses—for example, the fact that production functions may differ across different countries—are less unanimous in their conclusions and have trouble identifying the direction of causality (see Islam 1998).

This early literature suggested different channels through which exports can lead to higher growth. In the presence of underuse of existing capacities or factor unemployment, exports can generate greater capacity use and factor employment, leading to short-term growth. In countries with small domestic markets, increases in foreign demand can help take advantage of economies of scale. Higher standards in foreign markets and interactions with foreign buyers can bring technological progress and productivity gains and the need for a more skilled workforce (World Bank 1993). Although all these mechanisms can explain a positive link between exports and growth, this early literature was not able to disentangle which forces were at work. Its focus on aggregate or industry-level exports did not allow authors to examine the microdynamics involved. As a result, it generally failed to establish causality: whether exports lead to higher growth or growth leads to higher exports remained an unanswered question in this early literature.

More recently, an important empirical literature has developed that looks in detail at the microdeterminants of export activity at the firm level and their consequences (Bernard and Jensen 1995, 1999, 2004; Clerides, Lach, and Tybout 1998; see also Bigsten and others 2000; Hallward-Driemeier, Iarossi, and Sokoloff 2002; International Study Group on Exports and Productivity 2007; Van Biesebroeck 2003). A clear consensus emerged from this growing literature: exporting firms are better. They have higher productivity, hire more workers (particularly skilled workers), and pay them higher wages.

Using the Enterprise Surveys available for Latin American and Caribbean countries, this chapter estimated productivity and wage exporter premiums for each country and a pooled sample of all Latin American countries by running simple ordinary least squares (OLS) regressions of total factor productivity (TFP) and average wages on variables capturing firms' age, size (number of employees), foreign ownership, unique establishment, log of capital per worker, and region and industry dummies (country dummies were also included when running the pooled regression). The TFP model follows the analysis of chapter 2, where the dependent variable is value added, and capital per worker appears as an explanatory variable (see chapter 2 for additional details). The estimated coefficients on the exporter dummy and their standard errors in the TFP and wage regression in each country are reported in table 7.1.

Results by and large confirmed the idea that exporters are better. On the basis of point estimates, the analysis finds that in 14 of the 16 Latin American countries in the sample and in the pooled sample, a positive TFP exporter premium exists, signaling that exporters are more productive. Similarly, in 15 of the countries and in the pooled sample, a positive wage exporter premium exists, indicating that exporters pay higher wages.

Only about half these positive exporter premiums are statistically different from zero (8 in the case of TFP and 12 in the case of wages), which indicates they are not estimated very precisely. However, they tend to be very large. For Latin America and the Caribbean as a whole, the productivity exporter premium is about 40 percent, and exporters tend to pay wages that are 23 percent higher.

These large exporter premiums, however, which indicate that firms that export are much more productive and pay much higher wages to their workers, tell little about the direction of causality: do exporters become "good" firms, or do "good" firms become exporters?[1]

Table 7.1 Productivity and Wage Exporter
Premiums in Latin America and the Caribbean

Premium country	TFP	Log of wages
Latin America and the Caribbean	0.339*** [0.035]	0.203*** [0.026]
Argentina	0.597*** [0.111]	0.09 [0.074]
Bolivia	−0.353* [0.193]	0.084 [0.163]
Brazil	0.478*** [0.070]	0.274*** [0.054]
Chile	0.427*** [0.135]	0.262*** [0.090]
Colombia	0.304*** [0.083]	0.275*** [0.071]
Costa Rica	0.011 [0.009]	0.538*** [0.177]
Ecuador	0.091 [0.259]	0.017 [0.173]
El Salvador	0.357*** [0.126]	0.305*** [0.092]
Guatemala	0.153 [0.148]	0.347** [0.143]
Honduras	0.22 [0.163]	0.208* [0.126]
Mexico	0.001 [0.132]	0.124 [0.096]

(continued)

Table 7.1 Productivity and Wage Exporter
Premiums in Latin America and the Caribbean
(continued)

Premium country	TFP	Log of wages
Nicaragua	−0.02	−0.019
	[0.109]	[0.080]
Panama	0.024	0.257**
	[0.362]	[0.125]
Paraguay	0.485	0.052
	[0.297]	[0.179]
Peru	0.520***	0.297**
	[0.160]	[0.121]
Uruguay	0.678***	0.465***
	[0.185]	[0.105]

Source: Authors' calculations based on Enterprise Surveys data.
Note: * = significance at the 10 percent level; ** = significance
at the 5 percent level; *** = significance at the 1 percent level.
Standard errors are in brackets. An OLS regression is run for each
country, as well as a pooled regression labeled for Latin America
and the Caribbean. Only the coefficient on the exporter dummy is
reported. All regressions include as control variables firm-, region-,
and industry-level characteristics (see text for more details).

Under the first hypothesis, exporting improves productivity. The most
common explanation, known as "learning by exporting," is that exporters acquire information from foreign customers on how to improve the
product design, the manufacturing process, or the quality of the good
(Westphal, Rhee, and Pursell 1984).[2] Foreign demand also allows domestic firms—particularly in small countries—to take advantage of unexploited economies of scale.

Under the second hypothesis, the best firms self-select into export markets. One rationale for this self-selection is that important entry barriers
exist in export markets because of higher costs associated with selling in
foreign markets (transport, but also distribution, marketing, and even
production costs when firms need to adapt their product to foreign standards). Thus, only the more productive firms can enter foreign markets,
and the observed differences between exporters and nonexporters can
then be explained by preexisting differences.

These two hypotheses are obviously not mutually exclusive, but depending on which is the most important force, the policy implications can be
very different. On the one hand, export promotion activities, which are
quite common in Latin America, are often justified on the basis of the

learning-by-exporting explanation. On the other hand, the self-selection explanation would suggest that policy makers should focus their efforts on the internal determinants of productivity growth.

The existing literature offers no clear-cut answer regarding the relative strength of the self-selection hypothesis versus the learning-by-exporting hypothesis. By nature, this literature is country specific, and depending on the country examined, studies seem to reach different conclusions. This chapter's brief survey tries to unveil some patterns in the existing literature.

Regardless of whether exports cause firm-level productivity gains, exporters can boost growth through other channels. As mentioned earlier, another finding of the literature is that exporting firms hire more skilled workers and pay higher wages. As will be seen, however, the direction of causality in the existing literature is rarely explored. Higher wages or employment can simply reflect preexisting conditions in the industry (or firm) that may affect the decision to export, or confounding factors may affect wages and exports simultaneously, meaning that the wage premium should not be attributed to the export activity. An exception to this literature is a recent paper by Porto (2007), commissioned for this chapter. It carefully looks at the direction of causality in Argentina between exports, on the one hand, and wages and employment, on the other.

Exporting firms are also larger, and this characteristic implies more factor use, which can boost short-run growth in the presence of factor unemployment or capacity underuse. In another paper commissioned for this study, Casacuberta and Gandelman (2007) decompose the output differential between exporters and nonexporters in a small economy (Uruguay) into three determinants: TFP, factor use, and factor elasticity.[3]

The rest of the chapter is organized as follows. The next section reviews the existing evidence regarding the effect of exports on firm productivity and wages and examines some of the existing patterns in the literature. The chapter then explores in detail the direction of causality between exports and wages in Argentina and examines the determinants of the output differential between exporters and nonexporters in Uruguay. Finally, the concluding section offers some policy implications.

Exporter Premiums: What Is Known?

The now-common approach in examining differences in productivity or wages between exporters and nonexporters in the literature is to run a regression explaining changes in productivity or wages with a set of exporter dummies that captures different types of exporters and a set of control variables that measures firm characteristics (firm size, location, industry dummies, year/survey dummies, and the like). Three sets of exporter dummies are used in most studies (see Wagner 2005). The

first exporter dummy takes the value 1 when the firm has been exporting throughout. The second exporter dummy takes the value 1 if the firm
started exporting in the second year, and the third exporter dummy takes
the value 1 if the firm exported only the first year and then stopped. Firms
that do not export throughout serve as the reference category. A positive
value in the first exporter dummy indicates that exporters are more productive or pay higher wages than nonexporters. The self-selection hypothesis will be favored if the difference between the coefficients on the second
and the first exporter dummy is not too large, meaning that export starters
are as productive as those that have already been exporting (controlling
for quitters, which are captured by the third exporter dummy). Most studies use variants of this approach.[4] The first survey that follows concerns
the existing evidence regarding productivity premiums; then, the literature
on wage premiums is reviewed.

Productivity Premiums

For this study, 54 studies that looked at the productivity premium associated with export activity were surveyed.[5] In 86 percent of these studies,
exporters are found to be more productive than nonexporters. Most of
these studies—with rare exceptions (see, for example, the results for the
Republic of Korea in Aw, Chung, and Roberts 2000)—found evidence of
self-selection: good firms become exporters, suggesting that penetrating
foreign markets may require higher productivity. About 60 percent of the
studies test the learning-by-exporting hypothesis, but the evidence is mixed.
Half the studies found support for the learning-by-exporting hypothesis,
and the other half found no evidence of postexport entry differences in
productivity growth between exporter starters and nonexporters.

  Thus, the general messages coming from the literature are that exporters are indeed more productive that nonexporters, that firms do self-select
into the export market, but that exporting does not always improve productivity (or only does so half the time). These findings suggest that a lot
of heterogeneity exists across studies in terms of the learning-by-exporting
hypothesis and that this chapter may be able to take advantage of the
relatively homogeneous methodology used in the literature to try to disentangle in which types of countries exporting leads to productivity gains
at the firm level.

  A probit regression is run to disentangle this heterogeneity. In the regression, the explanatory variable is a dummy that takes the value 1 when the
study found that in a particular country exports cause productivity gains,
and 0 if the study found that exports did not cause productivity gains (any
study in which the question of causality was not addressed is excluded
from this regression). A regression is also run that explores in which types
of countries learning by exporting is more likely. The dummy is regressed
on country characteristics, such as the degree of trade openness of the

country, its level of development, its size, and different variables capturing the investment climate.

The intent is simply to illustrate the type of countries where causality running from exports to productivity is most likely to be found, but some priorities do exist. One would expect exports to be more likely to cause productivity increases in poorer countries with a smaller domestic market. Indeed, poorer countries tend to be further away from the technological frontier, and they have potentially much more to learn from foreign buyers.[6] Similarly, in small countries, firms may count on foreign demand to take advantage of unexploited economies of scale. Openness to trade and a good investment climate may have ambiguous signs. On the one hand, a better investment climate allows firms to take advantage of business opportunities more freely, but also it may become more difficult for exporters to appropriate these productivity gains when barriers to enter or exit are small. Obviously, this possibility does not necessarily mean that there are no productivity premiums or that exporting does not allow firms to become productive. The point is that it is difficult or impossible for the statistician to identify this effect if the benefits created by the exporter are easily captured by all other firms in the economy.

Table 7.2 reports results from these probit estimations. Each column is run with a different investment climate variable from the Doing Business reports. They were not all included simultaneously because they tend to be highly collinear, and the authors did not want to choose one to test for the robustness of the results.

The clear message of table 7.2 is that exporting is more likely to cause productivity premiums in small countries. This finding somehow gives more prominence to the economies-of-scale rationale for productivity premiums than to the knowledge-acquisition hypothesis, although this specification clearly does not allow disentanglement of these two forces.

Probably because of the conflicting forces, the level of development does not seem to be an important determinant of the causality between exports and productivity: poorer countries have much more to learn from foreign buyers, but absorbing this knowledge may be more difficult. The degree of trade openness is also always statistically insignificant. The investment climate variables give an ambiguous picture, but the only result that is statistically significant tends to suggest that a cumbersome business environment is not likely to help exporters take advantage of some of the potential benefits in foreign markets.

Finally, two important points should be kept in mind because the focus of this regional study is on the microdeterminants of aggregate growth. First, the determinants of self-selection remain an open question, and little work has been done to explain the sources of productivity growth before entry into the export market. As Yeaple (2005) argues, productivity is likely to be an endogenous decision, and trade opportunities may

Table 7.2 In Which Countries Does Exporting Lead
to Productivity Gains?

	Difficulty of entry procedures	Difficulty of closing a business	Difficulty in paying taxes	Difficulty of firing workers
Openness ([M + X] /GDP)	−0.47 [0.97]	−0.64 [1.01]	−1.73 [1.32]	−1.25 [1.19]
Level of development (GDP per capita)	0.05 [0.16]	0.01 [0.15]	0.05 [0.16]	0.20 [0.2]
Size (GDP)	−0.31** [0.15]	−0.41** [0.17]	−0.57** [0.23]	−0.38** [0.19]
Investment climate (see variables in top row)	0.13 [0.73]	−0.41 [0.36]	−0.98** [0.50]	0.40 [0.31]
Pseudo R-squared	0.22	0.15	0.25	0.22

Source: Authors' calculations.

Note: ** = significance at the 5 percent level. Standard errors are in brackets.
All regressions are estimated using probit where the left-hand-side variable takes the
value 1 when a study finds that export causes growth and 0 when it does not find
any evidence of causality. Each column runs this regression using a different variable
to capture investment climate. Each regression has 34 observations. All regressions
include a dummy equal to 1 when the period under examination is in the 1990s or
later. This dummy is never significant.

induce some firms to adopt new technologies. The expected future entry
into export markets may well encourage firms to invest in new technology
and product design and to benefit from the experience and know-how
of potential foreign buyers. Thus, the increase in productivity observed
before entering export markets may well be due to this export potential.
Alvarez and López (2005) called this *conscious self-selection*, and they
found evidence using plant-level data from Chile that self-selection is
indeed a conscious process, where firms increase productivity with the
objective of becoming exporters.[7]

Second, regardless of whether exports cause firm-level productivity
gains, the fact that exporters are more productive and larger (perhaps
exclusively because of self-selection) suggests that as countries increase
their export orientation, larger and more productive firms will produce
a larger share of national output. This reallocation of resources from less
productive and smaller firms to more productive and larger firms in itself
is a source of aggregate GDP growth. In the section "Explaining Output
Differentials between Exporters and Nonexporters in a Small Country,"

this chapter explores the determinants of output differentials between exporters and nonexporters in a small open economy: Uruguay.

Wage Premiums

For this chapter, 30 studies that explored wage premiums associated with export activity were surveyed. In two-thirds of the studies analyzed, there is evidence of an overall wage premium. In all but two studies, evidence existed of large skilled-wage premiums,[8] whereas unskilled workers in the export sector benefit from a premium in only 45 percent of the studies. Thus, the big-picture message emerging from this review is that exporters pay higher wages to skilled workers, and sometimes they pay higher wages to those workers' less skilled counterparts.

The issue of causality is seldom addressed in the literature, however. Although many of the papers are based on panel data that allow for controls of fixed effects and unobserved heterogeneity at the firm level, the issue of causality from exports to wages remains largely unsolved. One exception is Feenstra and Hanson (1997), who set up an instrumental variables estimator of the effects of foreign direct investment and outsourcing on wages and wage inequality. In the section "From Exports to Wages: Evidence from Firm-Level Data in Argentina," this chapter addresses the issue in detail and provides some new evidence.

Before turning to the causality problem, this chapter again explores the heterogeneity in the findings regarding overall wage premium and unskilled wage premiums to see whether some country characteristics are associated with a higher likelihood of finding a wage premium associated with exports (regardless of whether self-selection or causality is involved). Again, for the same reasons as before (the productivity channel), one may expect that the wage premium is more likely to be observed in small and poor countries. A better and more competitive investment climate should in principle help transmit these gains from firms to workers, but the same caveat discussed earlier applies. One would also expect that unskilled wages have a higher premium in countries that have abundant skilled workers. Indeed, because unskilled workers are the rare factor in skilled abundant countries, one would expect them to benefit later than skilled workers from these wage premiums.

Table 7.3 shows the results of the probit estimations. The first two columns explain the presence of an overall wage premium using two different investment climate variables; the second two columns explain the presence of an unskilled wage premium, again using two different investment climate variables. The regression could not be run for the skilled wage premium because almost all studies surveyed found that a skilled wage premium exists.

Again, the clear message coming from table 7.3 is that wage premiums are more likely to be observed in small countries. This finding again provides tangential evidence of the importance for firms in small countries of

Table 7.3 In Which Countries Are Wage Premiums Observed?

	Overall wages		Unskilled wages	
	Difficulty of entry procedures	Difficulty of firing workers	Difficulty of entry procedures	Difficulty of firing workers
Openness ([M + X]/ GDP)	−0.40 [0.96]	−0.23 [1.04]	−1.36 [0.86]	−1.53 [1.14]
Level of development (GDP per capita)	1.49 [1.37]	0.64 [0.65]	−0.90 [0.67]	−0.90 [0.68]
Size (GDP)	−2.43* [1.39]	−0.69 [0.54]	−1.45** [0.57]	−1.23** [0.61]
Unskilled abundance (unskilled workers/ skilled workers)	0.92 [0.95]	−0.24 [0.77]	−4.16** [1.45]	−4.51** [2.07]
Investment climate (see variables in the top row)	−2.76* [1.46]	−0.36 [0.56]	−0.55 [0.39]	0.05 [0.35]
Pseudo R-squared	0.36	0.13	0.38	0.35

Source: Authors' calculations.

Note: * = significance at the 1 percent level; ** = significance at the 5 percent level. Standard errors are in brackets. All regressions are estimated using probit where the left-hand-side variable takes the value 1 when a study finds that there wage premiums (overall wage premiums for the first two columns and unskilled wage premiums for the last two columns). Each of the two columns runs the regression using a different variable to capture investment climate: either the difficulty of entry procedures or the difficulty of firing workers. Only 17 observations in the overall wage regression and 26 in the unskilled wage regression reflect the number of studies surveyed that tried to answer these questions. All regressions include a dummy equal to 1 when the period under examination is in the 1990s or later. This dummy is never significant.

being able to take advantage of unexploited economies of scale in world markets. Also, unskilled wage premiums are more likely to be observed in skilled abundant countries. This finding may be because exporters may need to pay higher wages to attract the rare factor (unskilled workers) to their firms in countries where skilled workers are relatively abundant.

From Exports to Wages: Evidence from Firm-Level Data in Argentina

This section's main goal is to generate evidence—one of the first—on the causality of exports to wages with an application to Argentina.[9] The empirical strategy exploits the Brazilian devaluation of 1999. Argentina and Brazil are major trade partners, and the Brazilian devaluation greatly affected Argentine exports. Having an exogenous shock to exports is crucial in identifying a causal relationship between exports and wages. The combination of the panel data set and the devaluation shock is an important instrument to address this problem because the same firm can be considered before and after the devaluation to see how the wages paid by this firm change when an exogenous change occurs in exporting opportunities. This situation presents the opportunity to determine causality from exports to wages.

Table 7.4 reports the main destination of Argentine exports during 1998–2000. In the first panel, countries of destination are divided into three categories: Latin America, Organisation for Economic Co-operation and Development (OECD) countries, and non-OECD countries. The first column reports the value of exports in millions of U.S. dollars, and the second column shows the share of Argentine exports to different destinations. Half of Argentine exports go to Latin America and another 30 percent to the OECD. The third column reports the GDP per capita of the country of destination. The fourth reports export unit values. Unit values are highest when Argentina exports to the OECD, as expected. The final column reports import unit values (computed for overall imports, not imports from Argentina only). Import unit values are usually taken as a proxy for quality demand (see Hallak 2006). Notice that the export unit values of Argentina are always lower than the overall import unit values of the destination countries. This finding suggests that Argentina exports products of lower quality than the average import of trade partners. The same conclusions follow when partners are divided into low-income, middle-income, and high-income countries.

Table 7.4 provides the same information, disaggregating the major partners (such as Brazil) individually and the ones with smaller shares by region (East Asia and the Pacific, Europe and Central Asia, Latin America, and so forth). Brazil is the major trading partner, followed by Latin America, the United States, and Europe and Central Asia.

Table 7.5 reports the same information by years, for 1998, 1999, and 2000. Note how the share of Brazilian exports dropped in 1999, when the crisis hit and Brazil devalued its currency, as well as in 2000. Furthermore, Argentine exporters found replacement markets in the United States and Europe. This finding suggests that, following the Brazilian devaluation, Argentine exports were diverted mostly to high-income countries. Thus, data from the United Nations Commodity Trade Statistics Database (UN Comtrade) provide prima facie evidence of the changes in the pattern of Argentine trade that supports this survey's empirical strategy for identification.

Table 7.4 Argentine Exports by Destination

Destination	Value (US$ million)	Share	GDP per capita (US$)	Unit values (US$ per ton)	
				Exports	Imports
Latin America	22,982	0.55	5,832	0.72	1.39
OECD	12,750	0.3	24,399	0.89	3.1
Non-OECD	6,206	0.15	7,572	0.5	0.88
Low income	2,283	0.05	6,123	0.43	2.07
Middle income	26,291	0.63	6,123	0.69	1.21
High income	13,363	0.32	23,476	0.5	2.99
Brazil	13,406	0.32	7,058	1.16	1.62
United States	5,416	0.13	32,820	0.63	2.6
Chile	3,019	0.07	8,853	0.28	0.99
Uruguay	1,848	0.04	8,881	1.01	1.35
Paraguay	1,354	0.03	4,627	0.43	0.61
East Asia and the Pacific	2,520	0.06	14,722	0.88	3.79
Europe and Central Asia	6,552	0.16	20,503	1.17	2.05
Middle East and North Africa	1,494	0.04	9,874	0.44	0.33
North America	380	0.01	26,430	1.71	1.94
South Asia	1,969	0.05	2,165	0.43	5.36
Sub-Saharan Africa	625	0.01	3,386	0.44	0.62

Source: Authors' calculations based on United Nations Commodity Trade Statistics Database (UN Comtrade) data.

Table 7.5 Argentine Exports by Destination, by Year

Destination	Year	Value (US$ million)	Share	GDP per capita (US$)	Unit values (US$ per ton)	
					Exports	Imports
Brazil	1998	5,372	0.365	6,876	1.44	1.82
	1999	3,707	0.281	6,935	0.97	1.45
	2000	4,328	0.308	7,366	1.08	1.60
United States	1998	1,496	0.102	31,475	0.64	2.81
	1999	1,751	0.133	32,871	0.57	2.79
	2000	2,169	0.155	34,114	0.69	2.23
Chile	1998	926	0.063	8,730	0.35	1.10
	1999	913	0.069	8,631	0.24	0.98
	2000	1180	0.084	9,197	0.27	0.88
Uruguay	1998	631	0.043	8,984	1.28	1.51
	1999	614	0.047	8,827	0.74	1.16
	2000	604	0.043	8,832	1.17	1.40
Paraguay	1998	474	0.032	4,646	0.44	0.63
	1999	424	0.032	4,621	0.39	0.55
	2000	456	0.033	4,613	0.48	0.65

Source: Authors' calculations based on UN Comtrade data.

Data Sources and Descriptive Statistics: Industrial Surveys

Table 7.6 reports some summary statistics from the Encuesta Nacional Industrial (ENI, or National Industrial Survey). Panel a of the table lists the main variables from the survey that are used in the empirical analysis: wages, employment, foreign ownership, age, skill composition of employment, and exporter status. A first look at the data confirms some of the stylized facts of this literature. Wages are higher in exporting firms than in nonexporters. In the surveys, firms report the total wage bill and the total number of employees, so the measure of wages is the average wage across workers of any skills. Average wages are 57 percent higher at exporters in 1998, 54 percent higher in 1999, and 55 percent higher in 2000. Also, firms that export are larger and tend to hire more workers, and they use skilled labor more intensively. As expected, exporters have a much larger share of foreign participation.

Table 7.6 Industrial Survey: Argentina, 1998–2000

	1998			1999			2000			Total
	Total	Exporters	Nonexporters	Total	Exporters	Nonexporters	Total	Exporters	Nonexporters	
a. Firm data										
Wages (monthly) (US$)	1,005.8	1,207.9	699.4	1,014.4	1226.6	734.0	1,019.2	1,224.5	716.40	1,012.8
Log of wages	6.91	7.10	6.55	6.92	7.11	6.60	6.93	7.11	6.57	6.92
Workers	96.0	129.9	44.6	89.0	120.3	47.6	83.1	114.1	37.5	89.7
Foreign participation	11.8	18.3	1.9	13	21.3	2.2	13.5	21.7	1.4	12.7
Foreign dummy	0.14	0.23	0.02	0.14	0.25	0.02	0.15	0.25	0.02	0.14
Log of age	19.2	20.9	17.2	19.5	20.6	18.2	19.8	21.3	18.2	19.5
Skill composition	0.256	0.274	0.229	0.265	0.282	0.242	0.270	0.289	0.242	0.263

(continued)

Table 7.6 Industrial Survey: Argentina, 1998–2000 (continued)

	1998			1999			2000			2000
	Total	Exporters	Nonexporters	Total	Exporters	Nonexporters	Total	Exporters	Nonexporters	Total
b. Exports										
Proportion of exporters	0.56	n.a.	n.a.	0.53	n.a.	n.a.	0.56	n.a.	n.a.	0.55
Share of exports on sales	0.08	n.a.	0.15	0.07	n.a.	0.14	0.08	n.a.	0.15	0.08
c. Export destinations: share of exports										
Brazil	0.19	n.a.	0.31	0.15	n.a.	0.26	0.16	n.a.	0.27	0.17
HIE (1)	0.29	n.a.	0.49	0.31	n.a.	0.55	0.33	n.a.	0.55	0.31
HIE (2)	0.08	n.a.	0.13	0.08	n.a.	0.15	0.09	n.a.	0.15	0.09

Source: Authors' calculations based on ENI Argentina and customs data. See text for details.

Note: n.a. = not applicable. HIE (1) includes all high-income OECD and non-OECD countries, as well as upper-middle-income countries (according to the World Bank's definition of upper-middle-income countries). HIE (2) includes only high-income OECD and non-OECD countries (it excludes upper-middle-income countries) and is constructed to test the robustness of the results.

Panel b of table 7.6 presents some export statistics. About 53 to 56 percent of the firms participate in exports; however, the shares of exports to sales are relatively small. Exports account for only 7 to 8 percent of the sales of a typical Argentine firm when all firms are considered, but for those actually exporting, exports account for nearly 15 percent of total sales.

Finally, panel c of table 7.6 reports data on exports and export destinations taken from customs data. Argentine customs keeps records of exports, by country of destination, at the firm level. Using confidential information, one can match these data to the firm data from Argentina's ENI. About 53 to 56 percent of firms in the sample are exporters to varying degrees; the average share of exports on sales is only 8 percent. Conditional on being an exporter, the average share of exports is about 15 percent. Brazil is a major partner: on average, the share of exports to Brazil on total firm exports is about 17 percent. Notice that these shares declined in 1999 and 2000, after the Brazilian devaluation, from 19 to 15 and 16 percent, respectively. In addition, conditional on being an exporter, the share of exports to Brazil declined from 31 percent in 1998 to 26 percent in 1999 and to 17 percent in 2000.

This drop in exports to Brazil is the key feature of this section's empirical strategy. When Brazil devalued, Argentine firms had to seek new markets for their products. These markets were found mostly in higher-income countries. To show this change, table 7.6 reports the share of exports destined to high-income countries (HIE, for high-income exporters). The following World Bank classification is used: low-income, lower-middle-income, upper-middle-income, and high-income non-OECD and high-income OECD countries. In the benchmark models, high-income countries (HIE 1) are defined as those in the upper-middle-income and high-income non-OECD and high-income OECD categories. For robustness and sensitivity, a variant of this definition is used that includes high-income countries (both non-OECD and OECD) but excludes upper-middle-income countries.

Under the broader definition (HIE 1), the average Argentine firm ships about 31 percent of its exports to high-income countries. In contrast, the average exporter ships between 49 and 55 percent of its exports to those countries. Notice that, following the Brazilian devaluation, the unconditional share of exports destined for high-income countries increases from 29 percent in 1998 to 33 percent in 2000; furthermore, the conditional average share for those firms actually exporting increases from 49 to 55 percent. A similar pattern is observed when using the narrower definition of high-income countries. Overall, these data from customs (together with the information from UN Comtrade previously reported) support this study's empirical strategy, which uses the dynamics generated by the Brazilian devaluation to identify the effects of exports on wages.

Regression Model: Exports and Export Destinations

The aim of this section is to examine whether wages and the share of non-production workers (an approximation to the percentage of skilled workers) depend on exports and on the country of destination of exports. Some of the following hypotheses are to be tested: (a) whether exporting firms pay higher wages and have higher ratios of nonproduction workers than firms that produce for the domestic market; (b) whether the composition of export destinations of a firm matters (that is, whether firms that export to rich countries pay higher wages and have higher ratios of nonproduction workers than firms that either produce for the domestic market or export to low-income countries); (c) whether product quality is one of the factors behind the wage-employment effect of exports.

The following regression models are set up to test these hypotheses:

$$\ln w_{it} = \alpha_1 Exp_{it} + \mathbf{x}'_{it}\,\beta_1 + \phi^w_t + \phi^w_i + \varepsilon^w_{it}$$
$$\ln s_{it} = \alpha_{12} Exp_{it} + \mathbf{x}'_{it}\,\beta_2 + \phi^s_t + \phi^s_i + \varepsilon^s_{it}, \tag{7.1}$$

where w is average wage paid by firm i at time t, and s is the share of skilled workers (nonproduction workers). Controls in $\mathbf{x}$ are industry dummies; location dummies; year dummies; indicators of whether the firm is foreign; the percentage of foreign ownership; the firm size, as measured by total number of workers and, alternatively, by sales; materials consumption as a proxy for productivity shocks; and the age of the plant. The error terms have a firm fixed effect ϕ^w_i and ϕ^s_i. The variable Exp (from *exports*), which captures exports and export destinations (as explained in the next section), is of most interest.

Main Results

Table 7.7, which displays the main results from the log wages specification in equation 7.1, begins the exploratory analysis of wages, exports, and export destinations. The first three columns correspond to pooled OLS regressions; the last three, to panel data and fixed effects (FE) models. Two definitions of *exports* are adopted. First, instead of a dummy variable for whether a given firm exports or not, the ratio of exports to total sales is used as an indication of export participation. This approach has the major advantage of using panels and fixed effects. In the data, however, very few firms change status from exporter to nonexporter. In consequence, the use of a dummy to capture exporter participation is not useful. Using a measure of exposure, such as the ratio of exports to sales, which responds much more flexibly to changes in the economic environment, is much more convenient.[10] The first column of table 7.7 shows that firms with higher exports-to-sales ratios tend to pay higher wages. On the basis of an unconditional average exports-to-sales ratio of about 8 percent, exporters

Table 7.7 Exports, Export Destinations, and Wages: OLS and FE Regressions

	OLS	OLS	FE	FE
	Dependent variable: log average wage			
Exports/sales	0.252*** [0.093]	n.a.	n.a.	-0.074 [0.087]
High-income exports	n.a.	0.054* [0.032]	0.038 [0.032]	0.016 [0.019]	0.017 [0.019]
Log sales	0.178*** [0.010]	0.177*** [0.010]	0.175*** [0.010]	0.060*** [0.022]	0.060*** [0.022]
Percentage of foreign ownership	0.003*** [0.000]	0.003*** [0.000]	0.003*** [0.000]	n.a.	n.a.
Log age	0.055*** [0.018]	0.058*** [0.018]	0.055*** [0.018]	n.a.	n.a.
Year effects	Yes	Yes	Yes	Yes	
R-squared	0.55	0.55	0.55	0.01	0.01
Number of observations	2,502	2,502	2,544	2,544	2,544
Number of firms			901	901	901

Source: Authors' calculations.

Note: n.a. = not applicable; * = significant at the 10 percent level; ** = significant at the 5 percent level; *** = significant at the 1 percent level. Robust standard errors are in brackets. All OLS regressions include industry, district, and year effects. All FE regressions include firm fixed effects and year effects.

pay only 2 percent more than nonexporters in the data. With an average, conditional on being an exporter, of 15 percent, wages are 3.8 percent higher in those firms engaged in exports. At the other extreme, a firm fully specialized in exports pays 25 percent more than a domestically specialized counterpart.

The second definition of *exports* used in this section is designed to explore the export-destination hypothesis. In short, the ratio of exports to sales is replaced with the share of exports to high-income countries. (This variable is denoted as high-income exports.) Results are in the second column of table 7.7. In this specification, a positive and significant coefficient of exports on wages is also found. Firms that export to high-income countries at the unconditional average (30 percent) pay about 1.6 percent more than firms that either export to low-income countries or do not export at all. Firms that export to high-income countries at the conditional mean (55 percent) pay almost 3 percent more. Finally, firms that specialized in exports to high-income countries pay 5.4 percent more than fully domestic firms. Although this relationship is not causal, the results provide some preliminary support to the export-destination story.

To complete the analysis, the third column of table 7.7 includes both the exports-to-sales ratio and the exports-to-high income dummy in the same pooled OLS regression. In this model, the positive correlation remains between exports to sales and wages, while the positive association with the share to high-income countries is lost.

Because the study has a panel of manufacturing firms, the regression model can be improved by including firm fixed effects. The FE models allow control for unobserved heterogeneity at the firm level and for exit and entry into export markets. (In the FE case, industry and location dummies are not used, and time-invariant firm-level variables, such as the age of the plant, that are also absorbed into the fixed effects are dropped.) Results are reported in the fourth to sixth columns of table 7.7. The main conclusion from these regressions is that both the ratio of exports to sales and the share of exports to high-income countries lose explanatory power when the fixed effects are included. In other words, when unobserved heterogeneity is accounted for, exporters do not appear to pay higher wages. These findings are consistent with those in Bernard and Jensen (1999), Isgut (2001), and others: good firms become exporters, but exporters do not necessarily pay higher wages.

Why is this? There are two sets of explanations. The one advanced by the current literature is that firms that are to become exporters are more productive and more efficient—thus, they can pay higher wages—but when the exporter status is achieved, those productivity advantages tend to disappear (Clerides, Lach, and Tybout 1998). The idea is that the fixed effects partly capture the self-selection effect (more productive firms export and pay higher wages); so once a fixed effect that captures how productive firms are is introduced, there is nothing left for exports to explain, whereas before the fixed effect was capturing the fact that those firms exporting were more productive and therefore paid higher wages.

The second explanation is endogeneity or omitted variable biases. To see an example of the endogeneity story, think of a model in which part of the labor component comes from nontradable goods. In such a scenario, high wages may prevent firms from being competitive in international markets, thus making them unable to export much. Furthermore, if a country like Argentina has to compete with low-wage countries like China for markets in developed countries, then high local costs can wipe out exports to high-income destinations.

Several examples of omitted variables are available. Keep in mind that the fixed effect model can account for firm heterogeneity that is time invariant, but many other sources of time-varying heterogeneity may exist. One such source is imports. If industries that export a lot are industries that also import a lot, and if import competition lowers wages, then the positive benefits of exports on wages may cancel out the negative impacts of import penetration. Another reason could be productivity shocks that would allow firms to enter or expand their export operation and pay higher wages at the same time. Another reason could be changes in labor regulations, changes in labor contracts, and changes in union policies. If labor regulations change for different industries during this time interval, thereby forcing firms to pay higher wages, failure to control for this variable in the regression may lead to biases in the effects of export, especially if the changes in the regulatory environment affect exporters disproportionately. This problem could potentially be a serious one, because Argentina introduced significant labor regulations at the end of the 1990s. More generally, this reasoning applies to other policies as well. In fact, a weak aspect of the literature on wages and tariff reforms is often the impossibility of accounting for the effects of simultaneous reforms (see Galiani and Porto 2006).

Both the unobserved variable and reverse causality stories may lead to biases in the estimates of exports to wages even after controlling for the fixed effects.[11] An instrumental variable approach is followed to address these issues and the issue of causality. The strategy is to explain both the level of exports of the firms and their composition of countries of destination by the exogenous exposure to the Brazilian devaluation of 1999. Notice that heterogeneity exists in the exposure to this shock because firms and industries that exported more to Brazil before the devaluation were more likely to be affected by the shock.

Two endogenous variables are used in the model. One is the HIE variable—the share of exports to high-income countries—which is related to the export destinations of the firm. The other is the share of exports on sales, which is more closely related to export status.

The instrument for the HIE share is built with an interaction of a postdevaluation dummy with the share of the industry's exports that were destined to Brazil in 1998. More specifically, two specifications are adopted. In the nonparametric model with dummies, the impacts of the devaluation are allowed to vary from one year to the other (as the economy adjusted, exposure in 1999 was different from exposure in 2000). Consequently, this instrument is built by interacting the level of exposure to Brazil before the devaluation—that is, the share of exports to Brazil in 1998—with a 1999 dummy variable and a 2000 dummy. In the second specification, an alternative instrument is built, which is the interaction of the predevaluation share of exports to Brazil (at the firm level) with the exchange rate of the Brazilian currency in 1999 and 2000. This instrument is a parametric model of the exposure to the shock. Support for these instruments comes from the preview of patterns of exports in Argentina, as documented in tables 7.4 to 7.6. The argument is that, following the devaluation, firms that were most exposed to the Brazilian devaluation had to adjust and move away from this market, exploring new markets in high-income countries (see tables 7.5 and 7.6).

A similar strategy is followed to deal with the endogeneity of the ratio of exports to sales. More concretely, the share of exports to Brazil on total sales is used as an instrument for the share of total exports on total sales. Two arguments support this instrument. One claim is that firms with a larger share of exports to Brazil on total sales had lower shares of exports to sales because part of the effect of the devaluation was to make them retrench into local markets. Another argument is that, conditional on the share of exports to Brazil on total exports, firms with higher ratios of exports to Brazil on total sales had a lower base to divert exports to high-income countries. As before, exposure is measured nonparametrically with a dummy for 1999 and another for 2000, using the Brazilian exchange rates.

Good instruments have to be exogenous, help explain the endogenous variables, and satisfy the exclusion restrictions. The instruments used here satisfy all these conditions. First, the Brazilian devaluation is arguably exogenous to the firm. Second, as argued before, the instruments are correlated with the level of exports and their composition and destination. Finally, the exclusion restrictions require that these instruments do not affect wages beyond the indirect effect through exports and export destinations. One potential violation of the exclusion restrictions is given by the macroeconomic effects of the devaluation of a major trading partner. This possibility is accounted for by controlling for any direct effect of the devaluation with year effects. The strategy is to rely on variation in export destinations as identification of the effects of exports on wages.

First-stage regressions reveal that the instruments work well (see Porto 2007 for more details). They have substantial explanatory power and are statistically significant in all the regressions. Furthermore, the results imply that, in fact, following the Brazilian devaluation, firms that were more exposed to it switched to high-income destination countries but faced lower exports-to-sales ratios, as expected. Also, the correlations persist even after including year effects to account for the macroeconomic impacts of the devaluation (and other time effects that affected all firms in the same fashion).

Now this chapter turns to the main results: the instrument variable coefficients of exports on wages. These results are reported in table 7.8. The table lists the two potential endogenous variables and has nine columns. These columns correspond to the three models of table 7.7 (only exports-to-sales ratio, only share of exports to high-income countries, and both export/sales and HIE together), for specifications without year effects and nonparametric dummy instruments (columns 1 to 3), with year effects and nonparametric dummy instruments (columns 4 to 6), and with year effects and parametric instruments using exchange rates (columns 7 to 9). The major conclusion of this work is that although exporting to high-income countries improves wages, the ratio of exports to sales does *not* affect them. Thus, exporting per se is not really a significant channel toward higher wages, but exporting to high-income countries is. That is, what appears to matter is the composition of exports.

The magnitudes are important, too: firms with average shares of exports to high-income countries pay wages between 8.79 percent (29.3×0.30) and 9.51 percent (31.7×0.30) higher than firms with no exports to high-income countries. It is difficult not to overemphasize this fact: the results are very robust and survive the inclusion of firm fixed effects (using the panel data) and the use of instrumental variables.

Channels

What are the implications of the findings so far? From the tests, one may conclude that exporters to high-income countries pay higher wages than other firms in the sample, even after including controls for exporting status. However, the results are silent regarding the channels. As has been argued, the existence of a positive relationship between (a) exports and export destinations and (b) wages is compatible with two stories. One hypothesis is that exports and export destinations allow firms to make higher profits (by selling to more profitable markets) that are shared with the workers. In another hypothesis, higher-income countries have a higher valuation for high-quality exports so that exporting to those countries requires more skills, higher wages, and a higher skill premium. Can the results and data be used to explore which of these two hypotheses seems to be more relevant in Argentina?

Information on wages by skill levels is not available; the composition of skills of the firm's employment is. Thus, the question can be asked whether exporters—in particular exporters to high-income countries— have a different skill composition. Hence, regressions are run of labor

Table 7.8 Exports, Export Destinations, and Wages: Wage Regression and Instrumental Variables

	(1)	(2)	(3)	(4)	(5)	(6)	(7)	(8)	(9)
					Dependent variable: log average wage				
Exports/sales	-0.979 [0.638]	n.a.	-0.343 [0.478]	-0.735 [0.594]	n.a.	-0.259 [0.513]	-0.543 [0.546]	n.a.	-0.075 [0.495]
High-income exports	n.a.	0.365 [0.106]***	0.357 [0.111]***	n.a.	0.317 [0.108]***	0.305 [0.107]***	n.a.	0.296 [0.107]***	0.293 [0.110]***
Log sales	0.054 [0.019]***	0.054 [0.018]***	0.055 [0.018]***	0.064 [0.020]***	0.057 [0.020]***	0.058 [0.020]***	0.063 [0.021]***	0.057 [0.020]***	0.058 [0.020]***
Year effects		—			Yes			Yes	
Instruments		Dummies			Dummies			Exchange rate	
Number of firms	901	901	901	901	901	901	901	901	901
Number of observations	2,544	2,544	2,544	2,544	2,544	2,544	2,544	2,544	2,544

Source: Authors' calculations.

Note: n.a. = not applicable; * significant at 10 percent; ** significant at 5 percent; *** significant at 1 percent. Robust standard errors are in brackets. All regressions include firm fixed effects.

force composition on the share of exports to high-income countries and the ratio of exports to sales (as before), using the same instrumental variable setting. Results can be found in table 7.9.

The results suggest that, as in the case of wages, whereas the ratio of exports to sales does not seem to affect the composition of skills at the firm level, exporting to high-income countries does matter. In fact, the intensity of use of skilled labor in firms that export to high-income countries is about 10.1 to 13.8 percent higher than in other firms. These results provide some support to those hypotheses that require increases of the skill composition following exports (especially to high-income countries), like the quality story. Indeed, in the profit-sharing model, there is actually no reason to expect increases in the skill composition following a higher exposure to export markets. In consequence, these data seem to favor the quality hypothesis over the profit-sharing hypothesis.[12]

This conclusion is, however, weak. In fact, profit sharing as a valid mechanism behind the wage results cannot be ruled out. In an exercise to shed some more light on this issue, the wage specification is reestimated, adding the skill composition as one of the regressors. As before, a dummy of exports to high-income countries and the ratio of exports to sales are included, and the model is estimated with instrumental variables. Results are reported in table 7.10.

The previous findings are confirmed. In particular, although the ratio of exports to sales remains insignificant in all the empirical models, exporting to high-income countries still determines wages. The share to high-income countries, HIE, is positive and significant in all the specifications even though the skill composition of the firm is controlled for. This finding supports the hypothesis that other mechanisms, such as profit sharing, may be in place on top of the quality mechanisms. Moreover, the coefficient of the HIE variable is smaller: it ranges from 22.8 to 25.6 (when before it ranged from 29.3 to 35.7). This finding provides further support to the notion that quality considerations alone are not enough to explain the higher wages paid by exporters to high-income countries. Profit sharing is also probably part of the explanation.[13]

Explaining Output Differentials between Exporters and Nonexporters in a Small Country

Are exporting firms more productive?[14] A common methodology for answering this question is to obtain an estimate of TFP and to regress it on measures of export performance. Most papers find a productivity premium for exporters, although others fail to find productivity differentials (for example, Greenaway, Gullstrand, and Kneller 2005). Do firms become more productive as they engage in export activity? As has been seen, the evidence on the learning-by-exporting hypothesis is mixed, and

Table 7.9 Exports and Export Destinations: Labor Force Composition

	Dependent variables: share of skilled workers; share of hours worked by skilled workers					
Exports/sales	-0.111 [0.218]	n.a.	0.076 [0.179]	-0.141 [0.221]	n.a.	0.08 [0.207]
High-income exports	n.a.	0.129 [0.044]***	0.133 [0.046]***	n.a.	0.134 [0.043]***	0.138 [0.044]***
Log sales	-0.001 [0.008]	-0.003 [0.007]	-0.004 [0.007]	-0.001 [0.008]	-0.003 [0.007]	-0.004 [0.007]
Year effects	Yes			Yes		
Instruments	Dummies			Exchange rate		
Number of firms	901	901	901	901	901	901
Number of observations	2,544	2,544	2,544	2,544	2,544	2,544

Source: Authors' calculations.

Note: n.a. = not applicable; * = significant at the 10 percent level; ** = significant at the 5 percent level; *** = significant at the 1 percent level. Robust standard errors are in brackets. All regressions include firm fixed effects. Bootstrap replications: 500. Includes all firms.

Table 7.10 Exports, Export Destinations, and Wages: Wage Regressions Controlling for Labor Force Composition

	Dependent variable: log average wage					
Exports/sales	-0.682 [0.571]	n.a.	-0.295 [0.466]	-0.477 [0.515]	n.a.	-0.112 [0.458]
High-income exports	n.a.	0.256 [0.099]***	0.243 [0.098]**	n.a.	0.233 [0.103]**	0.228 [0.101]**
Skilled workers	0.472 [0.096]***	0.472 [0.093]***	0.471 [0.091]***	0.473 [0.096]***	0.472 [0.093]***	0.472 [0.095]***
Log sales	0.064 [0.019]***	0.059 [0.020]***	0.06 [0.020]***	0.063 [0.019]***	0.059 [0.019]***	0.059 [0.020]***
Year effects	Yes	Yes			Yes	
Instruments		Dummies			Exchange rate	
Number of firms	901	901	901	901	901	901
Number of observations	2,544	2,544	2,544	2,544	2,544	2,544

Source: Authors' calculations.

Note: n.a. = not applicable; * = significant at the 10 percent level; ** = significant at the 5 percent level; *** = significant at the 1 percent level. Robust standard errors are in brackets. All regressions include firm fixed effects. Bootstrap replications: 500. Includes all firms.

the section "Exporter Premiums: What Do We Know?" showed that the potential for learning by exporting seems to be stronger in small countries, suggesting that economies of scale could play an important role in explaining learning by exporting. This possibility explains the choice to undertake this section's exercise using firms in Uruguay, which has one of the smallest domestic markets in Latin America.

Productivity estimations, however, tend to be based on a specification that assumes common parameters of the production function for both subsets of firms. Other specifications (see Arnold and Hussinger 2004) undertake productivity estimations similar to that used by Olley and Pakes (1996), partitioning the sample by industry groups. Within a sector, common production function parameters are assumed between exporters and nonexporters. By ignoring the heterogeneity of production functions across exporters and nonexporters, one could obtain biased estimates of the contribution of TFP to explaining output differentials between these two types of firms.

Thus, this section, instead of considering a common functional form, allows coefficients to differ between exporting and nonexporting firms.[15] Differences in output can be explained (in a decomposition similar in spirit to the Oaxaca-Blinder decomposition for wage differentials) in terms of factor use, factor productivity (elasticities), and TFP (see Blinder 1973; Oaxaca 1973).

TFP is estimated using the Levinsohn and Petrin (2003) methodology. The estimation—for exporters (X) and nonexporters (NX)—is carried out in logs, and inputs into the production function are white-collar employment, blue-collar employment, and capital. In Levinsohn and Petrin's (2003) methodology, a productivity proxy (in this case, electricity) is used to control for unobservables. This method addresses two key problems: (a) in a panel, a researcher would observe only the surviving firms—hence, those likely to be the most productive (selection problem)—and (b) input choices of firms conditional on continuing in activity depend on their productivity (simultaneity problem).

Because the estimation procedure is not an OLS regression, residuals do not have 0 mean. Hence, there is a main difference between this procedure and the Oaxaca-Blinder decomposition: the latter involves only estimated coefficients and predicted levels and does not include residuals. The following results suggest that (a) exporters are larger in terms of output and input use but have lower factor elasticities than nonexporters, (b) the export premium increases with orientation to foreign markets, and (c) without allowing for different production functions, much of the export premium is lost.

Decomposition of Output Differentials between Exporters and Nonexporters

To graphically represent the decomposition, figure 7.1 presents the simple case in which production is a function of only one factor of production.[16]

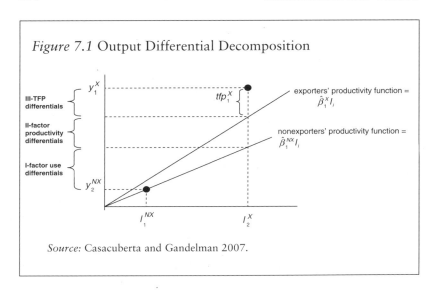

Figure 7.1 Output Differential Decomposition

Source: Casacuberta and Gandelman 2007.

The exporting firm's output and labor use are assumed to be larger than those of the nonexporting firm, and for ease of exposition, the TFP level of the nonexporting firm is assumed to be null. The decomposition introduces three terms to explain the percentage difference between an exporter and a nonexporter.

The first term of the decomposition is an output measure of the effect of the nonexporting firm's larger labor use. It is calculated as the difference between the predicted outcome for a nonexporting firm and the actual outcome of an exporting firm. This measure shows how much the nonexporting firm could increase its output if it decided to hire an amount of labor equal to that of the exporting firm. The second term captures the different labor productivity (or factor elasticities) between exporting and nonexporting firms, valued at the usage level of the exporting firm.[17] The third term captures the share of the output differential explained by differences in TFP (recall that the nonexporting firm's TFP level is 0, or alternatively, all TFP levels are normalized so that the nonexporting firm's TFP level is 0).

One can now easily see that if the TFP estimation procedure does not allow for different factor elasticities between exporters and nonexporters, the estimated contribution of TFP to explaining output differentials will be biased. Figure 7.1 will tend to show an upward bias because the higher labor elasticity in the export sector will be attributed to TFP. However, if the factor elasticities are lower in the export sector, then the estimated contribution of TFP to explaining output differentials will be downward biased, which may, in turn, explain why some studies have not found that export firms are more productive, or the absence of learning by exporting.

Data Sources and Descriptive Statistics

Establishment-level annual observations are used from the manufacturing survey conducted by the Instituto Nacional de Estadística (INE, or National Institute of Statistics) for 1988 to 1995. The INE survey is a representative sample of Uruguayan manufacturing establishments with five or more employees. According to the sampling criterion, all establishments with more than 100 employees were included in the survey. Moreover, a random sample was drawn from establishments with fewer than 100 employees until total employment of selected establishments accounted for at least 60 percent of the total employment of the sector, as reported in the 1988 census.

The data include domestic and export sales figures. The definition of *exporters* used in this section is based on the share of exports in sales across the sample period. In this sample, the share of establishments that show positive exports (regardless of the stability of their presence in foreign markets) increases with time (see table 7.11).

All establishments showing a ratio of foreign to total sales greater or equal to 5 percent in all sample years are included in the group of exporters. Descriptive statistics for exporters and nonexporters are shown in table 7.12. Exporters are clearly on average much larger firms than nonexporters. During the sample period, average blue-collar employment falls relatively more, and white-to-blue-collar ratios increase more sharply for the exporter group. Although the capital-to-labor ratio increases for all firms, the increase is also larger for the exporter group.

Table 7.11 Share of Establishments with Positive Exports: Uruguay

Year	Percentage	All
1988	35.0	671
1989	36.5	600
1990	39.3	595
1991	39.1	562
1992	42.3	530
1993	40.4	510
1994	41.1	491
1995	42.9	455

Source: Authors' calculations using the INE manufacturing survey.

Table 7.12 Descriptive Statistics: Exporter Criterion—Exports Greater than 5 Percent of Sales

Period	Blue-collar employment	White-collar employment	Capital stock	Capital-to-labor ratio	White-to-blue-collar ratio	Output per worker	Output-to-capital ratio
Nonexporters							
1988–90	59.0	20.6	149,706.1	1,878.7	0.35	12,636.1	6.73
1993–95	51.5	19.6	145,326.2	2,044.5	0.38	17,317.7	8.47
Percentage change	87.2	95.1	97.1	108.8	109.1	137.0	125.9
Exporters							
1988–90	218.8	50.4	441,115.7	1,638.7	0.23	13,638.9	8.32
1993–95	163.1	47.1	540,092.4	2,569.6	0.29	19,818.8	7.71
Percentage change	74.5	93.5	122.4	156.8	125.4	145.3	92.7

Source: Authors' calculations using the INE manufacturing survey.

Additionally, the increase in output per worker and the decrease in output-to-capital ratios are more pronounced in the exporter group. Capital and labor creation and destruction rates estimated by Casacuberta, Fachola, and Gandelman (2004) confirm the shift in Uruguayan manufacturing toward more capital-intensive production methods. According to the evidence presented here, that process was deeper in more export-oriented firms.

Results

The main results of the output differential decomposition between exporters and nonexporters are presented in table 7.13, where factor elasticities are allowed to vary between exporters and nonexporters, and in table 7.14, where factor elasticities are common. On average, the output of an exporting firm is more than twice the output of a nonexporter, but interestingly, the output gap tends to decrease as the definition of the exporter

Table 7.13 Output Decomposition by Definition of Exporter and Allowing for Different Factor Elasticities between Exporters and Nonexporters

Threshold value: definition of exporter (%)	Output differential: exporter-nonexporter (%)	Factor use term (%)	Factor elasticity term (%)	TFP term (%)
0	171	168	−19	21
5	155	149	−42	48
10	148	145	−27	30
15	150	143	−41	48
20	142	137	−43	48
25	134	131	−29	31
30	126	121	−42	48
35	127	124	−45	48
40	122	120	−37	39
45	118	112	−69	75
50	123	116	−73	80
55	95	89	−96	102
60	96	89	−113	120
65	94	86	−109	118
70	91	84	−111	118

Source: Authors' calculations using the INE manufacturing survey.

Table 7.14 Output Decomposition by Definition of Exporter and Constrained to Common Factor Elasticities between Exporters and Nonexporters

Threshold value: definition of exporter (%)	Output differential: exporter-nonexporter (%)	Factor use term (%)	TFP term (%)
5	155	160	–6
10	148	154	–6
15	150	155	–5
20	142	145	–3
25	134	136	–2
30	126	128	–2
35	127	129	–2
40	122	122	0
45	118	117	1
50	123	122	0
55	95	90	5
60	96	90	6
65	94	88	6
70	91	86	5

Source: Authors' calculations.

sector is stricter. This finding means that although, on average, exporters are larger than nonexporters, the largest firms in this study's sample are not the most export-oriented ones.

For thresholds of exports up to 50 percent of total sales, between one-third and two-thirds of output differentials are due to differences in TFP, while the rest is caused by factor use and factor productivity. The share of the output gap explained by differences in TFP increases with export orientation (see figure 7.2). Thus, not only are exporters more productive than nonexporters, but also the larger the export orientation, the larger the productivity premium.

The corollary of the larger contribution of TFP is that factor contribution (as the sum of factor intensities and factor elasticities effects) decreases with export orientation. This result is due both the lower input usage term (always positive) and the lower elasticity term (always negative). As was observed in the case of output differentials, the evolution of factor use gap with export orientation implies that exporters tend to hire more employees

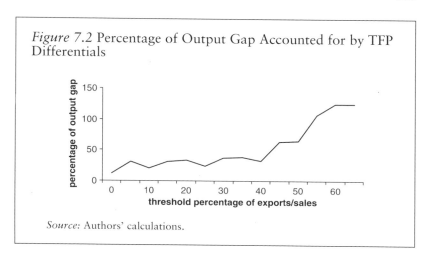

Figure 7.2 Percentage of Output Gap Accounted for by TFP Differentials

Source: Authors' calculations.

and use more capital, materials, and energy than nonexporters, but the largest firms in terms of input use are not the most export oriented.

If, instead of using the decomposition that allows factor elasticities to vary between exporters and nonexporters, one assumes that factor elasticities are common, the results are as reported in table 7.14, which disaggregates the output gap into only factor use and TFP differential. Because they refer to the same output gap (that is, the definition of exporter is the same), the second columns of tables 7.13 and 7.14 have exactly the same values, while the TFP column is different. In particular, when the production coefficients are restricted to be the same for both groups, the share of the output gap that is explained by productivity differentials is almost null.

Figure 7.3 presents the share of the output gap explained by TFP differentials, assuming equal and different production functions for exporters and nonexporters. At least in these data, when exporters and nonexporters are assumed to share the same technology represented by the production function, the result is that the productivity levels of exporters and nonexporters are basically the same. Conversely, when a more flexible approach is assumed, allowing the coefficients of the production function to vary between groups, then a sizable export productivity premium is found.

Conclusions and Policy Implications

Export firms are more productive and pay higher wages. These exporter premiums have two nonmutually exclusive explanations. Either more productive firms self-select into export activities, because only highly productive firms could face the entry costs associated with selling in foreign

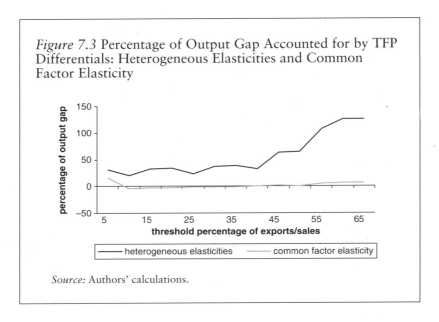

Figure 7.3 Percentage of Output Gap Accounted for by TFP Differentials: Heterogeneous Elasticities and Common Factor Elasticity

Source: Authors' calculations.

markets, or learning by exporting occurs, in which case the participation in the export market allows firms to become more productive.

The existing empirical evidence strongly supports the self-selection hypothesis; learning by exporting is observed in only some countries. More than 80 percent of the studies surveyed for this chapter found evidence that exporting firms were more productive before entering the export market, whereas only half the studies found that exporting firms' productivity grew faster than nonexporting firms' productivity after the former entered the export market.

Interestingly, learning by exporting was more likely to be observed in small countries, suggesting that the ability to exploit economies of scale in foreign markets may be part of the explanation behind learning by exporting. In contrast, trade openness, the investment climate, and the level of development could not help explain why learning by exporting occurs, suggesting that they are not important determinants of learning by exporting. Casacuberta and Gandelman's (2007) study, summarized in the section "Explaining Output Differentials between Exporters and Nonexporters in a Small Country," confirms the importance of firm size in explaining output differential between exporters and nonexporters in a small open economy (Uruguay). Casacuberta and Gandelman (2007) propose a novel decomposition of the output gap between exporters and nonexporters, inspired in the Oaxaca-Blinder decomposition for wage differentials. Differences in size (or *factor use*, as they call it) explain more than 80 percent of the output differential between exporters and nonexporters. Reorientation toward export markets could therefore be an important source of short-run growth in the presence of labor unemployment or capacity underuse.

Wage export premiums (that is, the fact that exporters pay higher wages than nonexporters) were more likely in small economies, whereas trade openness, the investment climate, and the level of development did not seem to matter. The existing literature stops at identifying whether or not a wage export premium is present and does not address the issue of causality.

In a paper commissioned for this chapter and summarized in the section "From Exports to Wages: Evidence from Firm-Level Data in Argentina," Porto (2007) seriously examines the issue of causality between exports and wages by providing convincing instruments for exports in a regression explaining wages paid by Argentine manufacturing firms. He uses as an instrument for Argentine firms' exports during the period from 2000 to 2002 their exposure to the Brazilian devaluation in 1999. Arguably, this factor is exogenous to Argentine firms' exports after the devaluation. He also controls for firm characteristics that could determine exposure to Brazil and direct effects of the Brazilian devaluation on Argentine firms (through macroeconomic effects, for example) by using firm and year fixed effects. The main findings are that exports per se do not necessarily cause higher wages. Rather, where countries export is what matters. Conditional on firm characteristics and firm fixed effects, the instrumental variable estimates suggest that firms that specialize in exports to high-income countries tend to pay much higher wages than their counterparts (including firms that export to low-income countries or to the domestic market). In other words, although exports per se are not necessarily good, the exposition of exports is a key engine for higher wages.

The results are consistent with both a quality and a profit-sharing story. High-income countries tend to demand higher-quality goods, a situation that allows firms to pay higher wages. However, Porto (2007) cannot rule out the existence of profit-shifting mechanisms, whereby firms that export to high-income countries tend to share part of the excess profits with their workers.

But what determines the rapid productivity growth observed by firms before they enter the market? Little is known about this growth, and some authors, such as Alvarez and López (2005), argued that an important part of the explanation—at least among Chilean manufacturing plants—is conscious self-selection. Firms become more productive with the objective of becoming exporters. So export activity may be the cause of the jump in productivity before firms enter the export market.

An important point to keep in mind, because the focus of this regional study is on the microdeterminants of aggregate growth, is that regardless of whether exports cause firm-level productivity gains, the fact that exporters are more productive and larger (perhaps exclusively because of self-selection) suggests that as countries increase their export orientation, larger and more productive firms will produce a larger share of national output. This reallocation of resources from less productive and small firms to more productive and larger firms in itself is a source of aggregate gross domestic product growth.

Depending on which is the most important force, however, the policy implications can be very different. On the one hand, offshore export promotion activities, which are quite common in Latin America, are often justified on the basis of learning by exporting. On the other hand, the self-selection explanation would suggest that policy makers should focus their efforts on the internal determinants of productivity growth. Evidence elsewhere indirectly suggests that the latter is probably more important in developing countries. In a recent paper, Lederman, Olarreaga, and Payton (2006) showed, with the help of a recent survey on export promotion activities, that in developing countries returns to onshore export promotion activities, such as technical assistance and training for (large) domestic firms on how to enter foreign markets, were much larger than returns to offshore export promotion activities, such as country image, fair participation, and other marketing activities abroad, including foreign offices. They also found that to maximize the effect on aggregate exports, export promotion activities should focus on large domestic firms that are not yet exporting rather than on established exporters. These findings are consistent with the idea that self-selection plays an important role in the explanation of export premiums.

Notes

1. One could envisage instrumenting the exporter dummy using variables similar to the ones used in the previous chapters, such as the share of firms that export in each region or the share of exports in total sales in each region, but in this case, whether these variables would satisfy the exclusion restriction is unclear. For example, the share of firms that export in each region is likely to affect a firm's productivity and wages through more direct channels than whether the firm exports or not. Knowledge spillovers from other exporting firms are likely to affect a firm's productivity and wages regardless of whether the firm is exporting or not, which would cast doubt on what the instrumented exporter dummy is really capturing.

2. Note that the expected effects from learning by exporting could occur either at the time of entry into exporting (a one-time effect) or every year after entry (a continuous effect).

3. Factor use can be seen as a size differential in factor demand, and factor elasticity is explained by the fact that it allows the production function of exporters and nonexporters to differ.

4. More recently, to disentangle the self-selection hypothesis from the learning-by-exporting hypothesis, some studies have started using matching techniques to create a control group of ex ante identical firms (Girma, Greenaway, and Kneller

2004; Wagner 2002). Also, some authors have focused on the difference between exporters and nonexporters over the entire distribution of firms and not only mean differences, using tests of first-order stochastic dominance (Delgado, Farinas, and Ruano 2002). Similarly, others have used quintile regressions to examine productivity effects at different points of the conditional output distribution to test whether they may be weaker or stronger for least productive firms (Yasar, Nelson, and Rejesus 2003).

  5. Some of these studies analyzed several countries; therefore, 70 individual country studies are surveyed. A detailed description of the methodologies used in all these studies is beyond the scope of the present section, which aims only at illustrating the larger messages coming from the literature (as opposed to performing a detailed meta-analysis on the subject).

  6. Absorption capacity may be an issue here.

  7. Iacovone 2007 and Hallward-Driemeier, Iarossi, and Sokoloff (2002) show that part of what self-selection may be capturing is the idea that exporters invest in retooling for foreign markets in advance of entering the market; therefore, self-selection may be actually associated with export activity.

  8. Interestingly, these two studies (Breau and Rigby 2006; Schank, Schnabel, and Wagner 2007) match employer-employee data, which allows controlling for workers' characteristics, such as education, age, and experience, that are unobservable when working with firm (employer) data only. It is probably too early to conclude anything, but a large share of what is captured as an exporter skilled premium seems to result from the "superior" characteristics of workers in the export sector.

  9. This section closely follows Porto (2007).

  10. Some papers in the literature find a significant exporter premium even after accounting for the fixed effects. Notice, however, that these cases correspond to larger panels, spanning several years, so that the possibility of switching is more pronounced.

  11. A third interpretation could be that fixed effects estimators identify parameters exclusively of intrafirm temporal variation in the data, which is typically small relative to cross-firm variation in the data. Thus, they are less accurate, and if variables are measured with error, signal-to-noise ratios are worse, making them more subject to bias.

  12. Porto (2007) includes a full review of the literature on quality and profit sharing.

  13. Furthermore, if one assumes that the quality channel is fully accounted for with the skill composition variable, then one can conclude that the profit sharing could even explain twice as much of the differences in wages between exporters to high-income countries and other firms.

  14. This section closely follows Casacuberta and Gandelman (2007).

  15. A caveat is needed here. By using a Cobb-Douglas production function, the exercise assumes the same returns to scale to all firms (regardless of output level).

  16. For the multi-input and algebraic decomposition, see Casacuberta and Gandelman (2007).

  17. Obviously, the distinction between factor productivity and total factor productivity is blurred in this example, with only one factor of production.

References

Alvarez, R., and R. López. 2005. "Exporting and Performance: Evidence from Chilean Plants." *Canadian Journal of Economics* 38 (4): 1384–400.

Arnold, J., and K. Hussinger. 2004. "Export Behavior and Firm Productivity in German Manufacturing." *Review of World Economics* 141 (2): 219–43.

Aw, B., S. Chung, and M. Roberts. 2000. "Productivity and Turnover in the Export Market: Micro-level Evidence from the Republic of Korea and Taiwan (China)." *World Bank Economic Review* 14 (1): 65–90.

Balassa, B. 1985. "Exports, Policy Choices, and Economic Growth in Developing Countries after the 1973 Oil Shock." *Journal of Development Economics* 4 (1): 23–35.

Bernard, A., and B. Jensen. 1995. "Exporters, Jobs, and Wages in U.S. Manufacturing: 1976–1987." In *Brookings Papers on Economic Activity, Microeconomics: 1995*, ed. G. L. Perry and W. C. Brainard, 67–119. Washington, DC: Brookings Institution Press.

———. 1999. "Exceptional Exporter Performance: Cause, Effect, or Both?" *Journal of International Economics* 47 (1): 1–25.

———. 2004. "Why Some Firms Export." *Review of Economics and Statistics* 86 (2): 561–69.

Bhagwati, J. 1978. *Anatomy and Consequences of Exchange Control Regimes: Liberalization Attempts and Consequences.* Cambridge, MA: Ballinger.

Bigsten, A., P. Collier, S. Dercon, M. Fafchamps, B. Gauthier, J. W. Gunning, J. Habarurema, A. Oduro, R. Oostendorp, C. Pattillo, M. Söderbom, F. Teal, and A. Zeufack. 2000. "Exports and Firm-Level Efficiency in African Manufacturing." Centre for the Study of African Economies, Working Paper 2000-16, Department of Economics, Oxford University, Oxford, U.K.

Blinder, A. 1973. "Wage Discrimination: Reduced Form and Structural Estimates." *Journal of Human Resources* 8 (4): 436–55.

Breau, S., and D. Rigby. 2006. "Is There Really an Export Wage Premium? Case Study of Los Angeles Using Matched Employee-Employer Data." Working Paper 06-06, U.S. Census Bureau, Washington, DC.

Casacuberta, C., G. Fachola, and N. Gandelman. 2004. "Employment, Capital and Productivity Dynamics: Evidence from the Manufacturing Sector in Uruguay." Documento de Trabajo 16, Universidad ORT Uruguay, Montevideo.

Casacuberta, C., and N. Gandelman. 2007. "Explaining Output Differentials by Export Orientation: Evidence from the Manufacturing Sector in Uruguay." Background paper for the Latin American and Caribbean Regional Study on Microdeterminants of Growth, World Bank, Washington, DC.

Clerides, S., S. Lach, and J. Tybout. 1998. "Is Learning-by-Exporting Important? Micro-dynamic Evidence from Colombia, Mexico, and Morocco." *Quarterly Journal of Economics* 63 (3): 903–47.

Delgado, M., J. Farinas, and S. Ruano. 2002. "Firm Productivity and Export Markets: A Non-parametric Approach." *Journal of International Economics* 57 (2): 397–422.

Feder, G. 1983. "On Exports and Economic Growth." *Journal of Development Economics* 12 (2): 59–73.

Feenstra, R., and G. Hanson. 1997. "Foreign Direct Investment and Relative Wages: Evidence from Mexico's Maquiladoras." *Journal of International Economics* 42 (3–4): 371–93.

Galiani, S., and G. Porto. 2006. "Trends in Tariff Reforms and Trends in the Structure of Wages." Policy Research Working Paper 3905, World Bank, Washington, DC.

Girma, S., D. Greenaway, and R. Kneller. 2004. "Does Exporting Increase Productivity? A Microeconometric Analysis of Matched Firms." *Review of International Economics* 12 (4): 855–66.

Greenaway, D., J. Gullstrand, and R. Kneller. 2005. "Exporting May Not Always Boost Firm Productivity." *Review of World Economy* 141 (4): 561–82.

Hallak, J. 2006. "Product Quality and the Direction of Trade." *Journal of International Economics* 68 (1): 238–65.

Hallward-Driemeier, M., G. Iarossi, and K. Sokoloff. 2002. "Exports and Manufacturing Productivity in East Asia: A Comparative Analysis with Firm-Level Data." NBER Working Paper 8894, National Bureau of Economic Research, Cambridge, MA.

International Study Group on Exports and Productivity. 2007. "Exports and Productivity: Comparable Evidence for 14 Countries." Centre of Excellence for Science and Innovation Studies, Working Paper in Economics and Institutions of Innovation 110, Royal Institute of Technology, Stockholm.

Isgut, A. 2001. "What's Different about Exporters? Evidence from Colombian Manufacturing." *Journal of Development Studies* 37 (5): 57–82.

Islam, M. N. 1998. "Exports Expansion and Economic Growth: Testing for Cointegration and Causality." *Applied Economics* 30 (3): 415–25.

Krueger, A. 1978. *Foreign Trade Regimes and Economic Development: Liberalization Attempts and Consequences.* Cambridge, MA: Ballinger.

Lederman, D., M. Olarreaga, and L. Payton. 2006. "Export Promotion Agencies: What Works and What Doesn't." Policy Research Working Paper 4044, World Bank, Washington, DC.

Levinsohn, J., and A. Petrin. 2003. "Estimating Production Functions Using Inputs to Control for Unobservables." *Review of Economic Studies* 70 (2): 317–41.

Oaxaca, R. 1973. "Male-Female Wage Differentials in Urban Labor Markets." *International Economic Review* 14 (3): 693–709.

Olley, G., and A. Pakes. 1996. "The Dynamics of Productivity in the Telecommunications Equipment Industry." *Econometrica* 64 (6): 1263–97.

Porto, G. 2007. "From Exports to Wages: Evidence from Panel Data in Argentina." Background paper for the Latin American and Caribbean Regional Study on Microdeterminants of Growth, World Bank, Washington DC.

Schank, T., C. Schnabel, and J. Wagner. 2007. "Do Exporters Really Pay Higher Wages? First Evidence from German Linked Employer-Employee Data." *Journal of International Economics* 72 (1): 52–74.

Van Biesebroeck, J. 2003. "Exporting Raises Productivity in Sub-Saharan African Manufacturing Plants." NBER Working Paper 10020, National Bureau of Economic Research, Cambridge, MA.

Wagner, J. 2002. "The Causal Effect of Exports on Firm Size and Labor Productivity: First Evidence from a Matching Approach." *Economic Letters* 77 (2): 287–92.

———. 2005. "Exports and Productivity: A Survey of the Evidence from Firm Level Data." Institute of Economics Working Paper Series in Economics 4, University of Luneburg, Germany.

Westphal, L., Y. Rhee, and G. Pursell. 1984. "Sources of Technological Capability in South Korea." In *Technological Capability in the Third World,* ed. M. Fransman and K. King, 279–300. London: Macmillan.

World Bank. 1993. *The East Asian Miracle: Economic Growth and Public Policy.* Oxford, U.K.: Oxford University Press.

Yasar, M., C. Nelson, and R. Rejesus. 2003. "Productivity and Exporting Status of Manufacturing Firms: Evidence from Quantile Regression." Department of Economics Working Paper 03-23, Emory University, Atlanta.

Yeaple, S. 2005. "A Simple Model of Firm Heterogeneity, International Trade, and Wages." *Journal of International Economics* 65 (1): 1–20.

Index

References to boxes, figures, tables, and notes are indicated by "b", "f", "t", and "n".